SKODA
LAURIN & KLEMENT

SKODA
LAURIN & KLEMENT

IVAN MARGOLIUS
& CHARLES MEISL

TO

Heda Margolius Kovaly and Jane Meisl
with love

PAGE 1 **Laurin & Klement ENS, 1910.**

TITLE PAGE **Škoda 420 Popular, 1934.**

Published in 1992 by Osprey Publishing
59 Grosvenor Street, London W1X 9DA

Cataloguing in Publication Data is available from the
British Library

ISBN 1-85532-237-4
Project Editor Shaun Barrington
Copy Editor Simon Morgan
Designer Gwyn Lewis
Filmset by Tradespools Ltd., Frome, Somerset
Printed in England

Contents

63

Acknowledgements

We wish to express our gratitude to a great number of people who made this book possible both in Czechoslovakia and the United Kingdom. The new atmosphere in central Europe made it possible for us to reach and research materials which would have been inaccessible in the old days of repression.

We would like to take this opportunity to remember our dear friend Robert Ives who died so tragically during the writing of this book.

We thank Amanda Bates and Jane Meisl for moral support and general advice, proofreading, word processing and helping with research, Daniel Margolius with word processing, Heda Margolius Kovaly with proofreading and translations, Peter Titterton of Škoda (GB) Ltd for advice, photographs and general information, Dr Jan Tulis, Dr Jan Králík, Dr Jan Hozák of National Technical Museum, Dr Vladislav Krátký of Škoda, Plzeň, Antonín Mocek of Škoda, Mladá Boleslav and Ing Roman Kratochvíl for supplying photographs and archive materials, John Haugland and Steve Iles for supplying photographs, Jane Williamson and Matthew Critchley from the RAC Library for supplying research materials, John G. Henry for technical advice, Paula and Sheila Bates for word processing and proofreading and the Škoda Owners' Club of Great Britain for their support and understanding. Finally we wish to thank Nick Collins of Osprey Publishing for his confidence in us and his encouragement during the writing of this book.

If the authors have missed out specific acknowledgements to the many who have helped, please forgive and understand.

Every attempt to trace the origins and copyright of the plates and illustrations has been made. Photographs and illustrations are reproduced with acknowledgments to the following:

ČSTK, Škoda, automobilová a.s., Škoda, koncern, Plzeň a.s., National Technical Museum, Prague, Karosa, a.s., Vysoké Mýto, Dr.Ing.h.c. F.Porsche AG, A.Bates, V.Bidlo, S.Iles, J.Haugland, J.Králík, Ludvigsen Associates, I.Margolius, A.Mocek, P.Titterton, Škoda (GB) Ltd, J.Tulis, V. Zapadlík.

Škoda 932 prototype, 1932.

Map of Czechoslovakia between 1918 and 1939.

Introduction

Škoda's history is a fascinating one, being closely linked to the fortunes of the company's home country of Czechoslovakia.

This is the story of the manufacture of motorized transport in Bohemia started by the firm Laurin & Klement and successfully continued by a world renowned industrial and armaments concern – the Škoda Works – to this day.

The Laurin & Klement/Škoda story is not one of sparkling individuals such as Ledwinka, Porsche, Maybach, Benz or Daimler, but of a collective; a determined team of like minds which created over a number of years one of the most successful collections of bicycles, motorcycles and automobile products to have come out of central Europe.

At the turn of this century Bohemia was still an integral part of the Austro-Hungarian Empire, but had developed a sense of its own culture and technical know-how, despite being dominated by foreign influences and traditions for many hundreds of years. It was only after the end of the First World War that a free Czechoslovak republic was established consisting of Bohemia, Moravia, Slovakia and Ruthenia – the remnants of the broken Austro-Hungarian Empire. From the beginning, the company of Laurin & Klement was a purely Bohemian enterprise, run by Czech entrepreneurs Václav Laurin and Václav Klement, unlike other concerns in Austria-Hungary such as the Moravian Nesselsdorf Wagenbau, or the Reichenberger Automobil Fabrik. Nesselsdorf, renamed Tatra in 1919, was in the hands of an Austrian, Hans Ledwinka, and backed with Austrian capital while the RAF, in northern Bohemia, was founded by a Sudeten German, Baron Theodor von Liebieg and was supported by German financial houses.

The firm of Laurin & Klement was based in the heart of Bohemia in a small provincial town, called Mladá Boleslav, some thirty five miles north of Prague. There the Czechs produced sturdy vehicles which were technically advanced and always had the rider or driver in mind. Laurin & Klement, and later Škoda, produced transportation and other products ranging from bicycles, tricycles, motorcycles with or without sidecars, automobiles, trucks, omnibuses, military vehicles, aeroplane engines, stationary engines as well as railway wagons, locomotives, and, during the wars, arms, ammunition, armoured cars and heavy artillery.

Its common sense attitude was richly rewarded as soon as the company entered into sporting competition. Laurin & Klement, and later Škoda, achieved countless victories at the hands of such famous racing riders or drivers as Vondřich, Count Kolowrat-Krakowský, Hieronimus, Bobek, Haugland and others in speed and long distance reliability trials, adding glamour, glory and sparkle to the firm's name in rallies and hill-climbs and placing it at the forefront of public consciousness as a successful enterprise. Up to 1904 Laurin & Klement motorcycle riders participated in 64 contests in which they gained 56 victories and 59 second and third places. Out of 146 motorcycles starting, 142 machines completed the competition courses; not a single one had a mechanical defect. Similar successes followed in automobile races, gold and silver trophies filling up the Laurin & Klement display cabinets in Mladá Boleslav.

When Škodovy závody, Plzeň (Škoda Works, Pilsen) took over Laurin & Klement in the mid 1920's, it was the second biggest armaments factory in Europe and also one of the largest heavy

Laurin & Klement A.-G., Motorfahrzeugfabrik, Jungbunzlau.

Fabriksniederlagen: Prag I., Náměstí Republiky 6. — Brünn, Ul. Dr. Raš.na 10. — Bratislava Justiho rad 10. — Warschau, Ul. Zlota 68. — Budapest VI., Andrássy út. 10.

Vertreter in der Č.S.R.: Pilsen: J. Waldmann. — Budweis: J. Škrlandt & Co. — Königinhof: Ing. Otto Schiel. — Königgrätz: Ing. J. Novák. — Ung. Hradisch: R. J. Starý. — Karlsbad: Franz Albert. — Reichenberg: Willibald Breuer. — Mähr. Ostrau: Wagini & Comp. — Pardubitz: St. Janotka. — Mähr. Sternberg: Richter & Berg. — Teplitz-Schönau: B. Pánek.

engineering concerns. Škoda (which incidentally means 'it's a pity' in Czech) was established in 1859 and began producing motor vehicles in 1919, starting with commercial trucks and later passenger cars, using licence agreements. One was with the French company, Hispano-Suiza, for luxury vehicles and the other with the British firm, Sentinel Waggon Works, for the manufacture of steam powered heavy trucks. Its subsequent decision to take over Laurin & Klement enabled the Škoda concern to fully expand into the automobile industry, designing and producing its own vehicles. With great success the concern inherited and used the Laurin & Klement expertise and skills. Soon Škoda's products proved their thoroughbred background on the world scene.

In the early thirties Škoda concentrated on promoting its cars by participating in long distance rallies and events. On one trip a Škoda Popular travelled from Prague to India, another round North America and Mexico effortlessly covering 25,000 km without mishap; and another ran from Algiers to Dakar across the desert. A Škoda Rapid

ABOVE **Laurin & Klement factory buildings in Mladá Boleslav in the nineteen-twenties.**

RIGHT **E.Škoda Plzeň works in 1899.**

made a round-the-world trip in 97 days and another completed a journey from the Ivory Coast to Madagascar. Škoda's fame spread across the world with its export markets reaching all continents. Only when Czechoslovakia unwillingly entered the dark age of the Cold War did the name of the company become obscure in the minds of westerners.

It slowly emerged again in the late 1960s with the re-establishment of world export markets for the new Škoda rear-engined, rear-wheel-drive models whose old fashioned design initially created an unfavourable reputation. It took some time, almost fifteen years, to correct itself. When the suspension of the rear-engined Škodas was redesigned and the manufacturing quality improved, the sales increased and some models, especially the 136 Rapid Coupé, gained almost a cult status and a great following among young and old alike. The improvement in the design was later confirmed by victories in reliability trials and cross-country rallies.

In 1988, 15,798 British motorists bought new Škodas, which was more than Jaguar or Mitsubishi cars and almost as many as Alfa Romeo, Lancia, Lotus, Porsche, Daihatsu and Rolls-Royce put together. Currently with the modern robot production line built in the main works in Mladá Boleslav and the release of the new front-engined, front-wheel drive model the Favorit, in whose engineering Škoda was helped by Porsche and whose body design was entrusted to Bertone, the Škoda image has entered a new era. No wonder that recently there was a queue of candidates for joint ownership, including Volvo, GM, Renault and VW. The interest of the western manufacturers was not only confined to the Czech motor car production. The well known German, British, French, American, Swedish and Swiss industrial firms were vying for stakes in the locomotive-making unit of the main works of Škoda in Plzeň as well as the great interest that was shown for the whole concern by the French company Schneider and Japanese firm Mitsubishi.

In December 1990 it was announced that Volkswagen had beaten the Renault-Volvo consortium in the final round of talks, resulting in a multibillion Deutschmark deal for a stake in the Škoda firm. Renault's negotiations with Škoda excited anguished comments throughout France; the factory team sent ten missions to Czechoslovakia to discuss their offer and even President François Mitterrand went to Prague. 'It would be suicidal if France let itself be outpaced,' warned *Le Figaro*. The Czechs, however, preferred the private German company rather than Renault which is owned by the French state. Volkswagen chairman, Carl Hahn, stressed that the arrangement with Škoda was part of a European partnership and not a takeover. Hahn further said that Škoda's traditional strength in central and eastern Europe, the skill of its work-force, its geographical location and capacity were the key factors for Volkswagen's keen interest. The intention was to increase production quickly to 400,000 cars annually.

Since November 1989, after the so called 'Velvet Revolution', Czechoslovakia, having freed itself from the repressive Stalinist regime, has begun to regain slowly but surely its position amongst the industrially and technologically advanced nations. Between the wars, Czechoslovakia was equal to Switzerland, both in terms of standard of living and industrial output, which put Czechoslovakia among the top ten nations in the world on both counts. In 1935, for example, the Czechs had the highest per capita domestic production of any country in Europe.

With Volkswagen's recognition of the great potential available and the highly skilled workforce in Mladá Boleslav and Vrchlabí, the Škoda factory branch complex, and a relatively low wages level in comparison with western European standards, there is no question but that the tradition of technical innovation and quality of the Škoda marque will continue into the next century.

1 The beginnings

THE STORY OF the Laurin & Klement company begins early in the 1890's in the small Bohemian town of Mladá Boleslav (Jungbunzlau). The town was located on the northern periphery of the Austro-Hungarian Empire and was dominated, like any other Bohemian town of that time, by German values, language and culture. It was in Mladá Boleslav that a young man, a committed Czech patriot, Václav Klement (1868–1938), owned a bookshop.

Klement was born on October 16th, 1868, in Velvary, the son of a travelling salesman. He was apprenticed as a bookseller in a town called Slaný and worked in several bookshops in Prague and Mladá Boleslav. After work Klement studied to complete his education. In Mladá Boleslav he bought a bookshop having just enough money from his savings. Being an enthusiastic rider of velocipedes and bicycles, apart from books, he also sold a lot of other items such as tyres, Simpson chains, acetylene lamps and Seidl & Naumann bicycles.

Since its invention by the Scottish blacksmith, K.Macmillan, in 1839, the popularity of the modern bicycle spread quickly and as elsewhere, caught the imagination of the Czechs who never hesitated in trying to adapt to progress in technology or art.

The German firm of Seidl & Naumann had its main works in Dresden and advertised itself as 'the biggest bicycle factory on the Continent'. Klement wrote to a Seidl & Naumann branch which was operating from the Bohemian town of Ústí nad Labem asking to have one of his bicycles repaired. Naturally Klement wrote his request in Czech, but the Seidl & Naumann official, Foerster from Ústí, arrogantly replied with a pencilled scribble on Klement's letter in German: '*Wenn Sie von uns eine Antwort haben wollen, dann verlangen wir Ihre Mitteilung in einer uns verständlichen Sprache,*' meaning that Klement should write again in a language they could understand. 'The Czech language they cannot understand but they are happy to take Czech money!' was Klement's instant reaction. The incident made him determined that he would make his own 'Bohemian' bicycles.

In 1894 Klement persuaded a trained mechanic, Václav Laurin to combine resources. Laurin was born on September 27th, 1865 in the village of Přípeře. Eventually he moved to the town of Turnov, where Laurin became a partner in Kraus & Laurin velocipede workshop. There Klement found him and offered a business partnership, having first convinced himself of Laurin's great technical skills. In Mladá Boleslav Laurin and Klement set up a small workshop, which they rented for sixty gulden (1 gulden = 2 shillings) per quarter. The workshop measured only 120 square metres and their machinery consisted of one steam engine of 2 hp and three tooling lathes. Klement looked after the business matters and Laurin was the technical and development brains of the company. In fact Laurin was responsible for the majority of the inventions and patents produced by the firm.

Soon the Laurin & Klement Bicycle Manufacturing Company was officially established and registered in the Company Register which was kept in the Empire's capital, Vienna. Initially the company's personnel consisted of three apprentices, two mechanics and the two partners. In 1895 it produced its first bicycle to be sold under the trademark of 'Slavia', which emphasized the Bohemian origin of its machines. Most of the materials and parts were supplied from local sources but some

ABOVE Photograph of Klement's original letter that began it all.

LEFT Václav Klement and Václav Laurin.

13

V. LAURIN & V. KLEMENT V MLADÉ BOLESLAVI.

Vzor „Slavia" číslo 6.

Dvousedlový stroj cestovní

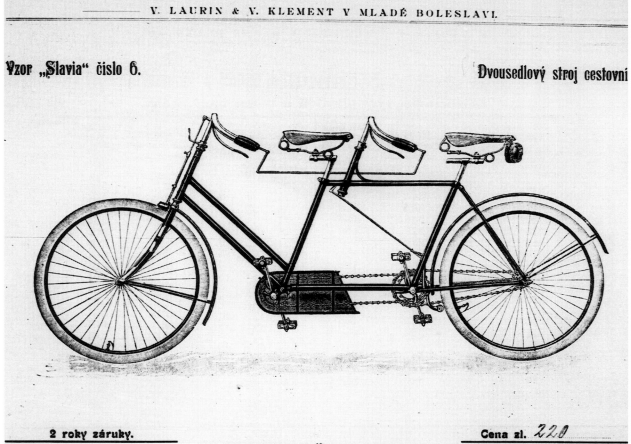

2 roky záruky.

Cena zl. 220

came from as far away as England. To begin with sales were slow, but soon the firm of Laurin & Klement became known for excellent workmanship resulting in good quality products. Its bicycles began to sell, the workshop needed to expand and new premises, 160 square metres in area, were found in the centre of town and the number of employees increased to 12. Then, in 1898, Laurin & Klement managed to buy a piece of land outside the town where a modest factory of 660 square metres was built employing some forty people working on 26 machine tools.

Bicycle frames were made out of lightweight tubes and a number of variations were offered. The bikes were sold in three sizes with optional equipment and colours to customers' orders. The range was completed by children's as well as ladies' bicycles. Manufacture expanded into goods-carrying three-wheelers, again sold in three versions; the price, depending on the model, was between 110 to 160 gulden. The closed goods boxes were made to order and were placed either in front of the rider or behind. The metal goods box could be substituted with a wicker basket. The third version had a low open basket positioned behind the rider. All the goods-carrying three-wheelers had, including the rider, a carrying capacity of 250 kg.

Václav Klement, a very ambitious man, soon tried to think of ways of extending from, and diversifying, bicycle manufacture. In 1898 he embarked on a study trip to France, having heard about motorized two-wheelers being used on the Paris streets.

The motorized bicycle, or motorcycle, as it is known today, was first produced in 1885. In that year Gottlieb Daimler made his experimental two-wheeler, the world's first petrol engined motorcycle. Daimler's *Einspur* (one-track) was a primitive wooden machine but it incorporated a number of surprisingly innovative features for that time: a handlebar 'twist' control, a float-type carburettor, fan cooling, same size wheels and a centrally located, single cylinder 264 cc, four stroke

ABOVE LEFT **Laurin & Klement 'Slavia' velocipede from 1896.**

LEFT **The 1897 'Slavia' type 6 tandem with connected steering. Price 220 gulden.**

ABOVE RIGHT **'Slavia' delivery tricycle.**

RIGHT **'Slavia' velocipede factory advertisement dating from 1906, mentioning manufacture of bicycles, motorcycles and motor cars.**

engine on flexible mountings. Motorcycle development was advanced by the British inventor, E.Butler, with his prototype called the Petrol-Cycle, in 1888; other pioneers quickly followed. In 1887 F. Millet made the first multi-cylinder engined motorcycle. The American E.J.Pennington invented a motorcycle with a two cylinder engine, each cylinder positioned above and either side of the rear wheel. Comte A. de Dion and G. Bouton produced a three-wheeler powered by a petrol engine in 1895. A year before them, the Germans H. and W.Hildebrand and A.Wolfmüller manufactured a motorcycle with a horizontal 2 cylinder engine of 1,489 cc providing 45 kph. This machine was called the *Petrolette* in France and was the first motorcycle produced commercially. This type of motorcycle was probably the first one to be driven in Austria-Hungary when it was bought by Baron Artur Kraus from Pardubice.

However the Hildebrand & Wolfmüller machine had a number of operational problems, the sales collapsed and the company had to close. In 1896, in Britain, Major H.C.L.Holden patented his single cylinder engine motorcycle. In the same year, in the next significant stage of motorcycle development, two brothers of Russian origin living in France, M. and E.Werner, also fitted a single cylinder petrol engine with hot-tube ignition to a pedal bicycle and, in this way, produced their very successful *Motocyclette*. At first Werner Frères positioned the engine at the front, then at the back, and later vertically in front of the steering post; a leather belt being used to drive a rim on the front wheel.

In Paris Klement encountered the Werner Frères *Motocyclette* and the then very popular motorized de Dion-Bouton three-wheelers. He especially liked the Werner machine. The de Dion-Boutons were more stable but unsuitable for the primitive Austro-Hungarian rough roads. The steered front wheel would not have withstood the strain.

Riding a motorcycle at that time was very much an adventure. Initially, with limited engine power and fixed gearing, the rider had to pedal to get over the crest of hills, while the position of the engine at the front or behind the rear wheel made stability and balance difficult to master, especially when rounding bends.

Klement went to the Werner works, bought one *Motocyclette* and brought it by train to Mladá Boleslav. There it was carefully unpacked, checked and analyzed part by part, put together again and thoroughly tested. The hot-tube ignition proved to be the most problematic element. When Laurin tested

the Werner machine on the roads outside the factory the hot tube kept blowing out. To start it again the rider had to get off the bike, pour methylated spirit in the tube, wait till the metal ignition probe was red hot and only then could he continue his journey. Laurin's first ride over a 9 km distance took almost two hours. In addition to the hot-tube ignition problems, all the levers operating the machine were positioned in such places that it was necessary to remove hands from the handlebars to move them. That particular manoeuvre caused Laurin a bad fall during his second test run when his front tyre unexpectedly burst. Another factory rider almost lost his eyesight when petrol splashed out of the canister, which was mounted on the front mudguard, onto the hot-tube ignition. In those days riding the motorized two-wheeler produced the same feeling as a few years later the aviators encountered when they ventured to fly the first flimsy aeroplanes.

Despite considerable difficulties with the hot-tube ignition, after much discussion the decision was made to start production of the first Bohemian made motorcycles. Laurin & Klement was faced then with the choice of following the Werner principle by mounting the engine above the front wheel or to search for other engineering solutions. Several prototype models (Ia, IIa, IIb, III, IV) with alternative engine positions were built and tested to destruction. Late in 1898 came the motorcycle prototypes type V and VI. From those Laurin & Klement developed a type A which started series production and was offered for sale to the public. Its construction was technically superior to its contemporaries.

This type had a one-and-a-quarter hp engine which was mounted centrally within the frame and the power was transmitted to the rear wheel by a flat leather belt via a tensioning pulley. The troublesome and messy hot-tube ignition was replaced by an electro-magnetic system specially developed by the factory. The centrally mounted engine, low in the frame, lowered the centre of gravity and improved the stability and handling of the machine. Other manufacturers then quickly adopted the same construction approach, yet Werner Frères patented this principle, ahead of Laurin & Klement in 1901.

Die Allgemeine Automobil-Zeitung stated in 1904, with the benefit of five years hindsight: 'The Laurin & Klement Company may be justly designated as the creator of a motorized two-wheeler, notwithstanding the achievements of the French designers, brothers Werner ... However, they only added an engine to a normal bicycle, without making any changes to its concept, while Laurin & Klement has been proceeding in the opposite direction. It matched the bi-wheel machine to an engine. Thus the idea was the same, but the approach different, the difference being that the French emphasized the principle of the bicycle, the Czechs the principle of the automotive machine. And the Czechs were right ... Only the shape of motorized two-wheelers betrays that its origin lies in the bicycle, but its substance is that of the automobile, as is substantiated by all recent constructions... The town of Mladá Boleslav should be grateful to the Laurin & Klement firm because no other product from this small Bohemian town carried the fame of its name into the world as did the motorcycles made by the above mentioned company.

'Everywhere the marque of Laurin & Klement found customers. For five years the firm toiled with really inexhaustible diligence improving its products and finding new markets. In many directions Laurin & Klement showed the way and today the company can be proud that it was the first to use the flat belt drive and the electro-magnetic ignition for motorcycles. The operating levers were arranged in such a convenient way that the rider could ride the machine without taking his hands off the handlebars'.

Significantly for a company working under a monarchy, the new Laurin & Klement two-wheel machines were called 'Republic' when exported. The choice of name showed the Czechs' quiet defiance of the old and corrupt Austro-Hungarian establishment. When offered locally however, the new motorcycles inherited the 'Slavia' name from the bicycles.

Having created the product, the new problem was marketing it. Selling this new form of transport to markets that were firmly stuck in their ways was a difficult task. In Germany, France and Britain marketing was easier as the public was more accustomed to new motorized transport technology. For some time the numerous orders Laurin & Klement received came mainly from abroad. This ensured the well-being and continuous production of the Czech company. It was at this time that Hildebrand & Wolfmüller's machines failed the public's expectations and Klement turned this to his advantage. He travelled around Germany where he performed exhibition rides. Audiences were fascinated and Klement's efforts were soon rewarded by the orders that poured in for the company's products.

Financial difficulties were one of the main prob-lems when Laurin & Klement began manufacturing. Any new business venture experiences these. When the 'Slavia' bicycles were the mainstay of profits, finances were so tight that Klement, having to pay his workers at the end of each week, was beset with immense worry. One of his strategies was in one way ingenious, but in another way disconcerting. The ready made machines were taken to the pawnbrokers. A customer wishing to purchase a cycle came to the works, Klement handed him the pawnbroker's ticket, the customer went to redeem the two-wheeler at the brokers and only then could he take his purchase with him! This strange financial system kept Laurin & Klement afloat while the two partners were sole owners, before they arranged bank credit. Later Klement used the town's savings bank for the same purpose. An article in Mladá Boleslav's newspaper of 1918, written by a resident judge recounted: 'I well remember the time when the factory built bicycles for stock during the winter and these were pawned at the savings bank for about 40 gulden per piece. The bank had a key to the stores and whoever wanted a cycle had to refund the pawned amount first, after which he could pay the rest by instalments to Laurin & Klement. The critical day at that time was generally Saturday when the perspiring Klement tried to get enough cash together to pay his workers, sometimes he even had to owe the book-keeper'.

Laurin & Klement's financial situation improved but the company still could not manage without substantial credit facilities. After failing to obtain finance from any Czech bank, Klement approached the Länderbank of Germany. After lengthy deliberation the bank agreed to provide finance but insisted on putting its own nominee on the company's board. The credit covered monies spent on manufacture. The motorcycles which Laurin & Klement now produced went into a storage depot which was a works store in name only. Its keys were held by a bank employee and whenever a customer appeared for whatever product, he again had to pay a deposit to the bank and the rest to Laurin & Klement. Only then could the customer wheel the machine on to the road and be on his way.

The selling technique of that time was very unsophisticated in comparison with today. The condition of the placing of orders was that the would-be rider had to learn to operate his new motorcycle within 5 minutes. Such a condition had to be fulfilled when Klement went to London to secure one of his first orders.

The would-be buyer was Henry Hewetson, the

first Englishman to have imported a Benz motor car into Britain in 1894. Hewetson later became a motorcycle and motor car dealer. The demonstration of the Laurin & Klement motorcycle was arranged outside Hewetson's showroom in Dean Street. Thankfully, due to the simplicity of the machine and the skills of the apprentice who was selected to demonstrate the bike, an order for 150 machines carrying the 'Hewetson' name was signed. In those days that was a very large order indeed!

Soon Laurin & Klement found that to encourage the sales of bikes at home, the purchasers needed to be educated in handling and operating this new and sensitive technology. Until then extensive correspondence or expensive demonstration was required to show that the motorcycles actually ran. Most of the customers lacked any form of technical ability and simply could not cope with correct carburettor settings and wrote furious letters to the manufacturers expressing their disappointment in being unable to operate their motorcycles. The Laurin & Klement company was not discouraged. It endeavoured to improve the situation by using the latest automotive technology to make motorcycle handling and operation as easy as possible.

In 1899 the Laurin & Klement factory had 68 employees, 36 lathes and other machinery. The working area had grown to 1,100 square metres. Production increased and in the following years a further nine single cylinder models were made – one having a water-cooled engine. Then a V-twin came and soon after the first Laurin & Klement four cylinder machine arrived. Motorcycles were produced in many versions, including tandems, military bikes and models with sidecars positioned either on the side or in the front following the principle of the trade bicycle.

In 1901, Laurin & Klement manufactured a prototype of a motorized four-wheeler with a front positioned, 2 cylinder engine. This was air-cooled

The 1904 V-twin motorcycle type CCR with coil spring suspension and belt drive.

by means of a side mounted multi-blade fan. This vehicle, of which only two or three were made, had a tubular chassis and was built using motorcycle components. One was exhibited at the *Automobil-Ausstellung* in Vienna in the same year. Laurin & Klement products gained first prizes in three other international exhibitions. In 1903 the number of factory employees grew to 204, there were 118 machine tools and the shop floor increased to 3,300 square metres. The growth of the company indicated the popularity of Laurin & Klement machines which went on into the following year. By then almost two thousand motorcycles had left the gates of the Mladá Boleslav works. The public soon called the Laurin & Klement product 'the Mercedes among motorcycles' and the same headline was used extensively by Laurin & Klement in its advertising.

Ironically Klement received a request from Seidl & Naumann's chairman, Mr Foerster. This was the same Foerster who used to run the Ústí nad Labem branch, and he asked to purchase a licence to manufacture Laurin & Klement motorcycles in Germany. Klement had an opportunity for revenge, but as a gentleman, he gracefully agreed. Soon Seidl & Naumann started to make these very successful motorcycles, which they called 'Germania'. On the machines and in all advertising Seidl & Naumann emphasized that these motorcycles were manufactured under licence from Laurin & Klement. This simple piece of information demonstrated how renowned Laurin & Klement products were and increased respect for the Germania motorcycles.

Even the British press was impressed, although confused where Laurin & Klement was based. 'A Powerful Racing Motor-bicycle' ran a headline in *The Motor* of August 16th, 1904. 'A machine which can easily touch a speed of 95 kph (60 mph approximately)... The makers are Messrs Laurin and Klement, a well-known German (sic) firm, reputed

The 1905 four cylinder motorcycle type CCCC with chain drive.

for racing machines. The engine is a twin cylinder type of 12 hp, driven by a V belt. The design of the frame is a very unusual one, but one possessing great strength. The driver sits right back over the rear wheel, and it will be noted that the steering bars are extended nearly the length of the frame, and are specially stiffened by tubes joining up to the front axle. The ignition is of the Eisemann high-tension magneto type, the dynamo being driven by a chain from the motor. The carburettor is a spray type. At the rear of the machine will be seen a wind screen and safety roller to be used when the machine is employed for pacing a racing bicyclist. The control levers are mounted on the curved top tube of the frame. There are no pedals, but a sort of stirrup rest is provided for the driver's feet'. *The Car* of October 26, 1904 commented on the recent Leipzig Show that 'the Laurin-Klement racing motor cycle attracted much attention, it being a 12 hp cycle of four cylinders for which a speed of 120 kilometres an hour is claimed'. The manufacture of Laurin & Klement motorcycles continued successfully in Mladá Boleslav until the end of the year 1911, and sales apart from clever advertising campaigns were helped along by numerous and triumphant achievements in the sporting field.

Václav Klement, the business mind of the firm in contrast to Václav Laurin's quiet technical and engineering leadership, was greatly aware of the importance of the factory participating in international and domestic race meetings. The anticipated victories would gain a valuable reputation for Laurin & Klement in the eyes of the general public. Even then the influence of advertising media was a powerful tool for promotion of manufactured products.

Then, as now, the races were organized cross country on hard roads over hills and mountains as well as on circuits. Apart from the obvious advertising advantage of promoting one's product and man's natural inclination to compete with his equals, racing also acted as a testing ground for the new products. Without the early hill-climbs and inter-city marathons today's machines would probably still have low revving engines like the old-time Daimlers and Benzes. If it were not for the racing riders and drivers stretching the abilities of their machines to breaking point and risking their lives in the process, very little progress in the motor car industry would have been made.

It took a few years for Klement to gain confidence in the quality and reliability of his motorcycles and make the decision to commit a factory team to prove the worth of Laurin & Klement

FROM LEFT TO RIGHT **Klement, journalist Heinz and Toman accompanying Podsedníček on his trip to Paris in 1901.**

machines on the race track. In 1901 he sent Narcis Podsedníček, his works test rider, to compete in the 1,196 km Paris-Berlin race, where 94 automobiles and 8 motorcycles took part. Henri Fournier won on a 70 bhp Mors in the automobile section. Podsedníček came second to a front-wheel driven Werner Frères *Motocyclette* ridden by Riviére.

In those days new tyres were not very reliable because of their poor construction and could be easily punctured with nails or sharp stones. Podsedníček came up with an interesting idea to make the tyres stronger. He placed between the inside tyre wall and the inflated tube a specially made strip formed by stitching together layers of cotton. 'This idea came about,' related Podsedníček 'when we came to Paris as participants in the Paris-Berlin race. I was worried that we would lose in this competition. There was a lack of money and we did not have much time to prepare ourselves for the race. It was difficult, this being the first time, to remember all we needed to have with us for these occasions. When we arrived in Paris and we saw how other riders were prepared and equipped I realized how inferior our setup was. I was not worried about the motorcycles, but the tyres were a different story. There was no money for new ones and I had to think how to succeed in the race with the old 'rubbers'. I slept with Klement in one bed as we could not afford a proper double bedroom in a hotel. It was two days before the start of the race. I could not sleep because sleeping was impossible. Klement kicked in his sleep and kept waking me up. I got up and went for a walk into the Paris night, pacing the

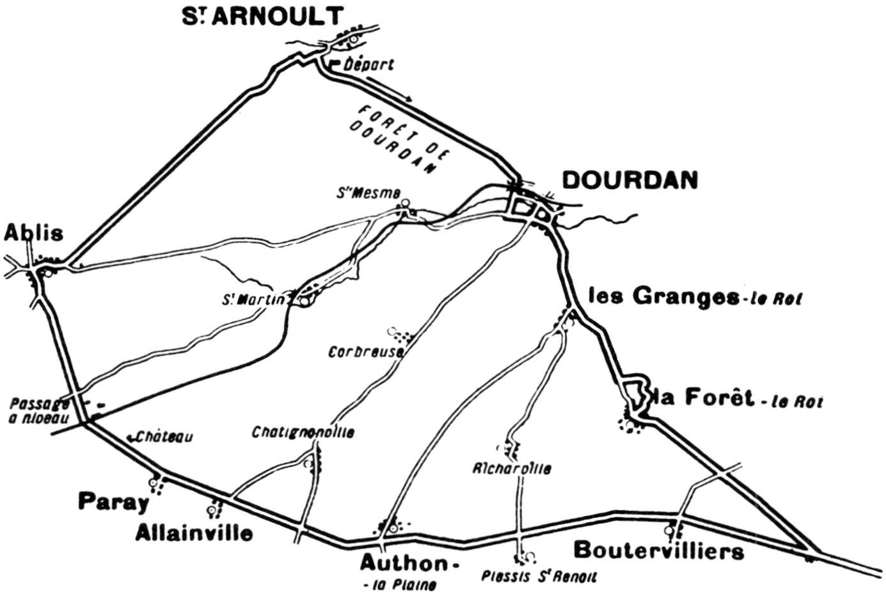

The Dourdan circuit in 1904 and 1905.

streets and thinking. Suddenly in an open uncurtained window I saw a woman sitting by her sewing machine. At that moment I had an idea and went to the window and tried to show that I needed something. She opened her door and let me in. I explained with difficulties what was needed. It took a little while before she understood. Then the seamstress sat by the machine with me next to her and made the first padded 'tyre strip insert'.' And this little trick worked like a miracle. Podsedníček completed this race and the following ones without a defect.

In 1902, eager to continue on the road to success, Klement entered himself and Podsedníček for the Arlberg hill-climb in Austria. To his great joy Klement won the climb on his own motorcycle and Podsedníček finished triumphantly in second place. The first Laurin & Klement victory was overwhelming.

The Laurin & Klement participation in the race on the Poděbrady circuit in Bohemia confirmed its strength when Václav Vondřich took the first place. The second and third places went also to men riding L & K machines.

As a young boy Václav Vondřich (Wondrich) was fascinated by velocipedes and bicycles while watching his father wheeling the boneshakers in the streets of Bohemian towns. As soon as he was allowed, Vondřich set off on the two-wheelers over the local countryside, quickly mastering the art of bicycle riding. To prove it he rode from Prague to Pardubice in four hours on a pennyfarthing. Soon his exploits came to Klement's notice and he hired Vondřich to become a Laurin & Klement factory rider. Before signing Vondřich agreed with Klement sums of money he was to be paid for participating in racing events and specified special bonuses in case of winning.

Vondřich was given a new 'Slavia' motorcycle and immediately scored his first success in competition, beating the established local riders Kohoutek and Vodílek. On the 330 metres Buben circuit in Prague Vondřich rode tirelessly around two hundred times and won. Further victories followed in the Viennese Prater Park where Vondřich defeated other European riders three times. On a two cylinder Laurin & Klement machine he achieved a speed of 75 kph in a flying kilometre race. On the Semmering Hill Vondřich participated six times and won every time.

A great success followed in the 1902 Paris-Vienna inter-city race of 1,430 km. This was held between 26th and 29th June, when apart from numbers of automobiles, eleven French and three Austro-Hungarian motorcycles took part. These races were difficult, with automobiles and motorcycles getting in each others way and causing many accidents along the route. Safety became problematical as spectators stepped onto the track, hypnotized by the sight of the powerful vehicles surging through clouds of dust as they raced over the primitive road surfaces. Only four motorcycles finished, two of which were Laurin & Klement machines. Podsedníček completed the journey, surviving a bad fall and a 9 hour delay at Arlberg. It took 31 hours and his riding time averaged at 50 kph. Podsedníček finished fourth just after the Werner Frères motorcycles and A.C.Rieger on a Laurin & Klement bike.

In 1903 further victories came Laurin & Klement's way in circuit and hill-climb meetings. But the pinnacle of Laurin & Klement's sporting success occurred when the firm entered the 1904 and 1905 Gordon Bennett *Coupe Internationale du*

Václav Vondřich, Dourdan Championship, 1905.

František Toman at Dourdan in 1904.

Motocyclette Club de France event. At that time a decision was made to improve the safety of races, abandon the inter-city marathons and to separate automobile racing from the motorcycle trials. A new form of racing came into existence, each type of vehicle racing round a closed road circuit.

The 1904 event was held on a road circuit near Paris. The circuit was 54 km long and was to be lapped five times. Five countries – Austria-Hungary, Denmark, France, Germany and Great Britain took part, each entering two riders. The French team had Demester and Inghilbert on Griffons. Other makes participating apart from Laurin & Klement were Terrot and Matchless.

On September 25th, 1904 Vondřich and František Toman on Laurin & Klement machines started off. This race, which was to have been considered as the first world motorcycle championship, was badly organized and consequently finished in confusion and chaos. Some riders did not abide by the rules, riding heavier machines than permitted and changing to spare parts made by other makes. To top it all parts of the circuit were blanketed by nails, possibly thrown by the distrustful villagers. Many riders were forced to retire with punctured tyres and related accidents. Vondřich ended that way, retiring with a holed petrol tank, having no tools to repair the damage. In the meantime Toman continued and despite the difficult conditions achieved a record time for the 54 km circuit of 38 minutes and 26 seconds. Toman went second through the finishing line, 3 minutes behind Demester. Only after the race was Toman's heroic achievement recognized when it was revealed that he completed the race without a saddle, having broken it off during a fall on the circuit. Toman wrapped his cap round the saddle carrier stump and completed the race on this rather inadequate and finally bloody seat.

The French magazine *L'Auto* commented:

'Toman rode an extraordinary race, he set a record for one circuit (averaging 84.3 kph thus becoming a record holder for the Dourdan circuit) and was placed second after the French racing rider Demester. The Laurin & Klement motorized two-wheelers are the only ones which placed themselves next to our machines and that for one hundred per cent. They are worthy opponents about whom we can say that we are proud to have beaten – they are opponents who have to be watched and taken account of in future'.

The 1905 Dourdan race was more controlled, better organized and became recognized as the first world motorcycle race of any major consequence. To qualify for the race, because of high interest, elimination trials were held. The Austro-Hungarian team selection was staged at Pacov circuit in Bohemia on May 28th, 1905. Vondřich, on a Laurin & Klement 2 cylinder 5 bhp bike, recorded the fastest speed of 102 kph. However Toman was first, Vondřich second and Nikodem, on a Puch, third.

Further local races followed, one only a week before the 'Dourdan'. The British magazine *The Motor* of June 20th, 1905 reported in an article headlined 'Some Fast Travelling by Laurin and Klement Machines'. 'On Whit Sunday motorcycle races took place over the Raida-Böhmisch-Leipa stretch, 16 kilometres in length. The Laurin and Klement men, driving two cylinder machines, put up to their credit some extraordinary times considering the weather and the fact that competitors had to double. In the single cylinder competition the following were placed: 1, Toman (Laurin and Klement), 10 minutes 48 seconds; 2, Klimt (Puch); 3, Wondrich (Laurin and Klement). Double cylinder events: 1, Toman (Laurin and Klement), 9 minutes 26 seconds; 2, Kalka (Laurin and Klement), 9 minutes 33 seconds; 3, Wondrich

Vondřich negotiating a bend in St Arnoult.

(Laurin and Klement). Thus Toman attained a speed of close upon 102 kilometres (roughly 64 miles) an hour! Toman's chances in the *Coupe de France* are not of the worst'.

The selections after the English heats were J.G.Campbell on an Ariel, H.A.Collier on a Matchless and Franklin on a JAP. The Germans had decided to send their team of Jahn, Müller and Menzel on Progress motorbikes. France, confident again of victory, with the local press predicting its inevitable success, prepared Demester on a Griffon and Giuppone and Cissac on Peugeots. The confidence of the French team was increased by bending the rules when its eliminating trials were held on the Dourdan course. *L'Auto* declared a week before the race: 'We can calmly count on the victory by our riders. We shall compete with good spirit but it is important that the cup gained last year stays with us. Both our excellent marques must win. Long live our modern three musketeers: Demester, Giuppone, Cissac'.

When the day of the race finally came the excitement of the crowds and riders knew no bounds.

The Czech riders forming the Austro-Hungarian team had confidently walked the race course the day before, removing any little obstructions along the route. However, the better quality tyres they had ordered failed to arrive and later anxiety befell the team.

Vondřich tried to offer his specially obtained Continentals to Toman, but Toman refused this grand gesture from his comrade. Vondřich, determined to win, was well prepared and had left nothing to chance. Apart from the best equipment he could get for his Laurin & Klement 5 bhp motorcycle, on the way to the start that sunny Sunday morning, Vondřich carried on his shoulders a leather bag full of all the tools he might need for an emergency roadside repair – including a soldering iron. He wanted to make sure that he would not be caught out this year. The astonished crowd shouted abuse and nicknamed Vondřich on the spot: *Le forgeron ambulant* (travelling blacksmith).

The starting numbers were as follows: Demester

Vondřich at full speed.

(1), Müller (2), Campbell (3), Toman (4), Giuppone (5), Menzel (6), Collier (7), Nikodem (8), Cissac (9), Jahn (10), Franklin (11), Vondřich (12). The Austro-Hungarian team had light blue sweaters, the French were sporting elegant red shirts with a white stripe, the English were in yellow and the Germans wore white pullovers. The riders were let out on to the course one by one at predetermined intervals. Vondřich set out last with a shoulder bag on his back to the merriment of the crowd.

The sequence of riders in the first round of 54 km did not change except that Toman dropped out after his tyre blew out resulting in a skid at 70 kph and a broken machine. Luckily Toman was unhurt apart from a few scratches. But the crowds were to be amazed further when the times were announced after the first round: Demester 35:55.; Vondřich 36:13! In the second round Vondřich was 3

seconds faster than Demester and the French crowds fell silent. Campbell and Müller, retired followed by Jahn and Franklin. Of the 12 starters only seven remained. In the third round Vondřich increased his pace to 105 kph, getting two minutes ahead of Demester. Determination to make up for the last year's failure encouraged Vondřich and his Laurin & Klement. He went like the wind, leaving others behind one by one. The fourth round entered only five riders – only the fastest and luckiest five – Vondřich, Demester, Giuppone, Collier and Menzel. During these 54 kilometres the Englishman and the German dropped out of the race for the trophy of the best rider in the world, leaving the Czech and the Frenchmen to battle it out in the fifth and final round.

Vondřich overtook Demester and Giuppone and sped through the villages towards the finishing line at 103 kph. At the last minute, just before he got to the stands, with all the dignitaries and spectators anxiously watching for the first rider, Vondřich's heart nearly stopped. A woman confused by the noise and cheering crowds started to cross the road in front of him. He managed to avoid her by the thickness of a tyre, skidding in the dust, but crossed the finishing line eight minutes before Demester, thirty in front of Giuppone. The first recognized world motorcycle championship went to a Czech, riding a Czech-made machine. A machine made by Laurin & Klement.

The well-known French motoring journalist Pierre Giffard commented on Vondřich's victory in the press the next day: 'Which one of our own riders would dare to carry a whole workshop with all the tools and spare parts? Which one of our own riders studied the track as carefully as Vondřich did. As a foreigner who does not know our country, who arrives in the evening before the race and defeats Demester, Cissac and Giuppone on their soil – such a man, my friends, deserves my deepest sporting respect'.

The Bohemian company Laurin & Klement and its riders had placed themselves in the record books. Vondřich's famous bag still exists and can be seen in the Škoda Museum in Mladá Boleslav.

The winner Vondřich at St Arnoult base camp with Václav Klement.

2 *The first Laurin & Klement automobiles*

LAURIN & KLEMENT car manufacturing began with the type A voiturette which was made from 1905 until 1911. The Czech company produced its experimental four-wheeler with a motorcycle engine in 1901, but it was only with real determination that Laurin & Klement started on this road in 1905. When questioned why Laurin & Klement suddenly decided to manufacture automobiles, Klement answered: 'We have not started to build voiturettes because the trade with motorcycles is not as good as it used to be, but because we wanted to keep our customers, who wished to change from the motorized two-wheelers to a more comfortable vehicle. It was a natural business decision'.

By 1905 the four-wheel transport concept was well established and many automobile manufacturers existed throughout the world. Karl Benz's first petrol powered three-wheeler had already been shown to the public in Mannheim in 1886 and the earliest motor car with a combustion engine to reach Bohemia was Benz's new four-wheel type Victoria in 1893. It was imported by a young textile manufacturer, Theodor von Liebieg, who was one of the first to buy a Benz motor car. Liebieg later persuaded Nesselsdorf Wagenbau, based in Moravia, to start producing cars in 1897. Nesselsdorf became one of the largest competitors to Laurin & Klement on home territory and had the advantage of beginning much earlier. When Laurin & Klement came on the scene the competition was much tougher.

The Laurin & Klement voiturette type A was fitted with a 1,005 cc, later increased to 1,100 cc, V-twin cylinder, water-cooled 6-7 bhp engine. It had a leather-faced cone clutch, three speed and reverse gearbox and could be ordered with chain or

an open propeller drive shaft. It was said to be capable of a top speed of 45 kph. Technically it was well up with contemporary products. The cylinders were cast with non-detachable heads, the crankcase was also cast in alloy and the pistons were fitted with three rings. Thermo-syphon cooling, with a gilled tube radiator was assisted by a four-blade fan. The exhaust valves were activated by a low mounted camshaft, while the automatic, suction-operated inlets had the usual return springs. The slide operated, spray carburettor was a Laurin & Klement design and, together with a separate ignition control, was operated from the steering wheel. Ignition was looked after by a low tension magneto, chain-driven from the front of the crankshaft. Splash lubrication was assisted by a hand-operated pump on the wooden dash board. Suspension was conventional, half-elliptics front and rear, the steering by worm and sector. The footbrake operated a band on the transmission, a side lever working on the 190x35 mm drums, the shoes being of bronze. A sprag could be lowered to prevent rolling back on steep hills. Acetylene front lamps and an oil lamp for the rear made night driving possible, with the acetylene generator mounted on the left running board.

The body was a simple, open two-seater with a folding top. Customers could choose the colours black, green, grey or blue - white cost extra. Altogether 55 cars were made. The type B of 1906 was identical, but with more power; still a twin, but of 1,399 cc and about 9 bhp.

The October 1905 issue of *Allgemeine Sport Zeitung* commented, 'Only a few weeks ago models of seven and nine hp two-seater cars left the Laurin & Klement factory and already these have proved

The 1905 type A open two-seater with a two cylinder engine of 6-7 bhp.

themselves as well worked out, reliable and fast (on a level ground a speed of 54 kph was achieved) that it is possible to put them side by side with the distinguished motorcycles made also by this firm. It is good news that this particular well renowned company began to manufacture small and cheap motor cars, which one can earmark as vehicles of the future and immediately the factory managed, with these first products in this field, to achieve a pretty good success'.

The change-over to automobile manufacture was taken seriously and the factory was purposefully striding ahead with its plans. In 1906 Laurin & Klement started to expand its workshops, machine shops, stores and paint shops resulting in a work area of 9,500 square metres and 500 employees. Laurin & Klement agencies spread across the continent reaching Prague, Vienna and London, establishing a network of distributors in Germany, Russia and Italy.

There had always been, even in its motorcycling period, the will to forge ahead with new and better designs. The story goes, and is factually confirmed in the factory's archives, that very early on there had been correspondence with Robert Bosch of Stuttgart requesting low tension ignition apparatus. Bosch himself replied that this was not far

enough advanced and therefore it could not be supplied. Laurin & Klement set about to produce its own system which provided a spark by means of make-and-break electrodes within the cylinder, without a condenser. Spark plugs came later.

The good driveability of voiturettes was confirmed by numerous stories published in the Bohemian daily press. One of the Prague newspapers reported on a trip made in August 1906 by a voiturette to the top of a very steep castle hill near a town called Pardubice carrying three passengers. After its successful ascent the car ran safely down hill. This was the first time that an automobile was a guest within the old castle walls.

In 1908 Mr and Mrs E.Kabát, with V.Vyšín, drove the B through the Alps and up to the Stilfser Joch in the Ortler region. Vyšín told the tale: 'While stopping in Trafoi to fill the petrol tank and replenish provisions, two other much larger cars came by. One had 40 and the other at least 60 bhp. Their happy owners looked with contempt on our little vehicle. When they found out that we also wanted to drive up to the Stilfser Joch they shrugged their shoulders and pulled faces when driving off to the mountains. Shortly, we were also on our way. The road to the Joch begins in Trafoi 1,520 metres above sea level and finishes at Hotel Ferdinande-höhe at 2,757 metres; it is 13.5 km long and has 52 serpentine bends. Already in the fourth bend we overtook one of the dignified automobiles and soon after that the second one. The Stilfser road had such sharp bends that these large cars had to reverse on every one to get round. And their drivers to their shame saw that this time we were shrugging our shoulders'.

Just as in the sphere of motorcycling, Laurin &

Klement considered racing its motor cars to be the best method of advertising. In the tough Semmering hill-climb in Austria in 1906, running in the 1.5 litre touring class, the type B achieved first, second and fourth places. The winning Laurin & Klement was driven by its designer Karl Slevogt, in second place was Kollarz, third place was taken by Joerns on Darracq, and in fourth place was Vondřich, the famed motorcycle rider now trying his luck with automobiles. Further success followed in the autumn in the German *Internationale Herbstprüfungsfahrt* when 900 km was covered in three days.

The type A/B chassis layout.

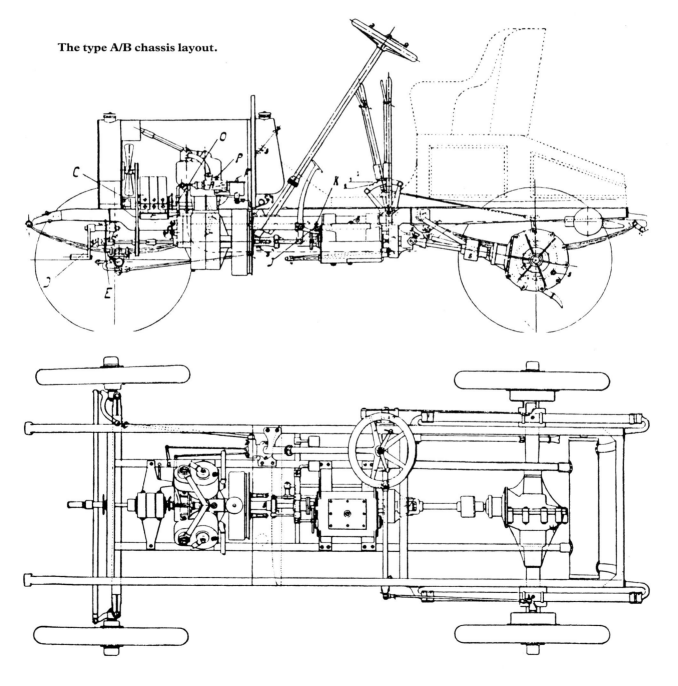

Early Laurin & Klement motor car advertisement extolling the flexibility and manoeuvrability of the company's products.

Laurin & Klement engineer Rezler was placed first in the class of cars priced from RM2,500 to RM3,500 and won the speed trial as well. The type B victory was underlined as the motorcycle class of up to 3.5 bhp was won by a Germania machine built by Seidl & Naumann under Laurin & Klement licence.

1906 was the last year of the pioneering era of the firm and its founders. Until then, the growth of the company and its further development was closely tied to the owners' personal means. This involved considerable risks. It must be said that in those early years, the profits from sales of bicycles and motorcycles only interested Laurin and Klement from the viewpoint of research, development and the enlargement of their works. Their will to prevail with new and specifically Czech products was so pronounced that although they were already making money there was still never enough to satisfy all the research that Laurin & Klement wanted to undertake. For the firm to devote itself to commercially viable manufacture of automobiles it was necessary to gain further investment, which

could not be supported purely by cashflow and borrowing. The discussions on how to resolve this issue were already tabled at meetings in 1905.

In 1907 a major step was taken, which not only established the factory among the foremost European automobile manufacturers, but also signified a year of internal re-organization. On January 1st, 1907 Laurin & Klement became a joint stock company financed by share distribution.

The new company of 2.5 million Austrian crowns capital took over the now famed Laurin & Klement name, Klement becoming managing director and Laurin technical director. The considerably increased financing enabled the factory to overcome the very last hurdles and expansion was top on the list of important issues to be tackled. The rebuilding of the factory, already begun in 1905, was completed in 1907. 13,400 square metres of working space was made available and many of the latest machine tools were installed. This meant that further vehicle types could be produced, such as the B2 with its longer chassis and more powerful engine which was also fitted with a taxi type body.

Next Laurin & Klement produced another model of a V-twin voiturette of 12 bhp, designated type C. From this model the new type C2 was derived. This had a four-seater touring body fitted for town traffic. Type D was the first Laurin & Klement with a four cylinder engine, but series production did not follow. Next came the type E of 28 bhp, its four cylinders, 110x120 mm, were cast in pairs.

The type F was a double phaeton with a 14 bhp 2,438 cc engine. *The Autocar* of October 3rd, 1908 carried this description: 'The motor has four cylinders cast en bloc, the casting being one which reflects the greatest credit on the firm's foundry work. Each cylinder has a bore and stroke of 84 x 110 mm, and the valves are all on one side. The ignition is by Eisemann H.T. magneto ignition with separate coil, the latter also serving for the reserve accumulator ignition. The water circulation is efficiently carried out on the thermo-syphon principle, which causes little or no loss of water, and maintains an equal temperature all day. The lubrication is by a mechanically driven pump delivering the oil to the engine through sight feeds on the dashboard'.

The Autocar continued: 'Having driven the car over 280 miles in one week-end, including two journeys of 127 miles each, we feel confident of expressing an opinion on its running. Previously we have covered the journey four times this year on a

is smooth in its action, and takes up the drive without shock or jerk. The control is by throttle and spark lever on the steering wheel and by foot accelerator pedal. The latter is rather awkwardly placed, but in the open country the hand lever is generally used. During our run to a village some eight miles north of Norwich, a certain amount of driving while there, and the return journey, the car behaved admirably, showing itself capable of maintaining a good average speed, despite an exceptionally heavy load and the fact that for many miles a terrific rainstorm dead ahead was encountered, and the hood had perforce to be erected. On the hills, which were on the whole of average severity, the extra 5 mm bore of the engine of the other car before referred to were missed, but the efficiency of the L and K motor for its size, which never required anything below second, in spite of the weight it had to propel – three adults, two children, a heavy collapsible basket brim full, a large hand-bag, a suit case, luncheon basket, coats, wraps, and several other items which cannot at the moment be remembered - left a most favourable impression in our minds'.

The type F became a base model of the Laurin & Klement production programme and was used in various modified forms in future manufacture.

In 1907 came a Laurin & Klement technical sensation – an eight cylinder car of 45 bhp. This was achieved by using two modified type F four cylin-

car fitted with an engine having a bore of 90 mm, and though the L and K felt the difference on several hills, it pulled remarkably well, despite the fact that it had been used continuously for about fifteen months, having in that time covered a considerable milage, and having been driven to Paris from the Laurin and Klement factory in Jungbunzlau, Bohemia.

'One of the car's best points is in the steering, which, though irreversible, is remarkably sensitive and easy, requiring practically no effort. The clutch

ABOVE **The 1906 type C V-twin cylinder of 12 bhp.**

BELOW **The 1907 type E four cylinder of 28 bhp in Roi de Belges body.**

der engines in line on a common light alloy crank-case. It carried the type number FF and was designed by engineer Karl Slevogt who in 1904, Klement had brought from Germany, where Slevogt had worked for the Ruppe company in Apolda, Saxony. Slevogt was responsible for Laurin & Klement car types A up to model FF. He left Laurin & Klement and signed up with Puch in 1907. Thereafter Hieronimus became the chief designer at Mladá Boleslav.

The type FF with its 4,876 cc eight cylinder engine installed, was sent off on a test trip at which a number of experts and motor journalists were present. Also there was an automobile racing driver and constructor, Otto Hieronimus, who travelled from Vienna. Behind the steering wheel sat the famous Laurin & Klement racing driver Count Alexander Kolowrat-Krakowský, who changed seats with engineer Rezler during the test. Straight after the test a demonstration journey from Mladá Boleslav to Paris and back was made and no defects were found. While only two prototype cars seemed to have been made, this model was the first attempt to manufacture an eight cylinder car in Austria-Hungary.

The eight cylinder engine did not come about by accident. After long deliberations its constructors came to the following conclusions: the eight would run quietly, top dead centre would be avoided and the engine would be more flexible and light. Vi-brations would be reduced, impossible to avoid with a four or six cylinder motor and this advantage would enable an increase in the number of revolutions. Because at each quarter turn of crankshaft one combustion occurred, the dead centre would be practically eliminated. Each of the two F type engine blocks used had its own magneto ignition. A cone clutch and four speed and reverse gate change gearbox transmitted power to a conventional rear axle. The crankshaft ran in 8 bearings and cooling was effected by a fan and pump. The footbrake acted on the transmission and the handbrake on rear wheel drums. A very large steering wheel was fitted. It appeared that Laurin's careful attention to the engineering side of things kept excellent pace with Klement's far-sighted commercialism. This car, however, was too expensive to manufacture to make it into series production.

As export efforts proceeded, a fascinating side issue was incorporated in the company statutes. Paragraph 4 stated that correspondence could be exchanged in German, Czech, French and English. Perhaps someone remembered the 'incident' of a letter in Czech to Seidl & Naumann!

No less than 250 cars and 100 motorcycles were produced in 1907 and these numbers, while tiny in comparison with today, established the company among the leading European automobile pro-

The 1907 type F town car.

The front cover of the British Laurin & Klement prospectus from 1907.

ducers. A good example of Laurin & Klement's export efforts was the number of taxis supplied to Moscow. The London newspaper, *The Daily Mail*, was distributed by Laurin & Klement cars fitted with a wooden box at the back.

The manufacture and sale of cars was of course incredibly different from today. The manufacturer demonstrated various models to the public of each of which, generally, only one machine existed. The purchaser then made known his personal preference, giving details which probably differed considerably from the vehicle demonstrated. For example, a longer chassis, or a more or less powerful engine might be wanted. These demands by the customer were considered as a normal part of the deal. Sometimes, only the chassis was supplied by the factory and the body and fittings were produced by coachbuilders who had previously built horse-drawn carriages.

In 1907 Laurin & Klement pioneered a form of series production for its A, B and F types. At first ten, then thirty and fifty cars of a model were made. This in turn required a network of representatives and also the necessary consumer confidence in the product. The established depots in Prague, Vienna

and Budapest expanded into factory branch agencies and workshops. Later F.Toman, the famous motorcycle rider, became manager of the London depot located at 255 Tottenham Court Road and Vondřich looked after the Prague branch. Laurin & Klement exhibited every year at various international exhibitions, in St Petersburg, Leipzig, Paris, Berlin and London. Seventy per cent of its products were exported, but it should be emphasized that some of the countries taking Laurin & Klement vehicles had their own motor manufacturing facilities.

After 1905, conditions for public transport began to become as viable in Austria-Hungary as on the rest of the continent. Before that poor road surfaces and the technical unsuitability of the vehicles caused great problems, as well as the lack of repair shops and servicing and unavailability of qualified and trained personnel. The general spread of passenger automobiles helped to overcome these obstacles and in 1910 omnibuses became a usual form of public transport in Austria-Hungary and abroad.

These conditions encouraged Klement's forward looking business mind towards public utility vehicle manufacture, Laurin & Klement lorries having already a limited success starting with the E type truck derived from the passenger model in 1907. Late in the same year a Laurin & Klement omnibus appeared, the HOP type (H stood for type H, O for omnibus and P for Prague where these vehicles were mainly destined for), which ran on many properly scheduled routes. The 22 passenger omnibus had a 116x140 4 cylinder H engine which produced 32 bhp at 1,000 rpm. Ignition was still on the make-and-break principle. A cone clutch, four-speed gearbox and two heavy chains drove twin rear wheels fitted with solid rubber tyres. Maximum speed was 26 kph, limited by an engine governor. On November 13, 1907 Prague council ordered four different makes of omnibus for testing as a substitute for a tramway route – the HOP, a Fiat, an Aries and a product of Süddeutsche Automobil Fabrik (SAF). None of the foreign vehicles generated as much attention as the Laurin & Klement omnibus. The omnibus line from the Old Town to Hradčany Castle ran for just over a year. The magazine *Sport* carried a story that the service had to be suspended due to an accident on the steep road up to the castle when the omnibus brakes failed and it slid back into a wall, demolishing it and putting its 15 passengers in danger of serious injury. Later the town council decided to adopt an easier route to the castle avoiding the

The 1907 type HOP Prague omnibus.

steep climb up the Nerudova Street. To this day there is no public transport running along this cobbled and picturesque way.

It is interesting that the domestic advances providing for internal scheduled bus lines also brought further export potential. Even remote Russian areas now supported omnibus routes. Incredibly, they ran from Turkestan to the Chinese border although 'roads' barely existed. That is where the relatively light Laurin & Klement omnibuses type FO of 8-10 seats with their 16 bhp engines triumphed. A high ranking military official commented in a Russian newspaper: 'Laurin & Klement automobiles are of such expedient design, withstanding all the obstacles and weather influences that even the Great Chinese Wall cannot be an uncrossable barrier for them for long. Soon these vehicles will breach it surely and victoriously, they will reach beyond it and will set out all over Asian Russia'. In 1908 four Laurin & Klement omnibuses HOS type were supplied for the inter-city route Pardubice-Holice-Bohdaneč. They had seats for 17 passengers and a special storage compartment for luggage and mail. In winter, heating was provided by a clever hot water installation which was warmed by the exhaust system. In the following years further models followed such as the FOD and DO.

The contemporary documents dealing with Laurin & Klement exports showed that Japan, China, Australia, Mexico and many European markets were very receptive to the excellence of the Bohemian products. In 1909 and 1910 a hundred taxis were supplied to Vienna and they ran satisfactorily until 1928. At the same time two hundred taxis were delivered to St Petersburg, an order of such magnitude for the time that no other European car manufacturer could have coped. As well as omnibuses Laurin & Klement also introduced a further range of commercial vehicles of various tonnages, carrying capacities, body and chassis sizes. The light one tonne truck type FL was derived from the basic passenger type F. The type H could carry four tonnes and had the same chassis as the HOP and HOS. Additional stronger models manufactured in 1910 were the DL and HL. The 6 tonne HL had a 7,363 cc four cylinder engine of 40bhp. Its strengthened chassis was later used to build large Laurin & Klement omnibuses.

Apart from standard trucks, special bodied versions for the Austro-Hungarian army were supplied for ammunition deliveries or ambulances. For beer and fuel deliveries cistern types were manufactured. Illustrated European magazines showed pictures of these vehicles and that free advertising brought more orders from Russia, Italy and the countries of the British Empire.

But business did not always proceed as smoothly as hoped. The British magazine *The Car* of January 20th, 1909, for example, showed a picture of the Laurin & Klement postal van and commented: 'Between the Montenegro Government and the

Laurin and Klement Company, of Jungbunzlau, Bohemia, a contract has been concluded whereby the latter firm is to establish, with the aid of the Montenegro Government, a motor postal service in Montenegro. By this contract the firm of Laurin and Klement have acquired for fifteen years the monopoly for the public automobile transport in the principality of Montenegro. Some days ago the cars were forwarded by railway to Montenegro in order to take up the regular postal service. When the vehicles arrived at Vienna, they were inspected by Ritter Wagner von Jauregg, the general manager of the Posts and Telegraphs, Court Councillor Hofer, Major Wolf, and Ritter Princig von Herwalt, general council to the Foreign Office. Soon after this inspection the despatch of the cars was prohibited by the Austrian Government, and only after much delay was the embargo removed, when it was decided that there was not sufficient motive to confiscate the vehicles.

ABOVE **1908 Laurin & Klement postal buses for the province of Montenegro with short chassis suitable for mountain roads.**

BELOW **Laurin & Klement A.G.**

'These cars are specially constructed for the hilly country of Montenegro (derived from the type DO with four cylinder engines of 4,503 cc of 105x130 mm, giving 25 bhp). The wheel-base is a very short one and the front wheels are so constructed that it is possible to turn the car in a very narrow road. Near the driver's seat there are two seats, and behind them there is a compartment which contains five seats, while behind this compartment is the postal box.'

The Laurin & Klement company was clever in knowing the specific needs of each individual market and had the manufacturing flexibility to adapt to most requirements demanded by its customers.

LAURIN & KLEMENT, A. G., MOTORFAHRZEUGFABRIK

JUNGBUNZLAU.

NIEDERLAGEN:
═══ PRAG I., Josefské nám. 6. ═══
WIEN I., Kaiser-Wilhelmsring Nr. 20.
BUDAPEST VI., Andrássy-utcza 10.

TELEPHON:
JUNGBUNZLAU . . . . Nr. 37.
PRAG . . . . Nr. 4620.
WIEN . . . . Nr. 8005.

Bahnsendungen: JUNGBUNZLAU-LOKALBAHN.

Lieber's Code Used.
ABC 5th Edit. Code Used.

JUNGBUNZLAU, den .... 191.

TELEGRAMMADRESSE:
„LAURINKLE".
POSTSPARKASSEN-KONTO:
Prag . . . . Nr. 44.823.
Wien . . . . Nr. 44.823.
Budapest . . . . Nr. 19.655.
BANK-KONTO:
Živnostenská banka, Prag. ─────
─ Länderbank, Filiale Prag.
Živnostenská banka, Filiale Jungbunzlau.

3 Hieronimus and Count Kolowrat

1908 BECAME A SIGNIFICANT year for Laurin & Klement. Otto Hieronimus joined the company as its chief engineer and designer and while he stayed a little less than three years, the imprint of his designs on Laurin & Klement production lasted over a decade. He was German, born in Cologne in 1879 and, without exaggeration, is an exceptional personality in the annals of engineering and motor car racing – one of those early enthusiasts prepared to give his all in the pursuit of technical advance. During his stay at Laurin & Klement he was the highest paid immediately after managing director Klement. Wherever he went in the world this twenty-nine year old was preceded by his technical reputation and his success in car racing.

Hieronimus' conceptual imagination exerted tremendous influence on the design of Laurin & Klement vehicles. Although theoretical design was in the hands of another man, engineer I.Rezler, Hieronimus provided the ideas, input and the 'fine tuning'.

He was fascinated by the art of flying and not only designed one of the first aircraft engines, but also became a well-known pilot. The first aircraft engine built during the reign of the Austro-Hungarian monarchy was the Laurin & Klement four cylinder 5,880 cc model EL of 50 bhp of 1910, designed by Hieronimus. It was tested in a Blériot aircraft near Mladá Boleslav on October 18th, 1910. Some of these engines were also used in airships. They were water-cooled, in-line, and only weighed 75 kg, twin magnetos provided the sparks and the steel cylinders had sheet metal water jackets. His other aircraft engine designs were also produced by Breitfeld, Daněk of Prague. Some of which were used in military aeroplanes.

Hieronimus learned to drive at fourteen, in one of the first Benz cars – his father was a Benz agent. From 1895 to 1899 he worked at Benz's factory; he left there to take a job at Gräf und Stift to build cars for Arnold Spitz, a Viennese car dealer. There he constructed his first two and four cylinder engines and a Spitz racing car of 24/30 bhp. Soon Hieronimus started racing, winning the Exelberg and the Semmering hill-climbs. On April 1st 1903 he drove a 60 bhp Mercedes racer at La Turbie hill-climb above Monaco and established a track record of 14 minutes 26.8 seconds. The last of the famous inter-city marathons, the Paris-Madrid event of 1903, found him at the wheel of a 90 bhp Mercedes. So many tragic accidents marred this race. When Marcel Renault, one of the three founding brothers of the great car-making dynasty died at Couhé-Verac, the French organizers stopped the race after the participants reached Bordeaux. Hiero, as he was sometimes named, was in the 62nd position at that time. On July 5th 1905 he participated in the Gordon Bennett Cup in the Auvergne, totalling 548 km, but dropped out because of persistent tyre problems. His Continentals were unable to cope with the great weight of his 120 bhp Mercedes. Leon Théry, on a 96 bhp Richard-Brasier, won this last Gordon Bennett Cup to be held and the following year the Grand Prix of France became the premier racing event. In 1905 Hiero participated in the first Herkomer Trial, which Germany organized in competition with the Gordon Bennett venues. In 1906 he received the Pötting Prize, an honour given for his engine designs.

Having left Laurin & Klement in 1911, Hieronimus went to work on aero-engines for Werner & Pfleider later renamed Warchalowski, Eissler & Co

in Vienna. We know little about his life during the First World War, but afterwards he seemed to have continued his activities at Warchalowski becoming a technical director. Hiero went on racing first for Austro-Daimler and then for Steyr. His sporting involvement brought this factory their biggest success when Hiero won his class at that great classic, the Targa Florio in Sicily. He died on May 8th, 1922 only 43 years old, while practising for the Ries hill-climb in Styria. An ironic stroke of fate, because it was said at the time that Hieronimus promised his wife that Ries would be his last racing event.

There were two versions of how the fatal accident occurred. The first one stated that at 5 o'clock in the afternoon a horse cart travelled up towards Ries. Hieronimus caught up with it by the school in Kainbach where the cart was stopped by gendarmes. Hiero, who just moments before developed tyre problem when taking a sharp bend leading to the gentler school bend tried to avoid the stationary cart. His hard braking caused a cloud of dust to envelop the car which turned over and both Hiero and his mechanic were thrown out.

ABOVE **Hieronimus at the wheel of the 1908 racing type BSC. Young Count Kolowrat sits beside him.**

BELOW **The open two-seater sports model BSC with dashboard oilers.**

RIGHT **The Laurin & Klement types FC at the end of the 1908 St Petersburg-Moscow event. The class winner Hieronimus is in the right hand car.**

The second description was put forward by the only eye-witness, a lady shop-owner, who stood about 30 metres away from the scene of the accident. She observed Hieronimus nearing the school bend. The race patrol signalled with a blue flag meaning 'take care!'. The racer skidded into the fairly easy bend, it slipped further and at that moment the rear left tyre burst. The car stood up on its end and turned over. The mechanic was thrown out, Hieronimus remained in his seat and the car turned over again.

In fact the bend was gravelled, Hiero went over 100kph and at the fateful time braked hard. The radiator was thrown several metres from the car, the magneto was torn out and found on the road. The front left tyre was flat, the rear left ripped out of the rim, the rear right wheel badly deformed. The brakes were in order. The car caught fire but this was almost instantly doused. The bursting of a tyre could not have caused Hiero's death considering the high quality of his driving skills, but the sudden hard braking in the racer with rear wheel brakes only could have made it turn over.

Following the laurels gained in motorcycle rac-ing, Laurin & Klement sporting efforts continued with great success. In 1908 the Zbraslav-Jíloviště hill-climb was inaugurated, an event that was to be enormously popular for many years to come. Laurin & Klement occupied first and second places in the 1.5 litre (Rezler 7:04.20 and Gotz), up to 2 litres (Kolowrat 5:58.60 and Vondřich 6:15.20) and up to 3 litres class (Kejr 6:56.40 and Exner). Laurin & Klement motorcycles also gained many medals.

Journalists described the scene: 'The view in the bends, where we were shown the neck-breaking art of driving skills, is simply unforgettable. The motorcycle riders' feet brushing the surface of the road, the teams in the sidecars leaning far out to keep balance to avoid turning over, and the cool calm of the drivers of automobiles who do not betray that one's life is in danger every second of the race – all is unique theatre, exciting and extraordinary'.

Over 20 motorcycles were entered including local makes Walter, Trojan, Nagl and Laurin & Klement and from abroad, Peugeot. The auto-mobiles included Opel-Beyschlag, Mercedes,

Minerva, Brasier, Benz, Züst, Laurin & Klement and Hansa – altogether 15 racing cars. Behind the steering wheels sat the best racing drivers of Europe: Joerns, Halphen, Kienle, Lauffer, Jonasch, Count Thurn-Taxis, Count Kolowrat, Vondřich, Hieronimus and others. The 5.5 km route started in the Zbraslav main square with the finish in Jíloviště with a maximum ascent of 8.25 per cent. The best overall time of 3:55.40 was achieved by Joerns in the Opel.

On June 1st, Hieronimus won his class in the very difficult St Petersburg-Moscow event. This win caused quite a stir in technical and sporting circles, not only had he beaten all the competitors in his class, but Hieronimus came fifth overall against many much more powerful cars. The Paris magazine *L'Auto* commented: '...Hieronimus in the Laurin & Klement car is the first in his class. . . This result cannot really surprise us because we know the driver's characteristics, a man who won Semmering. We know also the products of the Laurin & Klement firm, which always managed in motorcycles as well as in voiturettes to surprise with the best designs and constructions . . . But what makes this success so sensational is the reality that the light Laurin & Klement car was placed fifth in overall classification. In front of it are only four cars, two of which are from the first class! The winning

Benz (driven by Hémery) is the defender of Germany in this year's Grand-Prix, the second Darracq is the same one which Caillois drove in the Grand-Prix, the third place went to Wagner in the Fiat specially constructed for this year's Targa Florio and in the fourth place we see a member of the third category, a Fiat driven by Folkin'.

In December 1908 at the Brooklands track using a modified version of type F, the overhead valve FC, Hieronimus attempted and successfully concluded a record in the 86 mm bore class. Firstly Count Kolowrat managed an average of 112.26 kph, a week later after many modifications and much trouble, Hieronimus improved the speed to 116.15 kph, reaching 118.72 kph on one lap and earned Laurin & Klement a lasting inscription in the Brooklands record books.

The track at Brooklands was opened in 1907 and during its construction over two thousand workers were employed. When it was finished Brooklands was, without doubt, the best racing track in the world. The track measured 5.6 km and was 30 metres wide. The first race held there was on July

6th, 1907 and for its inaugural race the best racing drivers of the world gathered there, watched by five thousand spectators. A few months later, on October 9th 1907, a powerful eight cylinder Darracq of 200 bhp achieved an incredible speed of 185.678 kph.

The type FC, modified from the base model F by Hieronimus, had an engine with the bore of 86 mm and a stroke of 150 mm. The unusual bore/stroke ratio was dictated by the contemporary competition regulations, dividing cars according to cylinder numbers and their bore. Stroke was not limited. Hence the peculiar appearance of some racing cars.

A later Laurin & Klement racing version, the FCR had a bore of 85 mm and a stroke of no less than 250 mm! This car was powered by an OHC in-line four cylinder engine cast in two blocks with cast pistons and carefully machined hollow con rods, with walls that were only 1.5 mm thick. The crankshaft had three main bearings each with a separate oil feed. The valves were inclined at an included angle of 120 degrees in the cylinder head and operated by rockers. A vertical shaft at the front of the engine drove an overhead camshaft through two pairs of conical gears. At the lower quarter of the shaft further conical gears operated a magneto of aircraft type, with its drive shaft positioned at 45 degrees to the engine.

The hemispherical cylinder heads contained the plugs inclined at the same angle as the valves, but axially with the engine, protruding from both pairs of cylinder heads. The cylinder heads were non-detachable, which was the engineering practice at that time. Exhaust valves were on the left, inlet ones on the right and between the cylinder blocks ran the pre-heating tubing for the carburettor, placed low on the right. Slots at the top of the bonnet admitted cooling air to the open valve gear.

The engine could only be started by the handle. At the back of the engine was a sizeable flywheel with clutch and behind it a four-speed gearbox. The back axle was shaft driven. Gear change and brake levers were on the right hand side. A rectangular frame with U-shaped profiles formed the chassis with half-elliptic leaf springs attached to it. The front and rear axles were solid, the rear axle thrust being absorbed into the chassis by longitudinal arms and cup shaped bearings; the 22 inch wheels had mechanical rear brakes. The fitting of

motorcycle Michelin type tyres resulted in corners being taken by sliding. The front axle was fitted with adjustable shock absorbers with wooden friction discs.

The FCR driver could just see over the incredibly tall bonnet and he and his riding mechanic sat virtually atop the rear axle. The engine had amazing acceleration giving full power at 2,000 revs. This car was destined for record-breaking feats and therefore the position of its centre of gravity was not as important and behaved well even in the hillclimbs. The FCR, of which at least two were made, won races at Semmering, Gaillon and in the Zbraslav-Jíloviště climb.

There are several stories about the Brooklands record, indeed when considering these one must admire the determination and stubbornness of Klement who was present at this event. Shortly after the first laps, Hiero cruised the FC in with steam enveloping the bonnet. The verdict was very disappointing: water had entered the cylinders, the trouble was beyond immediate remedy, so it was back to the Brooklands repair sheds.

Klement despatched Toman, his manager at the Tottenham Court Road branch depot, to the post office with a telegram to Mladá Boleslav – 'send spare engine block by courier'. The track had been hired for this record attempt and the time-keepers were on the spot. Klement pleaded with the Brook-

lands officials to allow them another week. Now they had the anxious wait for the courier with the spare block. Days later Neumann, the Czech courier, arrived with the heavy block in a cardboard box. When he unloaded the box prior to embarking on the Dover steamer at Vlissingen, Neumann lowered the precious block a little too quickly to the ground. On unpacking the valuable cargo at Brooklands a sliver of metal broken from the block tinkled to the floor. Klement exploded: 'clumsy idiot, you heap of misery'! Neumann wanted the earth to swallow him up. But Hieronimus' mechanic Franta Krutský intervened: 'I'll mend the block – we'll have a go'. Less than a day remained before the extra week set for the record attempt expired. Krutský needed more time for the repair. 'Give us another 24 hours please,' Klement implored the organizers. Fortunately his request was granted.

We take up the story as described in 'On The Track' by H.C.Lafone, The Autocar of December 19th, 1908. 'We are getting to expect regularity in running nowadays, and especially is this the case at Brooklands, where outside conditions are practically constant, and it is merely a matter of consistency in the car's own behaviour. On Friday last week the well-known Continental driver Hieronymous (sic) came down to see what track speeds he could extract from the little 14–16 hp Laurin and

Klement racer, which had already distinguished itself during the past season at several foreign hill-climbing competitions, notably that held at Semmering, where the car won its class. There was no track record to establish, for there is no standard Brooklands class for anything below the 26 hp machines with cylinder bores of 100 mm, but Laurin and Klement's performance will need a good deal of beating by any car of equal engine dimensions. The four cylinder motor had a bore of 86mm, and a stroke – according to reports – of something like 150 mm, but the height of the cylinders certainly gave the impression of a longer stroke than this... Mr A.V.Ebblewhite hand-timed the Laurin and Klement's speed, for the RAC, over the flying half-mile, five laps (13 miles 1,456 yards) and 10 laps (27 miles 1,153 yards), the electric apparatus not being used at all. The actual time for the flying half-mile was 24 2/5 seconds, at the rate of 73.77 miles an hour, a decidedly fine achievement, considering the cold and blustering wind which swept the track. The five laps' time was 11 minutes 29 3/5 seconds, at the rate of 72.15 miles an hour; and the 10 laps were covered in 22 min-

ABOVE **Hieronimus in the FC after his success at Brooklands.**

LEFT **The FCR driven by Hieronimus.**

BELOW **Telegram sent to Mladá Boleslav announcing Hieronimus' record run on the Brooklands Track in December 1908.**

utes 58 2/5 seconds, at practically the same average speed. It is extremely interesting, as regards regularity of running, to note that the first and last laps were completed with a difference in time between them of 3/5 second only'.

Other British magazines did not miss this important news and the story was carried in *The Motor* of December 15th and *The Car* of December 16th, 1908. 'Record at Brooklands', announced *The Car*, 'Last week at Brooklands, Hieronimus, who some years ago was so well-known in racing circles, attempted to improve on the speed of 69.76 miles per hour for a 14–16 hp car recently attained by Count Kolowrat. He was quite successful in his attempt... His car was a 16–18 hp Laurin-Klement, which as the recorded times show, has a very good turn of speed'. So the record was Laurin & Klement's – a fine achievement for the time.

Laurin & Klement had a good reputation in Great Britain. As early as 1906, *The Motor* referred to 'a new light car made in Austria manufactured on the most up to date lines, priced at £175 for the 6–7 hp, £200 for the 8–9 hp complete with cape cart hood, lamps, horn and spares, and £285 for the 10–12 hp, with side entrance body'. The sole concessionaire for Great Britain and the Colonies was H.F.R.Engelhardt of 130 Fenchurch Street, London.

Clearly the agents for the Bohemian company were most anxious to popularize the make. *The Car* of November 28th, 1906 mentioned it as a 'small exhibit with very neatly designed grilled radiator and the body nicely got up' at the Stanley Show at the Agricultural Hall. In 1907 the 8 hp model was demonstrated and prospective buyers were given trial runs in the provinces. 'The car has been running remarkably well and has shown itself capable of making high average speeds. One day's run included a 100 miles non-stop run in five hours from Derby to Hull and 120 miles from Newark to London at an average speed that would surprise many people', said *The Autocar* of April 27th, 1907. '1st Blood at the Opening of the Continental Racing Season', in big black letters, ran a full page advertisement in *The Car* of April 14th, 1909. The 10 hp two cylinder cost £195 and the 14–16 hp four cylinder four-seater £380. Now, Laurin and Klement Motors had its quarters at Tottenham Court Road and 'they are open to appoint agents on liberal terms in districts where not represented'. Mention was made of a win in the 14–16hp class at the flying kilometre event in Cannes and a win at La Turbie hill-climb.

An article in *The Autocar* of May 18th, 1907

Adverts, and an intriguing offer.

called 'A Test of Reliability. Two 8–9hp Laurin-Klement Cars Made Non-stop Runs From London to Holyhead At a Legal Limit Average.' deserves to be quoted in full.

'To test the efficiency and general reliability of its cars, the Laurin-Klement Motor Agency decided to make a run, observed by some competent person, from London to Holyhead – a distance of some 260 miles. The car chosen for the trip was a standard 8–9 hp two-seater car (type B) driven by Toman, a well-known Austrian driver from the Jungbunzlau factory, who knows his car well and drives it like an artist. A young Austrian nobleman (Count Kolowrat), who is at present studying English in this country, and who is an enthusiastic amateur exponent of Laurin and Klement motor cycles and cars, having heard of this proposed trip, and being a thorough sportsman, was reputed to have declared that he would do better than Toman or break up his car in the attempt, with the result that he resolved to do likewise. He invited a representative of *The Autocar* to accompany him. Having previously met the Count, we gladly accepted the

LAURIN & KLEMENT MOTORS, 255, TOTTENHAM COURT ROAD, LONDON, W.

invitation, and at a few minutes to six, in company with Mr Douglas Leechman, who was to accompany Toman, we arrived at the Laurin-Klement depot. Only a few seconds later, the Count arrived, and at 6.10 both cars swung into the Tottenham Court Road, en route to the Welsh port.

'The weather did not look promising, and boded a showery trip. The roads out of London were in a shocking condition: the wood pavement was in a state of appalling greasiness, and the macadam was little better, while that between Swiss Cottage and Finchley was as bad, as regards surface, as any encountered on the whole journey. However, with never a slip, due to the Continental studded tyres we bumped over the abominable road to Barnet. Despite the appalling condition of the route, both the little cars pulled well, and sped along with a good stiff breeze behind them at a speed of which the casual observer would not think them capable. After Barnet, the roads were a good deal better, but it rained intermittently for many a mile. Much to the Count's chagrin, Toman's car managed to keep ahead, heaving a slightly heavier flywheel than the other, and consequently climbing hills rather better on the top speed. All things being equal, however, there was little difference in the speed of the two cars, but Toman just managed to keep ahead.

'Both cars ran with perfect reliability, and neither lost sight of the other till we neared Daventry. Here we knew the road to Atherstone, via Watling Street, while Mr Leechman thought he did, but did not. We besought the Count to take the right turning, but this he refused to do, fearing that by so doing, he might never see Toman again. So we 'hunted' him and 'hallowed,' but could not make him hear. Just beyond Braunston there is turn to the right, marked by a signpost to Rugby, and at this point the main road bears to the left. Consequently at the bend nothing was to be seen of the hunted one. Whether he had gone to the right or the left, we knew not, so we held a consultation, as our original intention had been to go via Watling Street to Wellington. Mr Leechman's error resulted in his finding a way on to the Roman road across country from a point near Braunston, while the Count and the writer plugged ahead to Coventry, proceeding through Allesley and Stonebridge to Castle Bromwich and Brownhills, where we again joined Watling Street. This is a really excel-

ABOVE **Laurin & Klement Motors managed by Toman.**

RIGHT **Young Count Alexander Kolowrat in the early days of his racing career on a Laurin & Klement BZN motorcycle.**

lent road for avoiding the Black Country, and we can thoroughly recommend it.

'Just beyond Castle Bromwich we stopped for a brief two minutes, just to stretch our limbs – the first halt after an excellent run of well over one hundred miles. Then, on arriving at Brownhills, we set to wondering what had become of our rivals. Near Cannock our gallant little engine showed signs of distress on the hills, the cause of which the driver was fully aware. Five minutes' halt served to fill the tank from the spare petrol tin, and fill the oil tank. Then off to the first petrol store, where we might fill up completely. This we found some few miles ahead, where we made enquiries as to the little red car, but with no result; either it had gone ahead unnoticed, or we were in front. Ah! should we ever see the gallant Toman again? With these thoughts in our minds, we started up the engine and bowled along to Shrewsbury, where we proposed to lunch. Beyond the stops for petrol, nothing had troubled us, and with the twin-cylinder engine pulling as well as ever we sped gaily along, the Count being in excellent spirits, in that an excellent average speed had been maintained, and the consumption had worked out to about thirty-two miles to the gallon. In Shrewsbury we stopped at the first respectable-looking hotel for lunch, only to be informed that nothing was ready, but a meal could be provided to order at half's hour notice. This naturally, did not suit. We wanted food badly, it is true, but should we ever see Toman again? Hardly had we decided to leave the inhospitable walls of this dead-alive inn, when – g-r-r-r-r! and the little red car, running as well as ever, came bowling up the steep hill. Before we were both seated, the Count was off, and ere we had reached the summit of the short, stiff rise he was back with the now 'conquered' Toman in his wake.

'Being directed to The Crown, we were in ten minutes busily engaged in devouring an excellent lunch. How excellent now, indeed, having bettered Toman's time by ten minutes. Mid-day at Shrewsbury, and 6.10 a.m. when we left London; hard to believe, it is true, but we did it, and beat the little red car, too. One hour and a half did we stay in Shrewsbury, and all that was done was to fill up with petrol and oil.

'In heavy rain, we set out on the last and most interesting section of our journey. Owing, however, probably to excess of oil, our engine started to misfire badly, but after a polite policeman had respectfully pointed out that our number plates were rather soiled and our law-abiding companion had carefully cleaned them, the car resumed its good behaviour, and ran like a clock to its journey's end. The other car did likewise, running with never a misfire, except, of course, for want of petrol, from beginning to end of the trip.

'We cannot remember having made a more delightful journey. Space forbids to say much respecting the good balancing of the engine, the ease of springs, and the reliability of the running of the two little Laurin-Klement cars, or of the gorgeous mountain scenery near Bettws-y-Coed and Capel Curig. But we conquered Toman, and arrived at Holyhead nine minutes before him, having ac-

complished the journey in 10h. 10m. running time – a truly splendid performance, considering the car was of ordinary standard type driven by an enthusiastic amateur. The Count obtained his wish, and to him great credit is due, but Toman's excellent performance is not to be neglected. In fact, in conclusion, we can only say that the run proved to be an eye-opener, and one on which the Laurin-Klement Motor Agency deserves the warmest congratulations'.

The young Austrian nobleman mentioned in *The Autocar* was to become the most successful and well-known Laurin & Klement racing driver and personality.

Count Alexander Kolowrat-Krakowský was a wealthy Austro-Hungarian aristocrat passionately fond of motoring, which he took up very much against the wishes of his parents. He was born in Glendale, New York on January 29th, 1886. His father Count Leopold had been banished to Cuba by the Emperor Francis Joseph for having killed Count Schönberg in a duel in Prague. In Cuba Count Leopold met and married the daughter of a

cigar manufacturer. Alexander was their son. The Kolowrat family, whose country seat was the castle Přimda in western Bohemia, was very much involved in automobile business. Count Leopold was one of the founders of the *Österreichische Automobil Club* in 1898 and drove the first private electric car in Vienna. The family owned shares in Laurin & Klement and in that way Alexander or Sascha, as he was known, became involved in its motor-sporting activities. Because his parents opposed his racing, Sascha often drove under the pseudonym Count Klatovský or Donald. As Count Klatovský he embarked on his racing career by entering motorcycling events as early as 1904 riding Laurin & Klement machines. After his father's death Sascha inherited the shares in Laurin & Klement and his considerable sporting successes materially assisted the company's export efforts.

Later Kolowrat also owned a glass factory in Harachov, Bohemia. A lucky meeting with Charles Pathé, the well-known pioneer of the French film industry, led Kolowrat to the cinematographic industry. He founded 'Sascha Filmstudios AG', which had its headquarters in Vienna. Although he first served in a motorized army unit in the war, Sascha then transferred to the press section, to film war-time action for the newsreels. After the war the Count made films that employed famous stars such as Marlene Dietrich. Kolowrat had grandiose ideas with his film company. He wanted even to rival Hollywood's monumental films thinking that they could be made better and cheaper than the American product.

In 1922 Kolowrat transformed the Laaer Berg in a Viennese suburb into a Hollywood studios replica and built enormous sets for 'Sodom and Gomorrah', a silent movie. Three thousand extras were employed and even more were used in some special scenes. To show the end of 'Sodom and Gomorrah', Kolowrat had the gigantic sets blown up to provide visual verisimilitude. The effects were quite amazingly dramatic but unfortunately a few extras were left seriously wounded, apparently some even died.

Sascha had a great personality and character, his only weakness being his overt superstition. When he raced in the 1913 Alpine Trial in his favourite Laurin & Klement, he carried a pet piglet on the back seat; at other times he had potatoes in his pockets for good luck!

Despite being chairman of a thriving film company, air ballooning and motor sport continued to hold his interest, which was mostly in car racing but also to a certain extent in car design. Kolowrat, as

ABOVE **Count Kolowrat celebrating ten years of his successful motor racing on two and four wheels.**

RIGHT **The legendary Alfred Neubauer in the 'Sascha' light car in the 1922 Targa Florio. Behind the '46' stands Ferdinand Porsche sporting a flat cap.**

an Austro-Daimler shareholder, knew Ferdinand Porsche who was a director of the company in 1922. Porsche had an idea to produce an easily affordable light car, realizing the economic need for a small vehicle. He and the Count put their heads together to design a new car, Kolowrat having had an experience of constructing a light 6/7 bhp cycle car in 1913. The Austro-Daimler company built excellent and large sporting cars before the First World War and ammunition during it. Now it was perceived that new vehicle designs were necessary. Eventually four cars were built – all called 'Sascha' – and Porsche and Kolowrat wanted to prove them in racing before the world.

These very light cars, powered by twin-cam 1,089 cc engines, were entered for the 1922 Targa Florio in Sicily. Three of the cars did very well, one handled by a driver destined to become a legend even in his lifetime – Alfred Neubauer, the famous racing chief of Mercedes Benz. Kolowrat blew his engine on the first lap. Sadly, for economic reasons, the Sascha light car project did not reach production stage. One car remains to this day in the Porsche Museum in Stuttgart.

Count Kolowrat married Countess Sonia Trubetzkoy in 1923, but they had no children. Kolowrat died in Vienna on December 4th, 1927.

In the early days of this century Laurin & Klement could not do without Kolowrat and his participation in motor car races was a foregone

conclusion. Klement was most anxious to do well in the forthcoming 1908 Gaillon speed hill-climb held against the clock as usual. This was the most prestigious and exciting event in France. Klement despatched Count Kolowrat there no less than fourteen days previously, complaining all the while how expensive that would be. Kolowrat and Franta Krutský, this time as his mechanic, eventually arrived there, after a certain amount of adventure. Klement, to save wear and tear on the FC racing car, had arranged for its transport by rail to Gaillon but the car did not arrive in time for the race. Kolowrat, after some hesitation was persuaded by Krutský to use the type F touring car in which they had arrived from Mladá Boleslav, Krutský arguing that the car had a non-standard higher powered engine. Krutský's confidence was justified, when Kolowrat won despite strong competition.

The night before the race Kolowrat and Krutský had transformed the dusty tourer into a 'racing' machine by stripping it totally, even the seats. They competed sitting on wooden tool boxes, which were attached to the chassis with wire and bolts. A problem arose on their return to base camp – their money had run out. The organizers paid only for their hotel and food and included no starting money or winner's purse. A guardian angel turned up in the shape of the man from the Speedolin lubricating oil manufacturer. 'If we can advertise your win on our oil, I can give you 500 francs'. Now

at least there was money for the return to Mladá Boleslav. The French journal *Les Sports* sponsored a race at Château Thierry immediately after Gaillon. The only Laurin & Klement entered won again and further Laurin & Klement victories followed, with P. von Satzger winning his class at La Turbie hill-climb.

In May 1909 the *Österreichische Automobil Club* held a reliability trial for light cars. The route went from Vienna via Trieste and Celovec then back to Vienna. Fourteen cars started out, of which twelve survived the difficult stage from Vienna to Trieste. In the second stage to Celovec there were difficult sections: one 14 km long, included an 18–20 per cent ascent which all the cars managed to overcome. In Vienna eleven motor cars finished and only Laurin & Klement managed to complete the course with a full team.

K. Kollarz was in a four-seater 14 bhp four cylinder type F, Kolowrat and Count Draskowich drove the two-seater versions.

A few days after this triumph, another followed in a hill-climb at Ries. The track measured 6 km and was lined along its full length with spectators. The famous Austrian factory Puch had two excellent cars in the race, a two-litre and a four-litre machine with both having a good chance of a win. Unfortunately they crashed, their remains littering the serpentine bends of Ries.

Laurin & Klement, in each of the categories they

entered, won every time. In the touring cars class up to 1.5 litres Hieronimus won in 6:12.40. In the 2 litre category Kolowrat gained the laurels with 8:11.60. In the 3 litre class Vokurka came first at 7:45.60 and in second place Hahn was six seconds slower. In the final class of up to 4 litres P. von Satzger won in a Laurin & Klement in 5:28.60 with this time breaking the standing record from the previous year. The Viennese newspaper, *Neues Wiener Tagblatt*, did not spare any praises: 'From industrial Bohemia the marque Laurin & Klement invaded the Ries. With this marque came Otto Hieronimus, Count Kolowrat with his chauffeur, Baron Hahn with his brother Otto, Mr Vokurka, Mr Friedrich and Mr Wetzka. It was a singularly excellent team which continued the winning campaign of Laurin & Klement cars, having taken four first prizes and one second prize in the green Styria... And it did not have to prepare for this race that well. The team took its old cars, with which it won so many battles last year, it adjusted the valves, put on new tyres and drove off to the battlefield. It could be said that the sign of victory is directly engraved into the Laurin & Klement marque'.

One of the most significant European touring car reliability trials was the Prince Henry Tour of 1909. In this *Prinz-Heinrich-Fahrt*, which the Germans founded to compete with the prestigious

French Grand Prix, Count Kolowrat finished second overall against powerful opponents. All cars had to carry a full complement of passengers. The length of the event extended to 1,842 km, from Berlin via Breslau over the high Tatra Mountains to Budapest, from there via Vienna, Linz, Salzburg to Munich – a truly international affair. In the first stage, at Guben, a speed trial was inserted. At the start in Berlin, 109 cars competed of which 103 got through the speed trial. Great consternation resulted when Kolowrat went through the trial in 3 minutes 10.2 seconds against the expected time of 5 minutes 3.5 seconds. This feat was a sensation because Kolowrat, in his light Laurin & Klement, defeated all the other machines of well-known marques and a variety of engine power.

In the Semmering hill-climb four Laurin & Klement cars competed in two classes, two cars won and two gained second prizes. Great interest was provided in the first category which included the light cars of up to 16 bhp. The class became a duel between the German and Austro-Hungarian marques. The Germans sent Mercedes, Opel, Adler and Oryx, which stood against Laurin & Klement and Puch representing the Empire. Hieronimus won in 9:3.4 and Kolowrat came second taking 9:14. Only the third place was conceded to Salzer in Mercedes and fourth was Lumer on Puch. In the 86 mm class Laurin & Klement automobiles had no serious opponents. Hieronimus and Wetzka fought a masterful battle, eventually a record in this category was reached by Hieronimus in 8:12.2 with Wetzka in second place.

Kolowrat's stripped type F touring car at the start of the 1908 Gaillon hill-climb. In this race Kolowrat drove under the pseudonym 'Donald'.

4 *The growth and progress of Laurin & Klement*

AFTER 1907 Laurin & Klement concentrated on the development of series production. Previously, cars had been built to the individual specifications of a single buyer, or at best in a small series of ten. It was now clear that the way forward was to follow the example set by manufacturers in the United States, where the motor vehicle was fast becoming indispensable in easing the transport problems posed by that country's enormous size. Countries in Europe, on the other hand, had efficient rail networks and consequently the European motorist only used his car for representative and sporting purposes or to demonstrate his wealth and place in society.

The development of heavy industry in the United States brought about an undreamed expansion in car manufacturing. This expansion will always be linked to the name of Henry Ford, whose model T, introduced in 1908, flooded world markets. Until 1927 over 15 million 'Tin-Lizzies' had left the Ford production line. Ford had developed the conveyor belt production system and it was now the manufacturers' turn to dictate what the customer could have. However, it was only the largest producers who could afford to follow Ford's example. In 1910 there were still 263 U.S. manufacturers of which thirty per cent made less than 75 cars a year. In the same year Ford made 34,858 units.

It was around 1910 that the European situation began to crystallize. The many hundred manufacturers became fewer. They either simply failed to remain competitive or merged with other companies. As a consequence of this consolidation, car producers were no longer considered as eccentrics, creating sophisticated toys for the rich, but became focal points of interest and investment. As a result they had to become more rational in production, marketing and publicity.

Klement, now the managing director of a major joint stock company and responsible to his board and shareholders had instinctively aimed towards these ends himself. He felt that mass production, as pioneered by Ford, could open up huge markets in Europe and the rest of the world. At that time he wrote: 'Although Austro-Hungarian production and sales increase satisfactorily, we must not be over confident in the future. Information gathered on the other side of the Atlantic is such that it must cause grave concern in all European plants. I believe, therefore, that other steps need to be taken to oppose the American danger. I propose a project which I have had in my mind for a long time and which you must have also considered. . . It is a well-known fact that specialized component manufacturers can produce cheaper than those works which make all the components themselves. But there are certain elements that no car factory can produce unless it increases the price of its own products. Therefore these must be bought from specialist manufacturers. This is very expensive in the long run, in import duty and freight costs. My idea aims to unite the Austro-Hungarian car makers with a view to found joint factories for cylinder casting in aluminium, bronze and steel, to make radiators, ball bearings, bodies, etc. These specialist factories would belong to all the vehicle makers and their profits would be distributed relative to the value of the products taken. The specialists would not be limited in their activities; they could also work for other car producers, thus their profitability might be considerable. . . We must be clear on this. The

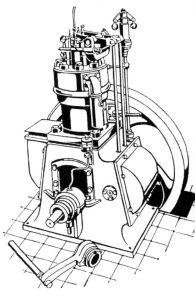

watchword is series production, no factory can be profitable unless it produces one hundred big motor cars or five hundred small ones'.

But Klement's efforts to unite the local manufacturers were unacceptable to the others. This was probably due to the fact that his ideas were a little too advanced and the benefits of such methods were beyond their understanding at that time.

In 1909 came further expansion at Laurin & Klement. Because of the very high fixed costs of production and the seasonal nature of motor car purchases, the company diversified into the manufacture of Brons stationary engines to be made under licence bought in Holland. These engines were favoured before the First World War and operated on a principle similar to the diesel engine. A number were made in Mladá Boleslav, from 4 to 32 bhp, and became very popular in small workshops and factories, as electric power was not universally available then. The Brons engine business grew to be so successful that a special building was needed to house the assembly plant.

The Car of April 14th, 1909 carried a very full one-and-a-half page description of a new Laurin & Klement 10–12 bhp model (type G) and it mentioned that 'Hieronimus, whose name is so well known in the continental racing circles, is responsible for the design of Laurin and Klement cars'. The journal continued that 'the four-seater cost £300 and the two-seater £280 complete; the 10–12 hp Laurin and Klement car as regards its initial cost as well as expense of maintenance, may be classed among those suitable for the man of moderate means'. The comment went on that it was a small four-cylinder cast en bloc, with a bore of 75 mm and a stroke of 88 mm and had Eisemann high

ABOVE LEFT **The 1908 type BS coupé with acetylene lighting and unusual windscreen.**

ABOVE RIGHT **The Brons stationary engine.**

RIGHT **The 1909 type L four-seater.**

BELOW RIGHT **The type L chassis layout.**

tension magneto ignition; a single camshaft operated both sets of valves, there were the usual compression taps, the cylinder head was non-detachable, access to the valves was obtained through caps into which the spark plugs were screwed. Most surprising was the absence of a throttle pedal, power being controlled by way of a lever on the steering wheel, the ignition control was also there. Forced lubrication occurred via a pump driven from the camshaft end and circulated through sight feeds on the dash. A cone clutch and four-speed gearbox fed power to an open double jointed prop-shaft with effective lubrication to the pot-type joints. The article concluded that 'the general finish is to be highly commended'.

New for the year 1909 was the type EN, meant to satisfy customers requiring a luxury touring vehicle. It was developed from the model E, the four cylinder engine was still cast in two blocks with 110 mm bore by 150 mm stroke giving 5,702 cc. The type EN carried a variety of bodies, all with luxury equipment. Another popular, but less expensive type, the L, was a four cylinder car of 25 bhp, available with factory made bodies, from two-seaters to six-seater limousines, the chassis length being determined by the body fitted.

Only five years after the first motor car was made

in Mladá Boleslav, Laurin & Klement products were to be found in all parts of the world, indicating the great marketing and managerial skills of the Czech directors. The increasing output and sales inevitably resulted in the enlargement of the works which continued in 1910. The most successful area of production was the export of motor cars to Russia. Two additional agencies were added, St Petersburg and Kiev. The other European states importing Laurin & Klement automobiles were Italy, Serbia, Germany, Great Britain and France and buyers could also be found as far as Egypt, Argentine, Mexico, Australia and New Zealand. Trade with Japan also flourished, with the Japanese imperial army placing orders for a number of Laurin & Klement trucks.

One of the trucks, the DL type, was made from 1909. It was fitted with a four cylinder engine of 4,503 cc providing 25 bhp at 900 rpm. Ignition was by magneto, cooling was looked after by a finned radiator assisted by a water pump and fan. A four speed gearbox and cone clutch transmitted engine power to a cross-shaft with a differential and to a chain driven rear axle. Either solid rubber or iron tyres could be supplied according to customer requirements. A speed of 16 kph could be achieved on the solid rubber tyres, but only 12 kph on the iron ones. The chassis weighed 2,400 kg for the 2 tonner version and 100 kg more for the 3 tonne truck. If required the customer could have larger carrying platforms fitted and special bodies, for instance, for delivering beer barrels were available. When towing a trailer which carried another two tonnes the DL type could only be used on level

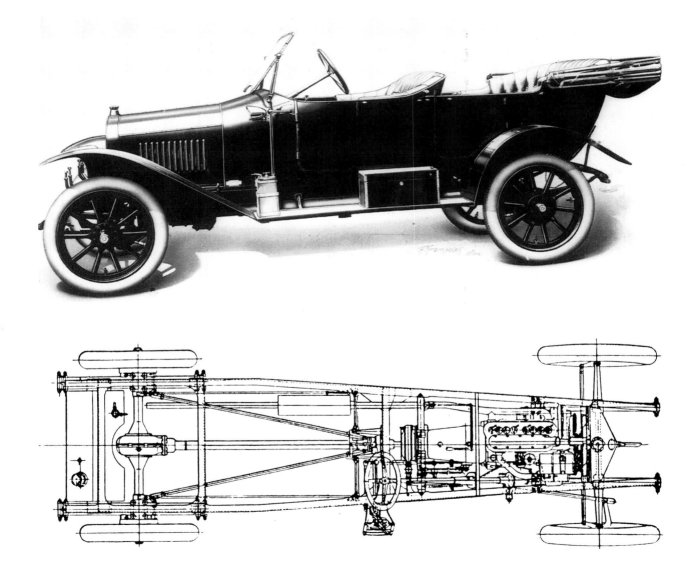

ABOVE **The 1910 type FN touring car with 'Auster' type rear screen.**

BELOW **One of the Laurin & Klement St Petersburg taxis, type GDV.**

ABOVE **The 1911 type S town car with unusual roof arrangement and electric lighting.**

BELOW **Type Sc roadster with a form of 'Stepney' type spare wheel.**

roads because engine power was barely sufficient to overcome a 5 per cent gradient.

The passenger car type F range was extended by the model FN which had a stronger 18 bhp engine, having the stroke increased to 120 mm and consequently the cylinder capacity to 2,660 cc. From the EN type derived the luxury ENS version. Again the power of the engine was enlarged to 60 bhp but this time with larger bore of 125 mm.

With the exception of the Alpine Trial Laurin & Klement cars did not participate in any other sporting events in 1910. This was not the result of fear of competition. On the contrary. In the previous year it was proven that in given categories Laurin & Klement motor cars had no serious contender in racing. At the same time the factory was deluged with orders to such an extent that shift work had to be introduced. From that point of view participation in racing only disrupted production and diluted resources without bringing any significant gains.

The Alpine Trial of 1910 proved the Laurin & Klement supremacy when Kolowrat, Draskowich and Hieronimus finished the course without penalty points, bringing new medals and trophies to Mladá Boleslav.

In 1911, Laurin & Klement concentrated on larger series and fewer automobile types with production amounting to 800 cars, 300 motorcycles and 268 Brons stationary engines. Demand was so high that deliveries could only be maintained by continued night shifts. Again considerable numbers went for export all over the world. Russia alone took 30 per cent of its products. Hieronimus shared the views of Klement that series production, rather than the building of individual cars to the wishes of customers, pointed the way ahead. His design imprint was particularly seen on the small type G. Its derivation, the type GDV, was the much exported taxi model and further variations, for standard use followed the types GDVT, GDVC and GDVR. The big automobiles EN and ENS were still made but only in small numbers. The A, B, C, E, and F models were gradually being phased out with the reduction of the stock of components. The last Laurin & Klement motorcycles were made in that year.

A new model, the K type appeared in 1911, the last year that Hieronimus led engineering design in Mladá Boleslav. The K had a four cylinder side valve engine of 95x150 mm bore and stroke, producing 32 bhp. It came open bodied or as a three-seater with one door called 'spider' or 3 door sports model with folding 'American' roof. The maximum speed was 80 kph. Then came the S type, a

technically interesting and later commercially viable product. It was made with detail modification and improvements until 1925. Initially the S had a 1,770 cc engine rated at 14 bhp. It differed from previous models by having its flywheel positioned at the front of the engine and the multiplate clutch and gearbox all in the same block. The whole arrangement was appealing due to its clearly thought-out detailing. To distinguish the future model variants, the type name S received additional small letters of the alphabet such as Sa, Sb, Sc up to Sp. The model S was preceded by a prototype bearing the same designation which had a flat twin 1,520 cc engine. No series production followed.

In 1911 negotiations started to take over the RAF (Reichenberger Automobil Fabrik) company, a northern Bohemian motor car manufacturer. Count Kolowrat was involved and much concerned in the takeover. RAF produced luxury motor cars as well as omnibuses and flat-bed trucks with short chassis and engines fitted below the driver's seat. Without doubt the RAF company's attitude to manufacture was instrumental in the takeover, because its high prices made its products increasingly uncompetitive; thus Laurin & Klement came, in a certain sense, to RAF's rescue.

1911 was also the year that Hieronimus left Laurin & Klement to work on aero-engines, but remained in the role of consultant, a fact Laurin & Klement proclaimed in its advertisements for such was his reputation. He also continued racing Laurin & Klement automobiles trusting implicitly in their unfailing performance.

In the same year a small series of ten petrol engined road rollers was produced, yet another vehicle destined for success at home and abroad. The rollers were of a light type, called VB. This was the British connection. The old established Ruston works had an agency in Prague and collaborated with Laurin & Klement on the VB project.

It was about this time that Laurin & Klement renewed its interest in sporting activity. It began with a then famous hill-climb in Opcina near Trieste where seven Laurin & Klement cars took part. All finished, Hieronimus making the fastest time of the day. This was a particularly important event for the factory because it provided points for the special industry trophy donated by Prince Erich von Thurn-Taxis and organized by the Österreichische Automobil Club from 1909 onward. This prize was aimed at car manufacturers in particular and Laurin & Klement set great hopes on the trophy right from the start. Winning became almost

certain with the success at Opcina. More medals came in the 1911 Alpine Trial, Laurin & Klement cars having for five years finished this very difficult trial without incurring penalty points.

Then the Russians organized a really tough event from St Petersburg to Sebastopol, 1,600 km on roads, 700 km on unmade tracks and the steppe. There were 57 cars at the start on September 22nd and only 25 finished without penalty points. Six Laurin & Klement K and S types competed. In the third class of 21 competitors Laurin & Klement won, and in the fourth class, Mladá Boleslav had another winner among the 16 runners.

After the St Petersburg to Sebastopol race Kolowrat won the *Coupe de Caucase* outright, beating fifty other participants. Another Laurin & Klement car driven by Knirsch was second and Doring finished fourth. To accommodate all these trophies, and the *Coupe de Caucase* trophy, being an enormous silver dish engraved with the Tsar's insignia, Klement had to order further showcases.

In the French Gaillon hill-climb Comanos, an Egyptian driver in the Laurin & Klement type FCR notched up another success in October 1911 by winning his class, the sixth category in 40 4/5 seconds, at the same time taking first position overall in the touring car section, beating Hispano-Suiza, Mors, Bugatti and others amongst the 45 cars of world famous marques making up the ten classes.

Also in 1911 engineer I.Rezler from Laurin & Klement constructed a special high-revving engine (3,500 to 4,000 rpm). The motor designated as type SR was installed in a special racing car in which Kolowrat won a first place in the Opava – Ostrava race in Moravia.

Hieronimus in the type K competing in the 1911 St Petersburg-Sebastopol long distance event.

1912 brought further expansion, increased production facilities and modernized plant and a new administration building was also erected. At the same time a gradual change began to occur as in other major European car makers. Manufacture aimed at more rational production meant concentrating on fewer but more successful models, made in larger series. Customers were slowly becoming used to the idea that the 'tailored' system was disappearing and their order had to be for a specific chassis of a certain type which was currently in production. It was of course still customary to choose a particular body type and equipment. J.O.Jech, V.Brožík and other local coach-builders bodied the chassis as required, although in the cheaper car ranges the Americans and some Europeans also propagated a degree of standardization of coachwork.

In 1912 came no marked changes in vehicle types, some of which had, bar certain detail improvements, been in production for five or six years. Main improvements meant quieter and easier running, make-and-break ignition was replaced by high tension magneto or coil ignition and the use of surface carburettors was discontinued. Acetylene lighting began to be changed for electric systems, even though the customer was charged for these 'extras'.

The production in Mladá Boleslav concentrated now on the types GDV, K and S and their derivatives Ka, Kb and Sa, Sb and Sc. The new type DN with a four cylinder 25 bhp engine was developed and eventually replaced the successful but out-

ABOVE **Comanos, the winner at the 1911 Gaillon hill-climb, in the type FCR.**

RIGHT **The 1913 type M with unusual coupé body and acetylene lighting.**

dated type GDV. The DN was in production for only two years.

Between 1909, the start of the Thurn-Taxis competition, and 1912 the factory had gathered nine main prizes and 24 points. The prize of 10,000 Austrian crowns and the well earned trophy was reluctantly awarded to Laurin & Klement by the *Österreichische Automobil Club*. Laurin & Klement, now the largest automobile producer in the Austro-Hungarian Empire had proven its lead in the quality and high engineering side of its products.

In 1912 Laurin & Klement repeated its successes in Russia at Simferopol, gaining first prize in the third category and snatching first and second places in the 100 km event organized by the Russian Automobile Club. In the Alpine Trial of 1912 Hieronimus, Kolowrat and Draskowich in Ka types again competed successfully. In October a 2,137 km long distance trial to San Sebastian took place. The route went via Linz, Munich, Strasbourg, Nancy, Dijon, Lyon, Clermont-Ferrand and Bordeaux. Kolowrat, on a fully loaded small type S, was positioned fourth overall out of 65 competitors.

The type M of 1913 had a four cylinder of 3,817 cc capacity with 40 bhp mostly bodied as a tourer. It became a base model for the subsequent variations MO of 50 bhp and MK with a Knight engine. The type M in sales brochures was designated as the M15/40 HP. Before 1925 the power of motor cars was expressed in fractions. The first figure gave the nominal, calculated power and the second number the actual effective performance of horse power measured on the brake. From 1913 a new tax formula was devised and the first number was based on so called 'horse power tax'. This was calculated for four stroke engines using a coefficient of 0.3 multiplied by number of cylinders, the stroke in metres and the bore squared in centimetres; in our case $0.3 \times 4 \times 0.15 \times 81 = 14.58$.

More important events followed in 1913. The Mladá Boleslav works finally took over the RAF company after two years of negotiations, an interesting move because RAF had originally been set up to compete with Laurin & Klement. This takeover brought Laurin & Klement not only RAF's fine reputation for well-engineered cars, but also its licence for the manufacture of the Knight sleeve-valve engine.

RAF had bought the licence to produce the Knight engines, renowned for their quiet running. In England these engines were very much in favour, being used by Daimler and other companies and fitted to big, heavy-bodied luxury limousines. John Henry Knight's sleeve-valve engine was so successful that Weymann & Hitchcock and the Engine Company of Cheltenham, the owners of Knight's patent sold the licence for its manufacture almost eight hundred times! The qualities of the Knight engine provided additional prestige to Laurin & Klement.

One could always tell a Knight-engined car, it ran without the customary camshaft clatter and the noise produced by the poppet valve operation. On the other hand it left behind a faint blue cloud as sleeve valves needed additional oil lubrication, the burning of which was visible.

At first Laurin & Klement continued to manufacture RAF's range and maintained its insignia. During the latter part of 1913, however, some of the original models were modified and sold as Laurin & Klement products – all this concerned the Knight-engined models.

As an experiment Laurin & Klement had already produced a prototype with a Knight engine in 1911 as a variation of the model L. The LK, of which only one or two were made, had a 4,084 cc engine of 25 bhp.

Laurin & Klement now used the Knight engine in the 3.3 litre type MK of 40 bhp and type RK of 50 bhp which was a modified type taken over from RAF. The type MK of 1913 had four cylinders cast in blocks of two, the shaft operating the sleeve valves which were driven by a wide chain at the engine's front. The crankshaft ran in five bearings

and there was magneto plus battery ignition. A gear pump ensured oil circulation, a sizeable fan plus a robust radiator looked after cooling. A Zenith carburettor with pre-heating of the mixture gave a rev range between 200 and 1,800 rpm. The U-shaped pressed steel chassis carried exceptionally wide and long leaf springs. The rigid front axle was forged from strong steel and the king pins ran in ball bearings. A multi-plate clutch and a four speed and reverse gearbox with direct drive on fourth led to a worm-drive rear axle, well protected from dirt.

Interestingly, there were three independent brakes. The two on the transmission were operated by the pedal, while the handbrake worked the rear drums. To stop running back, the driver could engage a safety ratchet and pawl working on the transmission brake. An air pressure pump transferred fuel from the rear tank.

Yet another feature of interest consisted of an automatic air pump built into the transmission for tyre inflation and this was standard equipment. At extra cost Laurin & Klement supplied electric lighting with an accumulator and dynamo, the latter driven by silent chain. Several body styles were made from 1913 until 1925; 904 vehicles were manufactured in that period.

After a preparation period of three years, which

ABOVE LEFT **Laurin & Klement advertisement, 1913.**

ABOVE **The Excelsior plough.**

RIGHT **The 1913 type Sd of 20 bhp advertisement pointing out car as well as body manufacture. The nickname 'Eska' was officially adopted but changed to 'Elka' for these models.**

involved cooperation with the firm R. Bächer of Roudnice, a motorized plough was put on the market under the name of Excelsior, type P4. For its time it was an unusually large piece of equipment with six plough shares. A three-wheeled chassis with an 80 bhp engine had two driven rear wheels, and a small front one which was used for steering. The P4 became very popular, even more so than the agricultural tractors which had also made their appearance then. The Excelsiors were not by any means cheap, costing 29,500 crowns in comparison to the luxury bodied Laurin & Klement ENS automobile which cost 17,100 crowns.

The years 1913 and 1914 provided concrete evidence of the increasing rationalization of production in response to the increasing threat of an American car invasion of Europe. Competitive European automobile makers started to defend themselves or, if possible, counter attacked. There was no chance to manufacture in American numbers, but it became of paramount interest to make rational numbers of small, cheap vehicles which would better suit national requirements.

To show the world-wide exporting abilities of Laurin & Klement, contemporary photographs depict a car being unloaded at a Japanese dock destined for Prince Higashi Fushimi, another saloon on the type S chassis in London, an L type on Place de la Concorde in Paris and a voiturette in New Zealand.

It would seem that the Mladá Boleslav designers really hit the jackpot with the S type. The market for this inexpensive, light, yet fast and well-built machine kept on growing and more production series were laid down. Originally with a stroke of 115 mm, it was increased to 120 mm in later series and the power lifted from 14 to 20 bhp. More type S (nicknamed 'Eska') cars were made in 1913 than

any of the other models. In 1914 for the series Sh and Sk the bore was increased from 70 to 74 mm and consequently the bhp rose to 24.

A new vehicle, the type T, was shown in the spring 1914. It was a small car, but both the public and the experts took note of it. Although only a small four cylinder of 1,198 cc with a mere 12 bhp, it achieved a speed of 60 kph and due to its light weight had sufficient acceleration and hill-climbing ability. The basic idea was to produce it in one type only but in large numbers, enabling the T to be sold at a record-breaking low price. It was intended to be the means of maintaining Laurin & Klement's recently attained leadership position as the largest automotive producer of vehicles produced in the Empire. Sadly the rapidly developing political problems soon put paid to these commendable ambitions.

1914 brought a new commercial vehicle, the MS, able to carry loads of 2,000 kg. It could also be fitted with omnibus bodies and many were exported to the postal authorities of Serbia. The rise of Laurin & Klement did not stop until the First World War, for apart from Russia, Austria-Hungary and other central European states, one could find the L & K marque represented in Amsterdam, London, Buenos Aires, Cairo, Rio de Janeiro and in Yokohama. It was at this time that production of the Brons engines was reduced. The general spread of electrification meant a reduction in demand for stationary engines. This made room in production capacity for the manufacture of road rollers and ploughs which became more and more in demand.

Sporting participation lessened during 1913 because reorganization of the works had to have priority and Laurin & Klement's excellent reputation was such that this way of advertising no longer much mattered. However, our trio of racing drivers, Kolowrat, Hieronimus and Draskowich were not happy with this non-participation policy and decided to enter the Tatra-Adria Rally privately. This reliability trial was organized by the

Österreichische Automobil Club. At the start the Laurin & Klement drivers were joined by Dr Julius Wermes in another L&K car. The route was 2,178 km long, which Kolowrat completed without any penalty points and collected a gold medal and a trophy in the competition. The bronze medal went to Dr Wermes and Draskowich this time had to be satisfied only with a diploma due to a burst tyre close to the finish.

An Austrian motor-journalist A. Schmal-Filius wrote about Count Pavel Draskowich in the *Neues Wiener Tagblatt*: 'In front of us drove Draskowich, who was also without any penalty points, similarly to us. Kolowrat drove up beside his friend and offered that they should enter Pest together... However, a few minutes later Draskowich burst a tyre... This really was bad luck because he only had 23 minutes remaining out of the allocated repair time of 60 minutes and not having a spare wheel, he had to change the inner tube – for that sort of job 23 minutes is simply not enough... We saw Draskowich and his mechanic put themselves to work in a great hurry. Ten kilometres before Pest our column of cars stopped in a shaded spot. We were very interested to see if Draskowich could make it within 23 minutes. The time passed and the grey Laurin & Klement was not in sight... Terrible luck, when one has been driving a car for seven days without a penalty point – and then to lose a tyre when the finishing post is almost in sight'.

In the same magazine appeared an interview with Count Kolowrat: 'The Tatra-Adria Rally suited me very well because it became an excellent training ground for the Alpine Trial. The car which I drove was an old one, the Alpine one, from the previous year, and because it endured this long rally, it gives me confidence that with this reliable motor car I can again participate in this year's Trial'.

The 1913 Alpine Trial was one of the most difficult. The route measured 2,667 km and was extended into seven stages, with one rest day. Again this event was entered privately without the official support of Mladá Boleslav. Out of the 43 cars starting, 31 completed the route and only 9 finished without penalty points. The greatest attention was paid to Hieronimus' driving effort, who was racing in a car entered for the touring trophy prize. Laurin & Klement had been successful in this competition in the previous year and considering that the prize was being given away under the condition of three annual consecutive victories Laurin & Klement were close to winning the trophy. However, Hieronimus drove his car without

V ALPSKÉ JÍZDĚ

1910 ✶ 1911 ✶ 1912 ✶ 1913

tedy

čtyři roky za sebou

dobyl

VŮZ LAURIN & KLEMENT

vždy prvého místa.

Four victories in a row for Laurin & Klement in the Alpine Trials of 1910 to 1913.

penalty points and received a silver plaque. Kolow-rat and Draskowich were honoured with bronze ones.

Yet 1914 seemed to reverse the tendency of the previous year, with renewed sporting appearances to advertise Laurin & Klement's newest products. In the Polish Reliability Trial, 1,215 km long, organized by the Warsaw Automobile Club, Ing. Heyne in a K type gained first place. He managed the whole route without a single penalty point and in the speed trial, which was incorporated into the event, Heyne won again beating the French Dela-haye into the second place. The other well-known marques defeated in this competition included Hupmobile, Panhard-Levassor, Peugeot, Nagant and Stoewer.

Count Kolowrat gained absolute victory in the Carpathian Trial in a type M. This trial of 2,500 km was very arduous, comprising steep and stony mountain roads. The organizers decided that apart from penalty points, bonus points would be given

to avoid the possibility of having to award several first prizes. Kolowrat gained so many points that he was proclaimed the undisputed victor.

In the Zirlerberg hill-climb, which was 5.2 km long with an average climb of ten per cent and maximum of 21.5 per cent, J.Bayer in a Laurin & Klement won in 10.05 min. In second place was Baroness Handel-Mazettio in another Laurin & Klement. Third was Hozer, again in a Bohemian made car. Only touring cars occupied by at least two persons could participate in this difficult hill-climb.

In the Alpine Trial of 1914 Laurin & Klement celebrated its greatest victory when Kolowrat received the touring trophy after five years of success-ive wins. 75 cars participated in this event but after the 2,932 km trial only 19 remained without penalty points. The Czech daily press commented: 'Five years without a penalty point scrambling along Alpine roads, to overcome the steepest ascents is not only the mark of a good car, but also proof that the production of vehicles is ac-complished, that the designers of the Laurin &

Klement factory are constantly at work, that the tooling equipment of the company is modern, that first class materials are chosen... Only this secures that kind of success over the whole series.

'The Laurin & Klement factory today is not only the largest automobile producer in the whole of Austria-Hungary, but also the most effective promoter of respect for our automobile industry as it is the only local marque which has won the touring trophy! The significant part in this success, next to the excellent characteristics of the car itself, is its driver Count Alexander Kolowrat, a real sportsman – courageous, enthusiastic, tough and prepared to go to the limit of human strength'.

Das Neues Wiener Tagblatt also enthused: 'For the large Mladá Boleslav factory to gain the touring trophy is a triumph. Laurin & Klement is the only Austro-Hungarian firm which has managed to compete on a par for this difficult prize. In the last three years of the Alpine Trial the Laurin & Klement cars were always without penalty points. And much more, two years before the announcement of the Alpine touring trophy, in the Alpine Trials of lesser complexity in the years 1910 and 1911, the Laurin & Klement marque was even then without penalty points.

'The Laurin & Klement firm with its successes in the Alpine Trial and its capture of the Alpine touring trophy proved not just for the first time – and surely not for the last time – that its vehicles are of the highest standard and can cope with the heaviest demands'.

Many other medals and trophies were brought back to Mladá Boleslav, perhaps one of the most important being the gold medal given by the town of Palermo for a sixth place gained by a type S in the dangerous Targa Florio race in Sicily. But this triumph and Kolowrat's Alpine Trial trophy marked the end of one competitive era. In Sarajevo, on June 28th young Gavrilo Princip shot the heir apparent to the Austro-Hungarian crown, the Archduke Franz Ferdinand (who was riding in a Gräf und Stift automobile) and Europe exploded into the terrible tragedy of the First World War.

Kolowrat wins the 1914 Carpathian Trial on type M.

5 The end of the Empire

THE OUTBREAK OF hostilities between the European nations in 1914, with Germany and Austria-Hungary on one side, Russia with its allies on the other, brought about a change of fortune for the Laurin & Klement company. The firm had experienced phenomenal growth in the twenty years since its inception. Everything indicated that with the planned enlarged production programme automobile manufacture would be even more successful. However, the war put a stop to all the justifiable hopes for the future and left the factory's directors with the stark reality of a war-time situation and all the problems associated with it.

Employment of the workers was not affected when the factory was ordered to start the manufacture of ammunition, but all the other technical research and development had to cease. Manufacturing ammunition had one benefit for the workers in that they were not required to be called up into service with the Austro-Hungarian army.

Soon after the outbreak of hostilities the future of the company was put in further jeopardy. Before the war a number of Czechs had worked in Laurin & Klement factory branches, workshops and agencies in Russia. 25 out of 36 employees, led by their director L.Tuček, volunteered for the Czech Legion during the first days of the conflict. The action of the Czech workers in Russia did not stay secret for long and as a consequence the Austro-Hungarian ministry of war decided to take the Laurin & Klement company under its own jurisdiction, on the basis that its workers appeared to be siding with the enemy. The directors of Laurin & Klement put up an enormous fight to prevent the ministry from taking over. After numerous discussions and appeals the threat of disaster was finally averted but the factory was nevertheless under military supervision throughout the war. Automobile production for civilian use almost ceased. Most of the vehicles manufactured between 1914–1918 in Mladá Boleslav were intended for the Austro-Hungarian army and models for passenger use were adapted for military purposes. In 1914 Laurin & Klement made 482 motorized vehicles which included ploughs and stationary engines.

The most numerous passenger car was the small model S of which 250 were made. In 1916 production decreased to only 384 units. This consisted of passenger types L, M, MK, OK, S and Sil; MS trucks and a small number of FO and MS omnibuses. On the chassis types O and M, Laurin & Klement mounted bodies for military ambulances. The production of MS trucks was increased and most were supplied to the army.

The only innovation was the use of four cylinder Knight sleeve-valve engines built into the former type O. The new model marking was changed accordingly to the OK type and sold for 18,150 crowns. This four cylinder car provided maximum power at 1,900 rpm. It had magneto ignition and water pump and ventilator cooling. The friction clutch transmitted power via a four-speed and reverse gearbox to the rear axle. Steering was by worm and sector. A conventional braking system worked on the transmission and rear drums. Acetylene lighting was provided including a lamp for the rear which also illuminated the number plate. 65 to

32 bhp Excelsior three share motor plough advertisement from 1918, just after the formation of the new republic.

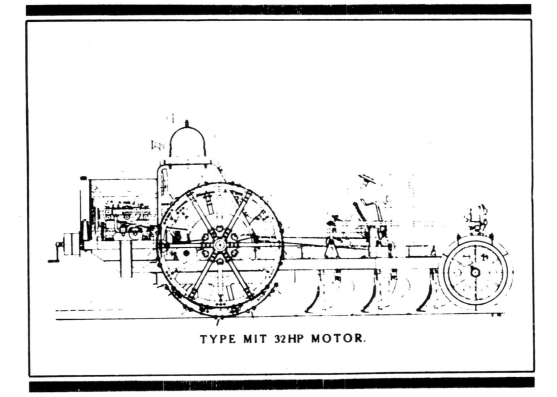

70 kph was the usual speed.

More successful than automobile production were the associated manufacturing processes in which the Empire was obviously more interested at that time – the armaments. The manufacture of stationary Brons engines practically ended in 1914 but orders for motorized road rollers and ploughs increased. The number of employees went up to 1,715, out of which 1,569 were manual workers. The main reason for the increase in labour was the continued demand for armament supplies rather than other products and that resulted in the decline of automobile manufacture. However, at least the demand for the motorized ploughs kept the automobile section in Mladá Boleslav in business.

There were not sufficient numbers of automobiles, trucks or even aeroplanes in the Austro-Hungarian army to cause a large shortage of fuel during the war. On the other hand agriculture was visibly affected by the reduced availability of shire horses, because the majority of the strong and healthy animals were requisitioned for the army. The situation on the farms was aggravated further by the army's requirement for compulsory supplies of fodder. The ministries tried to resolve these problems by supporting the introduction of motorized ploughs into agriculture. During the war came an organisational change in the way the ploughs were manufactured. The original firm, R.Bächer (now owned by Laurin & Klement), was renamed the Excelsior Factory for Motorized Ploughs after the departure of Mr Bächer. Bächer's forerunner, the six-share plough type P4 was too large and expensive for day to day use. Therefore a new model was developed. The new P5 type had only three plough shares. This plough was driven by a four cylinder 4,710 cc engine of 40 bhp. At the same

Type MK touring limousine.

time, within the framework of the military production, a large series of type 2TG engines were built which were intended to be fitted into Italian Fiat trucks. Motorized rope winches for observation air balloons were constructed for the army and factory-marked as types BW.

The Austro-Hungarian War Ministry continued to demand more and more ammunition, mainly 8 and 10 cm grenades. It became necessary to consider broadening the base of the special machine tool shop in Mladá Boleslav, but because it was not possible to obtain the specialist machines needed, director and engineer Rezler, together with engineers Samek and Řezníček, decided to design and construct their own. By the end of the war over 160 heavy machine tools were built at the Laurin & Klement works.

As automobile production was still restricted during that time, production continued to be reorganized for other purposes. The under-utilized capacity of the body shop was busy with military orders. The upholstery department made harness and the joinery section constructed military sledges. The manufacture of cars in the Reichenberg Automobil Fabrik, taken over by Laurin & Klement in 1913, was closed down at the beginning of the war and the tools, machinery and materials were moved to Mladá Boleslav. In 1916 the RAF buildings and other property of this famous marque were sold to a textile company also based in Liberec, marking the end of one of the pioneer automobile factories in Europe.

During the latter part of the war production in the Laurin & Klement factory began to suffer from a shortage of fuel supplies. Coal for steam power plants was running short, and its price constantly fluctuated. In the end the factory management decided to build its own power plant in order to supply all the energy requirements of the works. When the new station was completed in 1918 Laurin & Klement managed to supply almost all the electricity needed for production purposes.

At the end of the war in 1918 the besieged national economy was close to exhaustion and collapse. However, the orders for Laurin & Klement products did not diminish: on the contrary, they increased, but actual production was limited due to fuel shortages and lack of raw materials. Manufacturing was also adversely affected by disrupted imports of important production parts, including tyres and ignition components.

6 *The new republic*

LAURIN & KLEMENT'S struggle for survival was compounded by the total upheaval that was taking place in Europe. New national boundaries were being drawn and new states were being established. One such new republic, which arose from the dismembered and defeated Austro-Hungarian Empire, was Czechoslovakia. The aftermath of the 'war to end all wars' brought the most fundamental changes to the face of Europe.

However, the new republic of Czechoslovakia enjoyed several distinct advantages from the outset. It was democratic, and because there had been no indigenous Czech ruling class, a new elite had to be recruited from among the bourgeoisie and the workers. Its 13.6 million inhabitants represented one quarter of the former Empire's population and occupied one fifth of its area. At the same time the Czechs had on their territory two thirds of the former Empire's industry concentrated in Bohemia and Moravia rather than in the agricultural regions of Slovakia and Ruthenia.

Apart from several large industrial concerns like Škodovy závody, Ringhoffer, Českomoravská-Kolben, Tatra wagon works, Moser glass works, Kladno and Ostrava steelworks and mines, the most distinctive feature of Czech economic policy was its encouragement of small businesses.

The enormous and long-term political changes in central and Eastern Europe also changed the traditional trading patterns and markets which had been the speciality of Laurin & Klement.

Before 1914, Laurin & Klement sold only 30 per cent of its products on what was now Czechoslovak territory. Another 20 per cent went into other parts of what used to be Austria-Hungary and the other 50 per cent was exported elsewhere. After the war,

however, this pattern of distribution became nigh-on impossible to follow in the political and economic post-war chaos.

Nevertheless, there was a tremendous demand for vehicles of all descriptions in 1919 and 1920. Inflation and exchange rates were so unpredictable that those people who still had access to money turned to high value durables, such as cars, in an attempt to stabilize their assets. More orders came from beyond the Czech borders as foreign buyers took advantage of the weakness of the Czech currency, but despite the full order books, the high cost of raw materials brought a very unprofitable dawn to this new era.

These conditions were the same over most of Europe and motor car manufacture continued with only slight modifications of the pre-war automobile types. Production in Mladá Boleslav consisted of the Sh and the small type T. Real changes only came in 1920, when redesign of the previously produced models brought about the types So and Sp. They received enlarged engines to 2,412 cc and 25 bhp. Their chassis were used for private and commercial bodywork.

Changes were also made to the type M range – cars that sold very well. The new Mh retained its four cylinder 50 bhp engine with side-valve operation, while the MK6 received the sleeve-valve 60 bhp engine. The two were very similar in appearance and belonged to the luxury class. It was typical of the times to tend towards large and expensive vehicles. To bring out more popular vehicles, as planned before the war, was beyond economic and technical possibility. Even had those possibilities existed, the production cost would have been far too high for the broad public to afford

ABOVE LEFT **Type Sp light van of 25 bhp. Messrs F. Kňourek were 'Ham Exporters' from Hradec Králové.**

LEFT **The 1920 type Mh tourer of 50 bhp.**

ABOVE **The 1922 type 305 ambulance.**

BELOW **Elegant type 150 roadster with four wheel brakes.**

such vehicles. On the other hand, turnover in commercial vehicles and the motorized plough Excelsior was good. Interestingly, the Excelsior was shown at the international fair at Lyon in 1919. It was a valuable export for Laurin & Klement and its success was due to technical sophistication and quality. It even won first prize in a very demanding motor plough competition in Lerida, Spain.

The outlook in 1920 for the Czechoslovak motor industry was uncertain. Some of the public considered the motor vehicle an unnecessary luxury item. The press seemed to confirm this attitude and so did some parliamentary voices. Thinking was based on the fact that state finances were shaky and that new means of income had to be sought. If there was to be increased taxation, it followed that those owning luxury articles should be the first to pay. Cars were expensive, their running even more so and those who had them should pay extra taxes.

Vehicles and their components were subjected to luxury taxes. Imported vehicles were 'punished' by an import duty of 65 percent of their original cost. The home-produced machines were thus sensibly protected or so it was believed. Duties were also levied on components such as tyres, batteries and ignition systems, which were not manufactured in Czechoslovakia in sufficient quantities. These ill-conceived regulations resulted in the stagnation of motoring in Czechoslovakia, while in all other industrialized countries, even those without an automotive industry, car usage strode forward.

This unfortunate legislation worked against motoring in any form and made it excessively expensive. It sentenced the making of really popular cars to failure. Laurin & Klement continued with

ABOVE **Type 400 six-seater touring car with jump seats in back.**

RIGHT **Type 450 with four wheel brakes. Note the styling change to pointed radiator.**

its conservative manufacturing attitude and remained content with its modified pre-war models, producing more types but in less numbers. Between 1920 and 1925 Laurin & Klement produced a whole range of passenger cars, almost all of which were expensive. The main advantage of this range was the technical perfection and quality of finish. The use of the Knight sleeve-valve engine in several forms added to the factory's reputation.

An exception to this rule, in 1922, was a car which could respond to the demand for a relatively inexpensive but particularly solid vehicle. It was about this time the economic situation in Czechoslovakia began to improve, together with a firming up of prices and currency. The motoring situation had not really improved as yet, but the economic changes gave grounds for optimism.

With fresh hope in the air the new car was type-named A like the original voiturette in those far-off days of 1905. The new A was considered small by the standards of the day. A water-cooled four cylinder of 1,791 cc, it produced a mere 20 bhp and was fitted with a four-speed gearbox. This four-seater had, in standard form, an open touring body and became the cornerstone of Laurin & Klement's post-war small car production.

In 1923 the previously used vehicle type indication by letters was replaced by numbers: thus the A became the 100, the So was now the 200 and the Sp the 210, and so on. Then came the 150 which

had almost the same chassis as the 100 but with a sleeve-valve engine of 1,460 cc, 65 mm bore by 110 mm stroke, but its output was identical to the 100.

To suit the luxury market, the large type 445 was fitted with a six cylinder sleeve-valve engine of 4,962 cc and 60 bhp. The production programme also contained two types of commercial vehicles: a smaller type 500 carrying two tonnes and the four-tonner 540. A new licence was obtained to make the Martin articulated trailer which was offered to suit all of the commercial vehicles. Unusually, it was also made with a passenger carrier body of 50 seats and then attached and pulled by the type 540.

In 1923 turnover in vehicles increased over the previous year and the directors decided to reduce prices marginally to improve competitiveness. Exports slowly began again to Germany, Poland and Hungary, but the firm still only operated at about half its production capacity.

Management sought orders for other products and in 1924 bought a licence from the French company Lorraine-Dietrich to produce aircraft engines. These were twelve cylinder types with three banks of four, in W formation. Cubic capacity amounted to 24.4 litres with an output of 450 bhp. These engines were built into transport and military aircraft and this manufacture made use of the extra available capacity in Mladá Boleslav.

In those days the qualified personnel of Laurin & Klement belonged to the European automotive industrial elite, clearly demonstrated by their ability to manufacture not only aircraft engines but also the sleeve-valve motors which, due to their precision construction, needed a high degree of special skills and technology.

At this time Klement had again endeavoured, as before the war, to bring about production rationalization by getting the other vehicle manufacturers to co-operate with Laurin & Klement. These ideas were reintroduced in the twenties to respond better to the difficult national market needs. But again the negotiations came to nothing.

The position of Laurin & Klement in competition with the other major Czech automobile producers, Tatra and Praga, became increasingly more complicated. Both competitors were in fact departments of major engineering concerns (Ringhoffer and Českomoravská-Kolben respectively), which not only made possible advantageous technical co-operation, but losses or profits could be offset against other activities. Obviously these additional avenues were not available to Laurin & Klement which was totally on its own.

Since an agreement could not be reached with the other motor car manufacturers, Laurin & Klement was forced to negotiate a close relationship with another engineering concern. The partner was the well-known Škodovy závody (Škoda Works) in Plzeň, in western Bohemia. Negotiations began in 1924 and ended a year later with an agreement legally confirmed by the annual general meeting of the shareholders on July 20th, 1925. Škoda bought the whole of the Laurin & Klement company complete with all its branches and agencies. The agreement stipulated that all the original vehicle types made in Mladá Boleslav would carry not only the newly designed Škoda trademark of the winged arrow, but also the Laurin & Klement insignia. Only the types designed after the July 20th, 1925 would carry the Škoda marque exclusively.

7 Škoda before 1925

THE STEAM ENGINE and consequently the arrival of steam locomotives radically altered the industry and agriculture of mid-nineteenth century Europe. The railways spread across the continent connecting towns and villages and allowed easier transfer of goods and people and the opening of new markets. The town of Plzeň (Pilsen) in western Bohemia was connected by rail to Prague, the capital of Bohemia, in 1862.

The history of Škoda started in 1856 with a small ironworks in a town called Sedlec situated near Plzeň. The works were owned by the aristocratic Waldstein (Wallenstein) family. Increasing demand for machinery products enabled new and larger premises to be opened in Plzeň in 1859. This new Plzeň factory became the cradle of the future Škoda concern.

Count Christian Waldstein and later his brother Ernst, who decided to establish the Sedlec and Plzeň works, employed a number of workers which grew rapidly with the expansion of the factory complex. In 1865 sixty-eight workers toiled in long, twelve hour shifts. With the increased demand for goods disputes arose among the directors and engineers about decisions on how best to run the expanding business. The brothers František and Josef Belani who directed the works for the Waldsteins soon left and started their own business to compete with them. A new director, Emil Škoda, was appointed in 1866.

After three years of wrangling with the Waldsteins who rather shortsightedly were after maximum gain with minimum risk, Škoda convinced them to sell and on June 12th 1869 Škoda assumed the ownership of the Plzeň machine shop for the price of 167,642 gulden. This large sum of money was gathered partly from his own savings and partly as a personal loan from his uncle, Josef Škoda, a professor of medicine who lived in Vienna.

Emil Škoda was born on November 18, 1839 in Plzeň, the son of the town medical doctor František Škoda and Jana Rzihová, his second wife. Shortly after, the family moved to Cheb (Eger), a town in western Bohemia where Emil later studied at a local grammar school. When the Škodas eventually moved to Prague, Emil started his higher education in engineering and mining at the Prague Technical School. He completed his studies at the Technical School in Karlsruhe, Germany. After several years of practical training in German factories Škoda returned to Plzeň. In April 1867 his father František was knighted becoming Ritter von Škoda. Emil inherited the title after his father's death in 1888. By 1869 when Emil took over the Waldsteins' factory, 150 employees worked there. Škoda's dedication to his new company knew no bounds. He spent more time on the shop floor than at his home, woefully neglecting his long suffering family.

This single-mindedness of Škoda was reflected in the factory's success and the concern grew correspondingly with new workshops, casting shops, boiler shops and steelworks, allowing Škoda to produce quality steel products for civil and later military use. The machine shops assumed a secondary importance to the steelworks. Many famous ocean liners including *France*, *Normandie* and *Queen Mary* required large specialist heavy castings, refused by other makers for their complexity, which were made in the western Bohemian town. In addition, wholly equipped sugar works, breweries, distilleries and stationary steam engines were exported all over the world. Plzeň became known not only as

ABOVE **Emil Ritter von Škoda with his wife Hermina (née Hahnenkamm).**

BELOW **The arms of the Ritter von Škoda family.**

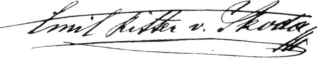

the place of origin of the best lager in the world, the Pilsner Urquell, but also for the E.Škoda, Plzeň and the marque ES on the company's products.

The next stage of development was crucial for the future of the firm. The armaments industry grew in Europe and Škoda did not want to be left behind. In 1879 Austria-Hungary signed a treaty of mutual cooperation with Germany which set them against France and Russia and gave reason for an increased demand for arms of various kinds. Škoda understood that under the prevailing conditions the armaments industry could be expected to expand faster than other types of manufacture. From 1886 Škoda made ship gun turrets and from 1889 a number of differing calibre guns. Armaments then became the predominant products of the company.

On December 12th, 1899 E.Škoda, Plzeň – Strojírna, ocelárna, kotlárna, slévarna a dělovka (machine, steel, boiler, casting shops and gun works) was turned into a joint stock company becoming Škodovy závody, a.s. v Plzni, or in German Skoda-Werke (Škoda Works joint stock company in Pilsen). The concern was valued at 7.5 million gulden (15 million Austrian crowns). E.Škoda himself received 2 million crowns and 65,000 shares of 200 crowns each. The banks kept 60,000 shares so the controlling interest was left in Škoda's hands with the banks taking part in the decision making. Personalities from the mainly German shareholding banks joined the Škoda Works board of directors which included T.Hoffmann and M.Feilchenfeld. Now the marque engraved on Škoda products was in the form of an encircled SW.

The end of the first stage and the beginning of the new era of Škoda's history and development was the sudden death of Emil Škoda on August 8th, 1900. He died on his way back from Bad Gastein in Austria, at half past two in the morning in a railway car compartment. His funeral in Plzeň was attended by almost all the contemporary workforce of 3,211 workers and 250 administration staff. The new directors were appointed and the company chairman became G.Mauthner and managing director W.Trappen. From 1902 G.Mauthner was replaced by J. Blum who remained in the chair until 1917.

The late nineteenth century was a time of new advances in technical sciences resulting in the application of scientific knowledge to manufacturing processes. The commercial emergence of the internal combustion engine in the late eighteen-eighties signalled the beginning of the second in-

LEFT **The main machine shop in Plzeň.**

ABOVE **Casting of dynamo rotor weighing 97 tonnes for London electricity power station.**

BELOW **Casting weighing 114 tonnes for the ocean liner La France.**

ABOVE RIGHT **The 1907 armoured car prototype, the first produced in Plzeň, with two machine guns.**

BELOW RIGHT **The Škoda gun shop before the First World War.**

dustrial revolution. In Bohemia the engineering industry flourished and tended by its nature toward specialization. Metallurgical and machine works concentrated on selected manufacturing programmes. Free competitiveness among production concerns gave way to monopoly and the rise of cartels, syndicates and trusts. The banks became the dominant players in the monopolistic economy. The capital of leading banks, combined with the capital of the large industrial firms, was used to monopolise individual branches of industry.

Soon, however, at the beginning of the century, an economic crisis occurred in Europe when large numbers of small companies flooded the market with similar products. The Škoda Works did not escape this slowdown, with the lack of orders resulting in unemployment and shortening of working hours. Only armaments production was on the increase and Škoda was fulfilling orders from the Austro-Hungarian Navy. During 1902–3 34.8 per cent of all Škoda's manufacturing capacity was devoted to arms manufacture. This predominant factor in production started Škoda on the journey toward becoming the largest armaments firm in Austria-Hungary. At that time new production was being established in steam turbines, by obtaining licence agreements from abroad. An electromechanical shop was also founded.

From 1904, G.Günther came to the head of the

company and the general and commercial directorate was moved from Plzeň to Vienna. Soon after Emil's son, Karel Ritter von Škoda (1879–1929), came to the forefront of his father's firm. The thirty-one year old Karel, having completed his studies in Stuttgart and Zurich, became managing director of Škoda Works replacing G.Günther in 1909.

In the period of 1905–13 the Škoda concern started to grow again, employing 5,000 workers and 580 administration staff. In 1913 the capital of the company was valued at 40 million Austrian crowns.

At the beginning of the First World War Škoda modernized its armaments manufacture and worked closely with the Austro-Hungarian War

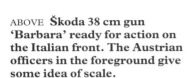

ABOVE **Škoda 38 cm gun 'Barbara' ready for action on the Italian front. The Austrian officers in the foreground give some idea of scale.**

TOP LEFT **Škoda 12 cm coastal defence gun.**

CENTRE LEFT **Škoda 19 cm ship's gun.**

LEFT **Škoda 30.5 cm gun.**

RIGHT **Škoda 42 cm howitzer from 1917.**

Ministry. The steel castings for ships armour, guns and munitions grew to become the most important items of the production programme, the main factor of balance and the stimulus for further growth of the company. Škoda became the steelworks and armament power base and was fully prepared to enter the war period. Škoda cooperated with its main European rival the German Krupp concern in the building of a new gun works at Raab in Hungary, where production started in July 1915. Škoda successfully penetrated the arms supply markets in the Balkans and Turkey, China and Latin America. In the middle of 1914 Škoda's sudden growth was indicated by the number of its employees which came to almost 10,000.

At the start of the war offensive the German army command requested from its ally, Austria-Hungary, 30.5 cm mortars and inevitably Škoda received the order. Overall, during the war in various campaigns on the French, Belgian and Russian fronts and in some naval battles, 117 of these heavy artillery pieces were used. Further guns of 21 cm, 38 cm and 42 cm helped to reach the strategic and tactical aims required by the German and Austro-Hungarian alliance. The highly valued efficiency of these types of artillery remained the pride of Škoda's constructors and designers. The skill involved in their development has been much

admired by generations of the company's workforce.

The long-running dispute between gun makers over the efficiency of steel or bronze as the main material of manufacture was thus settled with Škoda's proven results with its modern steel fire power.

Even in the early stages of Škoda's involvement in arms manufacture its approach was based on the use of modern materials and techniques: the employment of steel, recoil barrel design, quick-firing, speed of manoeuvre and the maximum strength of gun power. However, the Austro-Hungarian army's conservative command favoured standard field artillery and did not appreciate these innovations. As a consequence Škoda concentrated on the manufacture of a range of mountain guns which then became the main speciality of the company and sealed Škoda's reputation for having the most advanced armaments technology in Europe.

At the beginning of the war K.Škoda visited the German front to satisfy himself of the quality of his products. On his return to the Plzeň factory he ordered the construction of a new gun to be based on the well-established 30.5 cm mortar which was to have a firing range of at least 15 km and be fully motorized to achieve great speeds in its manouvrability. With this design K.Škoda went to the

LEFT **C-Zug tug and trailer on the road; designed by Ferdinand Porsche and manufactured by Škoda.**

ABOVE **C-Zug on rails towing a 24 cm gun in gun carriage mounted on a trailer.**

Ministry of War to sell his new idea. Only a year after his discussion with the minister von Krobatim the Italian front gunners received two new Škoda 38 cm siege-mortars called Barbara and Gudrun. These very heavy guns had the longest firing distance at that time – 3.6 to 15 km.

K.Škoda's order to motorize the transport of his factory's heavy guns was to be resolved by Ferdinand Porsche. He was then managing director of Austro-Daimler in Vienna, of which the largest shareholder was the Škoda Works. The designer of the 38 cm siege-mortar, which weighed 81,700 kg with each firing shell weighing 740 kg, was the chief engineer of Škoda, R.Dirmoser. He cooperated with Porsche to settle this problem in 1915.

The solution was to use the 'mixte' system – a petrol engine driving a dynamo which in turn ran electric motors placed in the hubs of wheels – already patented by Porsche in 1897. The new vehicle, which was later termed 'C-Zug' or BE vlak (petrol-electric train), could travel on road or rails. It consisted of a generator tug equipped with a Daimler six cylinder 20,309 cc engine providing 150 bhp at 1,200 rpm. This engine was connected to a dynamo with 99 kW capacity at 300 volts.

The purpose of the tug was to supply electric power to two tandem axles forming one bogie of a trailer. Each axle had 8 wheels with an electric hub motor in each wheel. These wheels could be changed from rail to road conditions in 50 minutes. The bogies then moved themselves, the tug supplying all the power to them as well as for its own movement to the two of its rear wheels forming altogether a ten or eighteen-wheel drive vehicle depending which type of trailer was used. The train was driven from the tug where all the controls were situated including the brakes, regulation of speed, lighting and starting.

The huge weapon was so heavy that it had to be dismantled into four parts for transportation. The barrel and breech weighed 20,700 kg, the gun carriage 17,600 kg and the two pieces of the gun bearings weighed 21,000 kg and 22,000 kg. Two parts were placed on each trailer.

The first test trials took place as soon as January 25th, 1916 in Wiener Neustadt and later on March 1st at Bolevec near Plzeň where the speed attained on road was 16 kph and on rail 27 kph, which later improved to 35 kph. The maximum road speed at maximum ascent (26 per cent!) was 1.35 kph.

The amazing C-Zug successfully moved the siege-mortars Barbara and Gudrun to the Italian front high in the Alps at Costalta, 1,395 metres above sea level. Later in May 1918 the guns were placed even higher at 1,600 metres, at Monte Erio again during the Austro-Hungarian offensive against Italy in the last desperate stages of the War.

Altogether 32 C-Zug vehicles were made by Škoda and were later used by the Czechoslovak army until the beginning of the Second World War when the trains were sold to the German army for 42 million Czech crowns. Sadly none have survived, though it is thought that one trailer may be on show in the Bucharest Military Museum.

In 1916 Hindenburg insisted that Austria-Hungary should increase arms manufacture. Škoda was prepared to comply with the order, but only on their terms. Consequently, for ten years from 1917, the company held a seventy per cent monopoly in gun manufacture up to 10 cm barrel diameter and 100 per cent monopoly for guns ranging from 10.4 cm.

Between 1910 to 1918 Škoda supplied the Austro-Hungarian army with 12,693 pieces of artillery. In 1917 alone 4,500 guns left the factory gates for the front. In the years 1916 to 1917 ammunition manufacture came to 1,200,000 rounds. The shareholding capital grew to 72,000,000 crowns by the end of 1916 and the profits during the war period came to 52.6 million crowns which must have made the holders of Škoda shares extremely proud of their clever investment. But the war was not to last forever.

The political situation in Austria-Hungary already had begun to change following the death of the Emperor Franz Josef in November 1916 and the accession of his son Karl I. As the war neared its conclusion the future became even more unclear. Similarly, in April 1918, the Škoda directorship changed when K. Škoda became executive chairman and a German, V.Salvator von Isenburg, was appointed as managing director.

Defeat for the German-Austro-Hungarian alliance saw the empire that had once dominated all Europe disintegrate into small independent sovereign states. Škoda, now a huge industrial concern located on the soil of the new Czecho-Slovak republic lost its main customer, the Austro-Hungarian army. It was said at the time that the small Czecho-Slovak state did not need or could not support such a large enterprise. Indeed, during 1919 the number of Škoda workers decreased by more than half to 15 thousand and armaments manufacture shrank to 29.5 per cent of total production. The Czechs, J. Šimonek as executive chairman and Ing F.Hanuš as managing director, replaced the German leadership and a new strategy for the future was desperately sought.

French capital came to the rescue in the form of an old established armaments firm, Schneider et Cie which had the main works at Le Creusot, Le Havre and St Chamond. To gain voting control of Škoda, Schneider obtained the controlling majority of shares. At the shareholders' meeting on September 29th, 1919, Schneider declared ownership of 60,000 Škoda shares which gave the French over 6,000 votes. Schneider's grip on Škoda was strengthened by the support of some longstanding investors such as the Czech financial house Živnostenská banka which held 43,000 shares. This gave the French company power to make sweeping policy decisions. The resultant disappearance of the German influence was distinctly approved of in government circles.

Schneider had also taken advantage of the First World War and expanded accordingly and one of the main reasons for the French interest in Škoda was to reduce the Czechs' competitiveness on the international arms market. However the influx of French capital and experience, and its influence on Škoda's future had fairly positive results in the difficult atmosphere of the postwar commercial crisis. For example, Schneider offered Škoda the benefit of its well established business apparatus and its extended contacts. In that way it was possible to fill up the order books to supply new equipment to sugar refineries placed in northern France and Morocco. A further positive effect was the mutual use of each others patents for arms manufacture in the respective countries, though Škoda had 25 patents in France and Schneider only six pending in Czechoslovakia.

Technical cooperation was mainly in the field of armaments technology. There was an agreement to divide the sphere of commercial interests – an agreement that was not always kept by either party. Nevertheless, even if Škoda was a junior partner in this arrangement which in the end lasted until the beginning of the Second World War, its newly developed international contacts helped the company to grow into a truly international concern.

Back in Czechoslovakia Škoda took a twenty per cent share in the Zbrojovka company, the makers of the famous Bren (Brno-Enfield) gun, and then forced the new acquisition to agree that only guns of up to 2.5 cm calibre would be manufactured there. Under the new control Zbrojovka could also not make armoured cars, grenades, mines, bombs airplanes and aircraft engines. In this way Škoda established an almost complete monopoly in Czechoslovakia of higher calibre armaments manufacture and all other military equipment, and that included military aircraft.

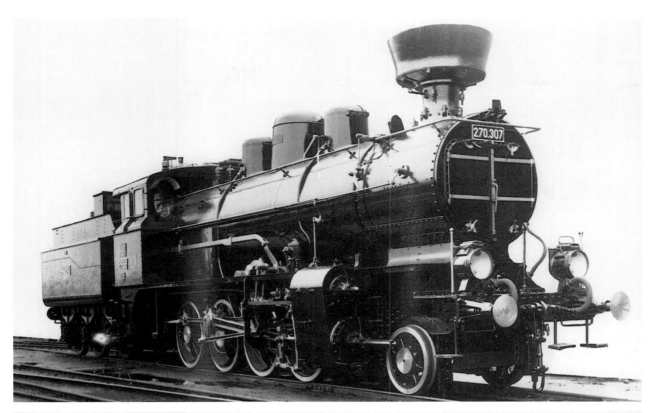

TOP **The 1920 twin cylinder goods locomotive for the Czechoslovak State Railways, 60 kph, 1,435 mm gauge. The first steam locomotive by Škoda.**

ABOVE **85 kph twin cylinder tank locomotive for passenger trains for the Czechoslovak State Railways produced from 1921 to 1938.**

TOP **Three cylinder express locomotive for the Czechoslovak State Railways manufactured from 1926 to 1937. Maximum speed of 110 kph.**

ABOVE **The first electric Škoda locomotive from 1927.**

TOP RIGHT **The 1947 three cylinder express locomotive for the Czechoslovak State Railways, 120 kph.**

CENTRE RIGHT **Twin cylinder locomotive for the South African Railways, 85 kph, 1,067 mm gauge, from 1938.**

RIGHT **Twin cylinder universal locomotive for the Czechoslovak State Railways, 100 kph, manufactured by Škoda from 1947 to 1951. Considered to be the most beautiful rail machine of the time.**

Between the wars Škoda found it necessary to expand into other markets and diversify the manufacturing programme. The departure from armaments led to the decision to start the manufacture of steam powered rail locomotives.

The locomotive division had already been planned during the war years and it did not take long for the first steam engine to be handed over to the Czechoslovak State Railways on June 16, 1920. The locomotives were soon exported abroad and from there came orders for the manufacture and repair of new and old stock. Production expanded in the two decades that followed and steam locomotives were delivered all over the world. The construction of these engines was an important part of Škoda's manufacturing activities for almost forty years. During this period, a total of 3,247 steam locomotives were built and several hundred engines were overhauled. In 1958 the production of steam engines finally ceased in favour of electric locomotives which varied in power and design. In 1927 the first Škoda electric locomotive type 1 Elo 1 was made. But only after 1958 were deliveries of large scale series of electric locomotives effected. Since that year Škoda locomotives have been produced in Plzeň, one leaving the factory every other day. Until recently its main customer was the Soviet Union as Škoda locomotives make easy going of the very hard, longhaul journeys across the former Union. The continued orders from Russia for these machines give proof of their longevity, low maintenance costs and good quality of design and production. Presently Škoda engineers are working on the third generation of electric locomotives; the 85E type, employing asynchronous traction motors individually driving the axles. There are various axle arrangements and the engines drive the axles directly without a gearbox.

As the nineteen-twenties progressed Škoda continued to enhance its good name at home and abroad with well finished and sensibly designed products and a distinctive trade mark was sought to stamp visually their origin and be instantly recognizable.

In 1923 an unknown designer employed within the company proposed the now famous Škoda logo which has been used on all Škoda products ever since. Its design was based on a unique concept. Emil Škoda when travelling in the United States late last century had a Red Indian servant. When Škoda returned to Bohemia he brought with him a plaque showing a relief of the head of an American Indian which he hung on the wall of his factory office. The story goes that the winged arrow motif

ABOVE **The image of a Red Indian which is said to have inspired the new Škoda logo.**

RIGHT **Motorized lighting generator with dioptical search light from 1932. Note the modern canvas seat tubular chair.**

BELOW RIGHT **The 1930-34 light tank prototype MUV-4. The first Škoda caterpillar vehicle powered by a 2,660 cc flat-four air-cooled engine of 40 bhp.**

is loosely based on the Indian and is interpreted sometimes as an Indian's head with an arrow at the level of his eye. At the same time the marque carries the following symbology. The large outside circle represents Škoda's all-round production; the wing, the upsurge in technical progress; the eye in the wing, exactness of production and sharp-sightedness; and the arrow-head, aiming at advanced methods of production. The Škoda symbol ranks even today amongst the most successful of creative concepts. It is registered and protected in 115 countries in all parts of the world.

Manufacture at Škodovy závody continued to extend in the inter-war period with a large number of heavy industrial products: steam turbines and generators, automatic machinery for tobacco industry and newspaper presses, special heavy tools, foundry equipment, rolling mill machinery, cranes, dredgers, pumps and compressors, hydraulic and crushing machinery and agricultural ploughs. It was only a short step into vehicle manufacture.

In fact a special automobile division existed in Plzeň from 1919. Initially this division of the company only built commercial vehicles. Later on it

TOP LEFT **The 1934 light tank prototype SU with a water-cooled 115 bhp engine. The tank was fitted with a 37.5 mm gun and two heavy machine guns.**

CENTRE LEFT **The 1926 Dewoitine light aircraft with a 450 bhp Škoda engine made under French licence.**

LEFT **The armoured car type PA II 'Turtle' of 1924. About 12 units of this vehicle, with an extraordinarily modern body concept for the time, were built. It had a water-cooled 5,200 cc engine and carried a crew of five men.**

TOP **The 1927 type PA XII armoured car which was equipped with two heavy machine guns in a rotating turret.**

ABOVE **The 1928 prototype of armoured car on a PA II chassis with a 7.5 cm field gun in front and a machine gun at back. This vehicle weighed 11 tonnes and was too heavy to go into production.**

ABOVE **Škoda experimented with licenced manufacture of the French Ballot motor car. The project was abandoned after one prototype built in 1923.**

RIGHT **After acquiring the Hispano-Suiza licence Škoda produced their own version - Škoda-Hispano-Suiza. This car has a limousine body by Václav Brožík & Sons of Plzeň and dates from 1925.**

diversified into the manufacture of agricultural and military tractors, armoured cars, light tanks, stationary and aircraft engines. Most of these products were intended for export or use by the Czechoslovak army. The military vehicles were of modern design and fitted with the latest equipment like the armoured car PA II which had four-wheel drive, an 85 bhp engine and could drive in both forward and reverse directions at 60 kph.

In the mid-twenties a decision was made to start manufacturing passenger cars and commercial trucks. Not having the time or resources for the necessary research and development, foreign licences from well-known manufacturers were sought. With the influence of Schneider et Cie the first discussions for a passenger car licence were with the French automobile producers Ballot.

Ernest Ballot made engines for various manufacturers before building racing cars in 1919 and passenger cars from 1921. Ballot benefitted from the publicity gained by the successes of his three litre, eight cylinder cars which were the fastest in the Indianapolis 500 miles race in 1919 and 1920 and in 1921, came second in the French Grand Prix and first in the Italian Grand Prix. The first Ballot passenger car was a two litre, four cylinder, sixteen valve twin OHC, the 2LS type, a racing car modified for road use. Power output was 75 bhp and maximum speed 92 mph. This was a rather special and expensive car and fewer than 100 were made.

On the basis of the initial negotiations with Ballot one prototype car was made in Plzeň by Škoda. However for some reason further development stopped and Škoda started to look for a new partner. More successfully, it forged cooperation with the French based company Hispano-Suiza and acquired its licence for manufacture of the luxury type H6B.

Only the rich Škoda concern could afford to build these expensive automobiles, initially intended to be offered for sale to its most valued customers.

The Hispano-Suiza enjoyed a very good reputation and its marque had a flavour of magic about it. At the beginning of this century the firm of E. La Cuadra y Cia of Barcelona tried to build electrically driven motor cars, but given the available automotive technology, the Spaniards had to overcome considerable difficulties in the production of their electric cars. The number of interested customers was limited and the company had to cease production altogether.

After that several partners of the defunct company got together and founded a new enterprise F. Castro y Cia. Its beginning was favoured with a stroke of luck in the form of a young Swiss technical director Marc Birkigt.

In 1904 Birkigt built his first combustion engined automobiles for this company. At first these were only small cars with two cylinder engines giving 4.5 bhp and later 10 bhp. Even so

the firm F.Castro was not spared the fate of its predecessor and it too was forced to close down.

The third attempt founded a firm under the new name of La Hispano-Suiza Fabrica de Automobiles S.A. Birkigt was appointed technical director and in 1905 Hispano-Suiza built its first four cylinder car; two versions of 14 bhp and 20 bhp were offered. These first cars aroused a great deal of attention and under Birkigt's leadership the new company finally got under-way. Numerous new types were developed which participated successfully in various races and competitions. The racing victories as well as the design concept aimed at reliability and precision. In this way the name of Hispano-Suiza became firmly established and became almost synonymous with other luxury automobile makers such as Rolls-Royce and Isotta-Fraschini.

During the First World War, Hispano-Suiza built aircraft engines of which more than 50,000 were produced. As early as 1911 a branch factory was set up in Bois-Colombes in France and registered under the company name Societé Francaise Hispano-Suiza. In 1923 it became independent.

Škoda prepared well for the new production, setting aside 13,000 square metres of its giant assembly halls in Plzeň. The car Škoda had decided to build was one of the best and most successful automobiles of its time – the Hispano-Suiza type H6B. The original automobile was presented to the public in 1919 at the Paris Autosalon and it was to retain its supremacy into the late 1930's. The first Škoda-Hispano-Suiza, as the Plzeň car was called came off the production line in 1925.

The first fifteen Škoda-Hispano-Suiza chassis were built from original parts supplied from France. Beginning with the sixteenth car all were truly Škoda-Hispano-Suiza and wholly manufactured in Bohemia. The first series amounted to fifty automobiles, including the fifteen original Hispano-Suizas. In fact Škoda only produced the chassis. The bodies were designed and manufactured by various Czech coach builders who enjoyed as good a reputation as French firms such as Saoutchik, Letourneur et Marchand and Million-Guiet. Václav Brožík & Sons of Plzeň delivered most of the bodies for the Škoda-Hispano-Suiza but others came from the Škoda works in Mladá Boleslav – the recently taken over Laurin & Klement, or well-known coachbuilders in Prague such as J.O.Jech, Pokorný & Beyvl and others.

When Škoda established the production of Škoda-Hispano-Suizas it employed 550 production staff working in two shifts. Director engineer Emil Rezler, who concluded and signed the agreement with the French company in Paris, was appointed managing director of the Škoda automobile division.

The six cylinder engine of the Škoda-Hispano-Suiza H6B was derived from the V12 Hispano-Suiza aircraft engine. The engine block, with its non-detachable cylinder head, was cast from light alloy and was given dry screwed-in cylinder liners. These were at first of steel, but later made of cast iron. The bore was 100 mm, the stroke 140 mm, which made for a total displacement of 6,597 cc. The car handled exceedingly well on the road and had marvellous four-wheel brakes, an efficient and reliable engine and luxurious internal fittings.

The first Škoda-Hispano-Suiza made in Plzeň was delivered to the country's President T.G. Masaryk. It was a black six-seater limousine with the type designation 25/100 and the body by the firm of Václav Brožík & Sons. Approximately 160 of these luxury cars were produced in the course of the following four years. This splendid machine carried a considerable price tag for the time – the sum of 206,000 Czech crowns, just for a plain limousine. For a dual limousine or cabriolet the price rose to 280,000 crowns. The plain chassis was priced at 155,000 crowns.

Prices for the Škoda-Hispano-Suiza were certainly very high, but these were in keeping with the excellent workmanship. The best materials went into these vehicles. Surprising above all was the extreme quietness of the engines and it is not an exaggeration that expert circles considered the Škoda-Hispano-Suiza superior to the original products from France and Spain.

The Škoda technicians and engineers were not only better qualified in the area of material processing but also possessed more progressive ideas. These attitudes reflected in the thermal qualities of

TOP **Škoda-Hispano-Suiza with a town car body.**

ABOVE **The 1925 Škoda-Hispano-Suiza H6B.**

the engine. The greatest attention was also paid to the camshaft drive, the valves and crankshaft. The connecting rods were made stronger, the main bearings were enlarged, the front brakes improved and the gear ratios were changed. The original Blériot lamps were replaced by ones made by Scintilla or Bosch. The Hispano-Suiza radiator emblem was removed and replaced by the round winged arrow of the Škoda marque. However the characteristic mascot of all Hispano-Suizas, the winged stork in silver placed on the radiator cap, was retained.

The production of Škoda-Hispano-Suiza was finally stopped in 1929 because there were too few buyers due to the economic climate. The Škoda-Hispano-Suiza was replaced by the newly developed, luxurious eight cylinder Škoda 860. Fifty cars were built but were superseded later by the six cylinder types 645 and 650, but more about that in the next chapter.

Similarly, as with the passenger cars, Škoda went abroad to obtain its licence for utility vehicles. A British firm called Sentinel & Waggon Works (1920) Ltd was selected and a production of steam powered trucks was established in Plzeň in 1923.

In 1868 Messrs Alley and MacLellan founded their engineering works in London Road, Glasgow and in 1873 moved to larger premises at Polmadie called the Sentinel Works. In 1885 they started to manufacture the Sentinel High Speed Engine which was used to generate electricity, drive machinery and for marine purposes. In 1904, encouraged by the upsurge in transport, Alley and MacLellan decided to develop a road waggon powered by a steam engine. Two years later they fitted a slow speed steam engine with a single chain drive to a differential on the rear axle to a flat bed truck. Thus the Sentinel Standard Waggon was conceived.

Various patents were taken out for the vehicle, the Sentinel patent steam boiler, the Sentinel patent steam engine, Sentinel patent road wheels, the Sentinel patent front axle and the Sentinel patent steering gear. Either steel or rubber-tyred wheels could be ordered. However it was easy to convert from steel tread wheel, as it was only necessary to remove the outside retaining ring, remove the steel tyre and rim and replace it with the rubber tyred rim and refit the outside retaining ring.

The popularity of these reliable steam trucks necessitated further expansion and a new factory was acquired in Shrewsbury in 1916 and a new company founded, called Sentinel Waggon Works Limited. In 1923 Škoda approached Sentinel for the licence to make steam lorries in Czechoslovakia.

One of the reasons to go to Sentinel was a decision in 1923 by the Czechoslovak Ministry of Defence to order several types of steam trucks of British make to be used in Prague in road trials. The main argument for selecting steam as the power was the possibility of petrol and diesel fuel shortages. It was explained that existing fuel reserves had to be assigned to the army and airforce; other fuels therefore needed to be found for public utility vehicles.

Steam engines, as opposed to petrol fuelled combustion engines, had several advantages. Steam engines were more flexible and could achieve instant acceleration; they managed substantial gradients without difficulties; coal was cheap and the vehicle was easily operational just with a single valve. By closing the valve the truck stopped instantly, because the engine worked like a compressor and automatically braked. The consumption of engine oil was minimal and due to the much smaller number of revolutions required (300), the engine parts had a longer life. The disadvantages were the weight of the vehicle and the time it took to get started because the water had to be heated first in the boiler. Additionally the driver had to pass a series of tests to check his skills not only as a driver, but as a boilerman and machine operator.

Škoda Sentinels were made in several versions as 3, 5 and 7 tonne trucks and with body variants, as street cleaning cars, omnibuses and refuse collection vehicles. Many survived the Second World War and were still used on Prague streets in the early fifties.

They were powered by a single valve engine for superheated steam, double-acting with crankshafts at 180 degrees. In the upright boiler with its vertical flame, the inner boiler tubes were sloped, aiding fast water circulation and preventing formation of scale and sludge. The boiler could be easily cleaned without the need of valve or pipes removal because the whole of the inner flue assembly was removable. For better operational economics, the exhausted steam was used to preheat the water in the storage tank. Power to the rear axle, where the differential was fitted, was transmitted by two Gall's chains.

The Škoda Sentinel had two brakes each acting on the rear wheel drums. One was operated by a foot pedal, the other by a hand lever. The water storage tank held 800 litres allowing a journey of 60 km without stopping for more. Fuel supply on board, such as coal, charcoal or wood, lasted 80 to 120 km distance.

In a test drive conducted in October 1923, a Škoda Sentinel carrying a load of 10 tonnes, needed 0.485 kg of coal per km per tonne. For comparison, a 5 tonne petrol engine truck with a 3 tonne trailer was also tested. At the contemporary prices the Sentinel's operational costs proved to be three times cheaper than the petrol fuelled vehicle.

RIGHT **The Škoda Sentinel truck.**

BELOW **The Škoda Sentinel driver's position showing the boiler and the controls.**

From the middle of the nineteen-twenties Škoda started to expand. Turnover and profits grew and achievements and successes followed on all production levels of the company. From the beginning of 1924 the forty-year old Dr K. Loevenstein became managing director. He established a strong administrative position, skilfully leading Škoda's complicated business strategy. Further expansion and takeovers were instituted, the most significant of which was most certainly the acquisition of the Laurin & Klement company of Mladá Boleslav in 1925.

80,000 Laurin & Klement shares were exchanged in a two for one swap for Škodovy závody shares. Klement, the managing director of the Mladá Boleslav works, was given the function of general consultant and became a non-voting member of the Škoda board, without the power to influence policy.

Large sums were invested in upgrading the Mladá Boleslav buildings for the intended increased production. With this move Škoda not only diversified its manufacturing base but, by the mid-thirties had become the largest passenger car maker in Czechoslovakia, beating Praga and Tatra into second and third places.

On the occasion of the last Laurin & Klement shareholders meeting Klement concluded: 'Today when the independence of Laurin & Klement ceases, a company which has been built up with love and to which I have dedicated 30 years of my life, I wish to announce that this loss is in the interests of faster growth for the company and will effectively combat the prices of the sharpened world competition and contribute in strengthening the important section of the economy which the automobile industry represents in this country. Let us hope that the Laurin & Klement automobile company will reach, under the flag of Czechoslovakia's biggest steelworking concern, a level of development to which I had hoped to bring it myself.'

8 Škoda as a major automobile producer

ŠKODA'S TAKEOVER OF Laurin & Klement opened up new vistas for Mladá Boleslav motor manufacture. This firmed up the capital structure and enabled larger investment. Considerable advantages arose from the purchase of castings and forgings from the main Plzeň steelworks which reduced overheads and the management and administration of both works were trimmed.

Obviously major re-organization had to follow: the lorry and bus chassis were now to be made in Plzeň as well as the production tools. In turn, Mladá Boleslav made all radiators and bodywork, which resulted in the decision to build a new, large body plant there. But what used to be Laurin & Klement became a branch of the mother company and all decisions and management structure came from Plzeň, which sometimes meant a long chain of command. Manufacture and sales were not sufficiently responsive to market needs and despite the considerable capital investment, by way of buildings and equipment, manufacturing capacity was under-utilized, resulting in a fairly undynamic balance sheet. This was reflected in a further organisational change which led to the reduction of the number of models to be manufactured. The Laurin & Klement factory programme was reduced to three passenger cars and two trucks.

The Škoda-Laurin & Klement 110 type of 1925, a descendant of the 100 or 105 was the most produced, with 1,945 being made. It had the same stroke and bore as the 100, but due to its new construction the power increased to produce 25 instead of 20 bhp with a maximum speed of 85 kph. It was fitted with four-wheel brakes and came with a variety of bodies including an open four-seater, cabriolet, Weymann limousine and coupé. The next was the 120. Its parts were largely interchangeable with the 110 but the engine of 1,944 cc had 30 bhp. A longer chassis enabled even six-seater bodies to be fitted. Altogether 553 cars were made over the next six years.

The production of the large type 350, with a six cylinder sleeve-valve engine based on the Laurin & Klement type MK6, continued until 1927. In 1926 it became Škoda type 360 with a 3,969 cc engine but with four cylinders and overhead valves. This engine was of an exceptionally clean design and was fitted with a mini-compressor for tyre inflation. The 360 also had a ratchet and pawl system to prevent running back when starting off on a slope.

As far as the commercial vehicles were concerned, the 115 could be had as a platform lorry with a carrying capacity of 1,500 kg, or as a light bus for 13 passengers. Its engine was that used in the type 110. The heavier types were represented by the 545 which arose from the older model 540. Again with a platform body, it could carry 4,000 kg or made into a 30-seater bus. It could also tow a trailer, which, when designed as a passenger carrier, could transport 50 people. The Excelsior plough continued in the production plan as did licence manufacture of the Lorraine-Dietrich aircraft engines.

In the second half of the nineteen-twenties the motor car business began to show an upward trend. Demand increased in the small car market, but particularly where commercial vehicles, coaches and buses were concerned.

In 1926 the new body workshop was completed in Mladá Boleslav. This new building helped substantially to increase the works manufacturing facility. Its four floors were planned for assembly

line production: the basement housed the stores and locker rooms for the workers, the ground floor was the carpentry shop, first floor was for the upholstery and leather workers, on the second floor was placed the construction of timber body frames and on the third the car bodies were clad in metal which were then painted on the fourth floor.

This building was only the beginning of extensive enlargement in Mladá Boleslav between 1925 and 1930. A modern assembly hall was added in 1928 and the subsequent modernization in all respects enabled Škoda to advance beyond the other Czechoslovak vehicle producers and stand equal among its European competitors, particularly as far as assembly line production was concerned.

When car production started evolving in the early days of the century, it brought about changes in manufacturing methods. Early on in automobile history, making a motor vehicle meant building it piece by piece to individual order. To produce a substantial series of cars was rare prior to 1910. In the following years the successful makers laid down series of perhaps a hundred cars. But still the individual components, engine, chassis, body could be traced to one workman or a very small group. That was the European way. In the United States however, due to the Ford-originated system, cars were produced on conveyor belts in very considerable numbers and could be sold relatively cheaply and therefore be financially accessible to a much wider public. The obvious reason why these systems were not copied in Europe lay in the limited local market and the very individual customer requirements.

Only in the twenties was there a tendency towards mass production. The Škoda takeover of Laurin & Klement led to more investment and better production rationalisation, but the market was still too limited to mass-produce in central Europe. The Škoda plant was modern and well organized, however its manufacturing programme still lacked the sort of vehicle which would really take off with the general public.

To design such a car was difficult, but despite this the factory managed to increase sales year by year, notwithstanding the old Laurin & Klement model range. In 1926 the rise in sales amounted to 30 per cent and no less than 100 per cent in 1927.

In 1928 the Škoda directors in Mladá Boleslav sought to replace the old models with newly developed ones – types 4R and 6R. The first was meant to satisfy the demand for a small to medium vehicle. It was given a four cylinder engine of 1944 cc with 32 bhp. The bore and stroke (75 x 110 mm) were identical on the 6R but this had two more cylinders, therefore it had a capacity of 2916 cc and 50 bhp. The latter car was in the very comfortable class, but not quite luxury. Both vehicles were conservatively designed, very robust and of lasting quality. Sadly they were not a commercial success, and two years later were taken out of production.

The demand for utility and commercial vehicles rose after Škoda's takeover. Apart from the light lorry type 115, there was also its very similar derivative, the 125, to which a more powerful engine from the type 120 passenger car was fitted. The heavier commercial trucks continued to be based on the original Laurin & Klement designs but became more powerful. The new 5 tonne truck type 550 had a stronger engine of 6786 cc and 50 bhp.

In 1928 a small series of 9 railcars using the engine and transmission from the 550 lorry were produced. The Czechoslovak railways introduced these vehicles later for local traffic. Their construction and interior equipment was not so different from the buses of the period, in fact they were called rail-buses. At the same time the motor plough manufacture was reduced and the production of agricultural tractors began. The first was the model HT 30 with a four cylinder OHV engine and an output of 36 bhp, running on kerosene. In the next few years came the development and sale of a further range of tractors and all the tractors were made in Plzeň; Mladá Boleslav cooperated in supplying certain parts.

In 1929 the first new heavy trucks appeared, the Škoda types 504 and 506. The engines of the 504 and 506 had the same bore/stroke ratio, the four cylinder capacity coming in at 4,849 cc, the six to 7274 cc, both using a number of interchangeable parts. The type numbering was no longer haphazard: the first two numbers, in this instance 50, referred to the weight carrying capacity, i.e. 5000 kg. The third referred to the number of cylinders.

Later in 1928 the Škoda engineers worked on the development of an entirely new range of passenger vehicles. This range was gradually put into production in 1929.

This new range of passenger cars was of similar construction yet provided a wide range of types to satisfy all manner of customers. The smallest, type 422, had a 1195 cc engine with 22 bhp and a three speed gearbox connected to the rear-wheel drive; a pressed steel frame was suspended on half-elliptics and had solid front and rear axles. It carried a four-seater standard body. Again, the type numbering proceeded according to a predetermined code: 4 for four cylinders and 22 for the horse power rating. The next type, the 430, had 30 bhp. This was also a four-seater but with more room for passengers. The six cylinder type 645 had an engine of the same cylinder size as the 430, but was intended as a luxury vehicle and could be chosen from two chassis lengths providing four- or six-seater bodies.

For demanding customers, the type 860 provided not only the biggest vehicle but also luxurious trim. It compared favourably with other European equivalent products. The 860 had a six- to seven-seater body and was fitted with an eight cylinder 3888 cc 60 bhp engine. This car was the first 'eight' in series production since the Laurin & Klement type FF prototype. The 860 was manufactured until 1931 and was fitted with phaeton, limousine and cabriolet bodies. Light commercial vehicles and small buses for 12 people were derived from the 860 pssenger car chassis.

This range of models did not show much of an advance on world motor car design developments; nevertheless, it set good competitive standards for

LEFT **Škoda tractor type HT 33/1 from 1933.**

BELOW LEFT **The 1933 tractor type HT 33 S with an 8.8 litre engine of 55 bhp.**

RIGHT **Škoda caterpillar tractor type STH of 60 bhp from 1934.**

the times. The cars were still too expensive but it must be realized that the market was very tough. There were too few buyers because of the enduring expense of personal transport. The industry endeavoured to create what today is called 'brand loyalty'. So if a customer wanted or needed to trade-up, the right vehicle had to be provided to prevent him from going elsewhere. The largest number of sales was in the smaller types, the 422 and 430.

Until 1929 production figures in Mladá Boleslav were still rising and so was the number of employees – 3278 in that year, the biggest number since production began there. This brought about its own internal problems which again threatened the viability of the company. The main difficulty was the delegation of decisions from the mother company in Plzeň, which was slow in responding and totally out of touch with the needs of the Boleslav works.

In 1929 it was resolved to completely re-organize Škodovy závody and to this end a joint stock company for automotive products was set up in January 1930, within the framework of the main Škoda enterprise. Its initials in Czech formed the letters

ASAP (Akciová společnost pro automobilový průmysl – Joint Stock Company for Automobile Industry). The new company took over the Mladá Boleslav works, the automotive department in Plzeň, the factory repair works in Prague, and a number of smaller repair shops and branches. However, the Škoda marque was retained. This decision proved to be correct and helped the works towards a better position in the years to come.

The worldwide economic crisis in 1929 did not at first affect the Czechoslovak automotive industry and Škoda vehicles sold well enough. Mladá Boleslav continued to concentrate on the design of passenger cars and commercial vehicles. The older 1928 types were still made but were at the end of their useful life and nothing radically new made its appearance. The type 650 came in 1930, more powerful than its sister the 645, with bore enlarged from 72 mm to 75 mm resulting in a 2,704 cc capacity. The stroke remained unchanged and the horsepower rose, as the type number implied, to 50. In the same year, the 650 engine was also used to power the two-tonne truck. This model became one of the most successful Škoda vehicles of the thirties.

Yet the dark clouds of the world-wide crisis, while delaying its impact on the automotive industry, eventually affected Škoda. From 1930 on, a considerable fall-off in production was recorded until its lowest level in 1933.

Short-sighted bureaucratic interference now added to the problems caused by the nervous economy. The Czechoslovak railways were in such a loss-making situation that it was seen to adversely affect the already shaky state budget. Some government officials believed that by drastically limiting road transport the railway situation could be improved. In 1932 a law was announced, known to the people as the 'anti-motoring' law. This put severe limitations on commercial and bus transport. Another anti-motoring blow was the enforced addition of alcohol to petrol which was meant to help with the sales of agricultural products. However this decision only brought about more expensive fuel.

Contemporary sources state that without exaggeration, these dispositions caused a veritable

ABOVE LEFT **The six cylinder Škoda 645 with Sodomka luxury body.**

ABOVE **Škoda 633 with a six cylinder side-valve engine.**

LEFT **The refined two-seater fixed head coupé type 650.**

BELOW **Auto Škoda letterhead.**

AKTIENGESELLSCHAFT
FÜR AUTOMOBIL-
INDUSTRIE

WERK ML. BOLESLAV.

Postsparkassakonto: 44.823.

AUTO ⊛ ŠKODA

DIREKTION ML. BOLESLAV.
Telefon 37, 73, 198, 373, 374.
Telegrammadresse:
ASAP ML. BOLESLAV.

Ml. Boleslav, den

No:

Verkaufsstelle:

catastrophe. A number of transport-connected businesses went under and thousands of cars were laid up. The sales of new trucks practically ceased and buses were no longer manufactured. Obviously, all remaining firms connected with the automotive industry were in great difficulty and not surprisingly the number of unemployed rose even further.

Another point that the law-makers had not considered was the reduction of the defence capability of the country. No modern army can make do with-out widespread civilian motoring, which, in case of war, could supply competent back-up. Only later, around 1936, did the government realize its mistake, when the spectre of another international conflict appeared on the horizon.

This lamentable situation had a dampening effect on the development of new types of vehicles. The exception was the broadening of the Škoda 633 range which gradually became a success due to its styling concept. A six cylinder four-seater of 1792 cc and 33 bhp, the 633 was very supple and

The 1929 Škoda 422.

easy to drive, yet still orthodox with solid front and rear axles. Then a longer wheelbase model of 1961 cc with a bigger body came along, the type 637, having many identical components to the 633.

The 430 continued to be the best-seller of the whole range and much favoured for taxi transport. A modified and longer diesel-engine version became the 430D. Its 1802 cc engine produced 32 bhp. From 1930 the commercial range could also be supplied with diesel engines, such as the heavy lorry type 606D with its 8553 cc, 100 bhp motor.

At this time a little known but interesting episode should be mentioned. Škoda's main competitors were the other major Czech automobile manufacturers – Praga and Tatra. Praga was founded on March 27, 1907 as Pražská továrna na automobily a.s. (Prague Works for Automobiles, joint stock company). From 1909 the marque Praga was established and wholly owned by První českomoravská továrna na stroje a.s. (First Czech-Moravian Machine Works, joint stock company). In 1921 the company combined with another engineering concern becoming Českomoravská-Kolben. In 1928 a firm Breitfeld, Daněk a spol. was added to the partnership and the industrial concern called ČKD was instituted. Its manufacture was initially based mainly on motor car models made under licence and later its own designs were used. Tatra, previously known as Nesselsdorfer Wagenbau and located in Moravia, started making cars in 1897 and was the first car manufacturer in the Austro-Hungarian Empire. Right from the outset Tatra became well-known for its innovative car designs. Even when times were relatively normal the three firms always competed hard for their market share. It follows that these manufacturers offered vehicles that were conceptually similar, even to the number of types made.

For comparison the 1929 sales figures were:

Praga: 8454 passenger cars, 4401 trucks and 745 buses.
Škoda: 4158 passenger cars, 2323 trucks and 623 buses.
Tatra: 5034 passenger cars, 842 trucks.

This rather unhealthy competitive situation, given the prevailing market conditions, brought the leaders of the three firms together. They decided to amalgamate their companies. Tatra, at this stage of the negotiations, toyed with the idea of joining the new venture but at a later stage pulled out. So matters were left to Škoda and Praga and they set up a new company naming it 'Motor', in January 1932.

This joint venture was to divide the production programme, thus getting rid of the unhealthy rivalry. The idea was basically sound but foundered on the marque loyalty of the personnel, particularly the sales people. It was too much to expect. How could they collaborate suddenly when for years they had been rivals? The contemporary press wrote: 'This marriage collapsed after two months and the divorce came after three months'. That is to say that on March 31st, 1932 both companies reverted to the status quo.

Some people feel that the golden era of motoring was firmly anchored in the nineteen twenties. Those were the days of great European automotive expansion, but most of the automotive technical problems had already been resolved. Technicians were concentrating on improvements in performance, suspension, braking and comfort. Cars became heavier and ever more powerful, which

1929 Škoda 430; not surprisingly, it was the smaller models such as this which sold in the greatest numbers.

lead to ever increasing fuel consumption. Actually the basic European car had not really changed: a pressed steel chassis with solid front and rear axle suspended on leaf springs with a separate, rectangular-shaped body on steel or timber frame, panelled in imitation leather and only lately wholly clad in pressed sheet metal. Only a few pioneers considered streamlining or lessening the air resistance of the big square rigged bodies. Though ASAP experimented, producing several interesting aerodynamic prototypes, they were mainly used in sporting events rather than sold to the general public. Some manufacturers took the plunge. Hans Ledwinka, for example, broke totally new ground with his aerodynamic Tatra type 77, but cars like these were sold in very small numbers.

To manufacture truly popular new cars meant enormous development costs, to say nothing of expensive publicity campaigns. There was also the possibility of financial catastrophe if sales of the new design did not meet development costs. So production plodded on with few risks and an acceptable level of profit.

Whether or not to make a quality small car became the basic question for the majority of vehicle producers. This was their very survival in the

Škoda's new concept of a small car - type 420. It had a central square section frame chassis forked in front to carry the engine on rubber mountings.

The 420 Popular represented great value for money in comparison with earlier models.

face of the deepening economic crisis. Manufacturers also realized that a commercially viable small car could not be designed by simply scaling down a larger one. The brighter brains saw clearly that weight was a key issue. Less weight meant less fuel consumption and a lighter vehicle could be powered by a smaller engine and work well in everyday situations competing easily with heavier vehicles. Lighter weight also equated to less material, resulting in lower costs. On the other hand the new model needed better suspension to increase comfort.

During 1931 and 1932 Škoda did not bring anything new to the market, but intensive work was going on in the design and development departments.

In 1933 came the introduction of a radical new vehicle, the Škoda type 420. It was destined to be a real bench mark in design. The fact that production of the original was short-lived does not diminish its true value, for it demonstrated new design principles and established a basis for further development.

The 420 type's fundamental novelty lay in its central frame. This was welded from steel U-shaped profiles and forked in front to cradle the

engine. This idea was based on the pioneering work of Hans Ledwinka in his Tatra 11 of 1923. Škoda's rear wheel drive arrangement and suspension was also a totally new concept, allied to rear independent swing axles. The front suspension was a solid tube on quarter-elliptics. The 995 cc side-valve engine (65 mm bore x 75 mm stroke) produced 20 bhp at 2,800 rpm with Ricardo-type cylinder head.

Towards the end of 1933 the type 420 was replaced by a new model, the 420 Popular. From that year ASAP gave up numbering its new products for a time and used proper names instead. The main reason, of course, was advertising. After all, a name is always easier to remember than a number.

The new Popular had a smaller engine of 903 cc (65 x 68) giving 18 bhp. The chassis was now made of steel tube with the engine fitted to the fork on rubber mountings. At the front was a split axle with a transverse leaf spring, with upper ends that were connected to friction shock-absorbers. The three-speed gearbox was actually located within the rear

ABOVE **The 1932 Škoda 'people's car' prototype 932 with an air-cooled 1,498 flat four rear engine and a very advanced innovative body design. The front end is certainly reminiscent of something . . .**

RIGHT **The well conceived rear engine compartment of the 932. Unfortunately no production followed.**

transmission and fixed to the central chassis tube. The overall weight came down as low as 650 kg. The first series cars were two door four-seater saloons and cabriolets or two-seater roadsters. The bodies dispensed with the use of running boards for the first time.

The cabriolet cost 18,800 Czech crowns and the two-seater 17,800 – a sensationally low price for the time. The following table shows the terrific progress made both in weight and price savings:

1927 type 110, open body, 1,450 kg, 50,000 crowns.
1931 type 422, closed body, 1,050 kg, 42,000 crowns.
1934 type 420, cabriolet, 650 kg, 18,800 crowns.

Contemporary exchange rate was 31 Czechoslovak crowns to US$1.

The Popular was a successful design, but more importantly the car represented an extensive rationalization at Mladá Boleslav. That the concept was correct was proven by the fact that this chassis design remained basically unchanged and used by Škoda for almost thirty years.

Škoda designs were always developed by a team of dedicated people but some more talented engineers stood out. A.Raška, director of the automobile shop, was responsible for the very successful Popular design. J.Káleš was employed by Škoda in the late 1920's and made a speciality of air-cooled engines. In 1930 he joined Dr Ing. F.Porsche to develop the first Volkswagen prototypes.

In the early thirties Škoda undertook some very interesting experiments with rear positioned air and water-cooled engines in streamlined car concepts. These ideas followed along the same innovative path and even ahead of contemporary research and progress made by others such as Ganz, Ledwinka and Porsche. One very advanced rear engine prototype, the Škoda 932 from 1932 which had a rear 1.5 litre air-cooled engine was very similar in concept to the Tatra V570 and the type 12 Porsche-designed prototype for Zündapp. Another experiment, the Škoda 935 of 1935 had a horizontal water-cooled 1,995 cc engine positioned at the rear and its body design based on the Jaray-Tatra principles. It is a pity that the Škoda experiments

ABOVE LEFT **Another 1932 prototype, this time with a water-cooled vertical four cylinder engine.**

LEFT **The 1935 rear engine prototype 935 with a modern aerodynamic body.**

did not result in series production. The only air-cooled Škoda passenger car taken further than the prototype was the 1937 Sagitta which had a front two cylinder engine in V form of 844 cc.

In 1934 the Popular received the 995 cc engine previously fitted to the type 420 but now with the higher output of 22 bhp. Apart from the Popular, Škoda also launched the more powerful 420 Rapid in 1934. This model was of the same concept as the Popular with a central tubular chassis and four-wheel independent suspension. Its 1,195 cc engine was lifted from the older type 422 with few modifications. The Rapid also had a three-speed transmission, synchronized on the upper two ratios as in the Popular, but this time the gearbox was situated in the vehicle's centre. Top speed was 90 kph.

Another novelty for 1934 was the completely re-designed 637 type, now designated 637D. This medium sized six cylinder car had a similar layout to the Popular and Rapid but with a modernized engine located on three rubber blocks and fitted with a down-draught carburettor. Horse power was increased to 45 and the gearbox synchronized. However, due to the prevailing economic circumstances, production was limited. The vehicle was expensive considering its lack of fittings and consequently the car was never a commercial success.

The 637D type never really made the grade because it fell between two classes of buyers. ASAP decided to develop its concept further into a larger car. The chassis was lengthened and received the six cylinder engine from the 206 truck in which it had been successfully used for some time. The bore was reduced by 3 mm and the cubic capacity became 2,492 cc providing 55 bhp. The new car was called the Superb 640 and was marketed as a luxury saloon. Other bodies were later also bolted onto this chassis. The engine had eight main bearings, a torsional vibration damper and pressure lubrication with a double oil filter. A twelve volt coil ignition with an automatic advance control and either a Solex or Zenith carburettor completed the engine equipment. A single dry-plate clutch was allied to a four-speed gearbox, fourth gear being direct drive, with third and fourth synchronized. Steering was by worm and sector, hydraulic brakes and shock absorbers were fitted and the central tubular chassis concept with four wheel independent suspension was maintained. In the saloon form the Superb could attain 110 kph. Two years later the engine was enlarged to 2,703 cc with 60 bhp or an even larger unit of 2,916 cc of 65 bhp was used. The Superb became a long-term success and was manufactured until just after the war with modernized body work and an OHV 3,137 cc engine of 85 bhp.

In 1935 the Rapid was launched with a more powerful 1,385 cc engine. It had four cylinders of 70 mm bore and 90 mm stroke, side valves and produced 31 bhp. A Cotal electric preselector gearbox could be fitted to order and Lockheed brakes acted on all four wheels. The Rapid came in a basic two door saloon version and cost 31,400 crowns. The four door four-seat version came to 33,100 and a two door four-seater cabriolet to 34,200 crowns. The British magazine *The Motor*, bringing news of the 1937 Geneva Motor Show, printed the photograph of a Škoda Rapid as the only illustration to its report of the Show. The caption read: 'The Škoda – a small car of pleasing appearance and built with independent suspension throughout. It comes from Czechoslovakia'.

In 1934 and 1935 the commercial vehicle market slowly began to revive and Škoda's competitiveness increased with the help of low prices and a good reputation. No exception was the new type 656D. This vehicle normally had a 105 bhp diesel engine and its chassis was usually fitted with coach bodies for town use.

Around this time Škoda's commercial vehicles found new markets among the emerging economies of the oil-rich nations in the Middle-East, particularly in Iran. With the exports on the increase, the range grew to the 8 and 10 tonne type 806DT. This truck had a three-axle chassis, only one being powered. It could be fitted with two alternative engines, either the 105 bhp diesel or, for the European market, with the 135 bhp motor, which was used in vehicles equipped with gas generators.

These generators were very significant in the mid-thirties. Fuel supply had been a major factor in the outcome of the First World War and with Hitler now gazing wistfully towards the East, all Europe had to secure a reliable fuel alternative to oil. Of course, no substitute was ever totally ideal. Using gas or charcoal generators decreased power output, increased vehicular weight and the need for engine maintenance. However, these generators were economical.

The Škoda works provided charcoal burning units on demand for its heavy commercial vehicles. The generators were made in-house under licence from the French Panhard-Levassor company.

The 404D truck was a smaller version of the 606D unit. It had a four cylinder diesel (110 mm x 150 mm) with 67 bhp and could carry 3 to 4 tonnes. The smallest Škoda commercial vehicle, the 254D was very modern and fast giving 60 bhp from its diesel engine of 3,770 cc. It even had hydraulic brakes.

In the nineteen-twenties and early thirties ASAP did not undertake much sporting activity other than the Monte Carlo Rallies and a few long distance local events. Until 1914 speed events were mainly contested by ordinary touring cars, modified to a small degree. The factory engines were lightly tuned and the bodywork was stripped to the barest minimum. This meant that virtually every manufacturer could participate in racing. But the early twenties brought about increasing technical differences between sporting and touring cars. Since Mladá Boleslav was mainly orientated towards production of fairly heavy touring machines, there was little point in entering major competitive events.

The prevailing mood of 'anti-motoring' in Czechoslovakia was a further determining factor in ASAP's reduced competitiveness. The change only came when new car construction concepts were introduced and it became necessary to convince the buyers of their abilities and characteristics. When the Popular appeared the general public had doubts about its real possibilities, capabilities and endurance. The sceptics had to be charmed and in May 1934 four Škoda Populars of the first series completed a journey of 14,800 km from Czechoslovakia to India without any mishaps. The seven drivers, mainly students, were lead by a Canadian, Dr Z.Peters. This expedition was big news for the foreign press and its success brought the factory applause from the entire world.

Any further lingering lack of confidence in the Populars vanished when two standard models covered the difficult 1,800 km 1934 Alpine Rally, bringing home two Alpine cups and two gold plaques.

The Popular was also successfully tested by Ing. J.Hanuš who drove one from Algiers across the Sahara to Gao and Dakar.

ASAP came back to racing with a vengeance. In

Škoda-Popular wins in the 2nd Alpine Rally!

Škoda lists its successes achieved during 1935.

1935 the factory built three aerodynamic coupés in light alloy on the production chassis of the Popular. The engines had a higher compression ratio and a bigger output from the oil pump. These special racing coupés managed a maximum of 125 kph on the longer straights, which was a fair performance. Weight distribution was good as was the tough chassis. Its small Hardy-Spicer universals had to be in good condition, otherwise propeller shaft vibration set in. Zdeněk Pohl, a well known racing driver, managed a few local successes with this sporting Škoda coupé. Small series of Populars with aerodynamic bodies were made and sold at higher price to regular customers and were called Popular Special.

1936 became a particularly significant year for Mladá Boleslav. The earlier high investment in the development of design began to bear fruit. Sales figures of 3,912 vehicles that year represented an increase of 55 per cent compared to 1935 and ASAP overtook its competitors in Czechoslovakia. Škoda also made another breakthrough selling 250

cars in one week at the Prague Autosalon. The mainstay of this upward swing was the Popular but the sales of commercial vehicles also rose. The sales levels attained before the time of the world economic crisis were reached and kept steadily rising further. Interestingly, this steep increase in sales did not abate until the outbreak of the Second World War.

A new vehicle for 1936 was the Favorit type 904, which was meant to bridge the gap between the Rapid and the luxurious Superb. The Favorit had the capacity of 1,802 cc and 38 bhp and was usually fitted with a four door 5 to 6-seater body. Its engine had a cast iron cylinder block with nitride liners and light alloy pistons. A Scintilla BP4 12 volt installation with automatic advance looked after the ignition and a Zenith 30 VEI carburettor was fitted with a fuel filter and an intake silencer. A dry single-plate clutch separated the engine from the four-speed and reverse synchro gearbox and the propeller shaft was statically and dynamically balanced with two universal joints. The front and rear

LEFT **Škoda Popular at the finish of the 1936 Monte Carlo Rally.**

RIGHT **The classic Škoda chassis with central backbone frame forked at front to receive the engine with four wheel independent suspension. In this case, a 1937 Popular OHV, the gearbox is integral with the rear axle. This basic design was retained by Škoda for thirty years.**

BELOW **Škoda Popular Monte Carlo with a 1,385 cc engine from 1936.**

BOTTOM **Another Popular Monte Carlo roadster from 1937.**

BELOW **The 1937 Škoda Popular Monte Carlo coupé. Note the headlamps incorporated into the body.**

suspension was independent with transverse half elliptic springs and hydraulic shock-absorbers. The chassis, based on the same principles as that of the Popular, consisted of a central backbone tube which was forked in front for the engine. Steering was by worm and nut, hydraulic brakes acted on the four wheels, with the handbrake operating the rears. The 43 litre fuel supply was fitted with a 10 litre reserve. This was controlled by a three-way fuel cock situated close to the driver's controls. Equipment was lavish for its time, complete with sun visor, newspaper net, ceiling lamp, a small hand lamp fitted to the A post to enable the driver to light up obscure direction signs (a very necessary fitting in those days), two glove compartments and even a cut glass crystal ashtray. Ride comfort was ensured by rubber mounting not only of the engine but also the body. In its six-seater guise the Favorit was publicised as particularly useful for larger families.

1936 brought ASAP not only increased exports but also success in the sporting field.

The Monte Carlo Rally, the 'world championship for sports and touring cars' took place for the first time in 1911. 23 competitors participated and the prescribed average speed must have been around 10 kph. This seems ridiculous today, but then the drivers were really in it up to their necks. The Rally was then, as it still is, typically run in January. The event was an amazing winter adventure, involving the crossing of the European continent in appalling blizzards and on poor roads. There were no ploughs to clear the snow and no regular maintenance of the roads in those days. In the Alps there was even the threat of being attacked by wolves. The course warranted a car of outstanding endurance and reliability and drivers of supreme skill and physical stamina. They were four days and four nights on the road, without proper sleep and as nearly non-stop as humanly possible.

Two drivers alternated at the wheel while the other snatched some sleep in the car. In view of the terrible weather conditions car crews carried carefully prepared special equipment: snow chains, spades, skis for the car, fog lamps, windscreen defrosters, food warmers and central heaters for the car interiors. If you imagine that most of the cars then had roadster bodywork one shivers at the thought of this marathon.

The rules of the competition changed with the times, but the basic arrangement remained the same. A route was selected starting from various distant European capitals and cities. For each route a set of points was awarded depending on the scale of the terrain difficulty. All routes were roughly the same length, but should a competitor fail to reach his starting point it was possible to start from a nearer control on his chosen route. However, this meant fewer bonus marks and in addition carried a penalty of five points. The average travel time was established and time controls were placed along the route.

In the nineteen-thirties, entrants were required to average not more than 65 kph and not less than 40 kph and for the last 1,000 km this was increased to not less than 50 kph. The controls were set at various points along each route, and, provided one did not exceed an average of 65 kph, it was possible to gain a bit of time in the stages between them, for rest and refuelling of car and crew. For the latest permitted hour of arrival based on an average of 40 kph from the previous control, was the time set for departing on the next stage. Obviously, the longer the stage, the more time in hand one could build up. Once at the control nothing could be done to the car. Arrival times were stamped on the drivers' road books and these books were not given back to competitors until the time of departure. Apart from the Channel crossing, for competitors starting from a town in Britain and for which a special allowance was granted, all delays at frontiers, sleep, meals, refuelling and permitted repairs had to come out of the time scheduled between controls, and therefore had to be made up.

At the finish, as soon as the drivers checked in, their cars underwent a strict scrutiny for condition, and points were lost for any defects which might have developed en route, such as starters out of order, lamps not working and also for damage to wings. Then a special eliminating test in acceleration, braking and reversing took place which decided the order among competitors who finished with equal points. Here the competitor could lose points or gain bonuses.

The test, against the clock, consisted of a route from point A where cars had to drive forward 200 metres to point B, reverse round a pylon, enter an area nearby and perform a figure of eight, dash off back to the start and reverse round a pylon there, and then again flat out to point C and to the finish 300 metres ahead.

According to the engine capacity in the 1936 Rally, the cars were divided into two groups, one below 1,500 cc, the light car category, and one above 1,500 cc, the general category. The main parts of the engine such as the cylinder head, cylinder block, chassis, radiator and front and rear axles were sealed to prevent dismantling for repairs or substitution. After the finish even the bonnet was sealed to prevent the drivers making changes or carrying out repairs before the special test. During the journey no competitor could accept help from a factory support team. Therefore there were no accompanying convoys. The only concession allowed was that drivers could help themselves.

The Rally prizes were many and various. In the general category the first prize was a cup and 50,000 French francs (about £600 in those days) with further cash awards for the next nine places. In the light car category the first prize was 12,000 francs. In addition to those there was a galaxy of special trophies awarded for the most comfortable car, cleanliness and appearance of engines and for the highest marks in the eliminating test.

The first Czechoslovak who reached the finishing line of the Monte Carlo Rally was Ing. Rechziegl in a Praga Piccolo in 1931, finishing ninth in the light car class. A year later he was twelfth in the higher classification in a Praga Alfa. This was, in fact, a bigger success considering the much stronger competition in that particular field. Until 1936 the best position attained by Czechs had been achieved by the racing driver B. Turek in an Aero 1000 when in 1934 he was placed second in his category.

1936 was the fifteenth anniversary of the Monte Carlo Rally and Mladá Boleslav decided to participate with its most successful commercial product – Škoda Popular. They prepared a special prototype with a roadster body using the engine from the Škoda Rapid of 1,385 cc and in this way better utilizing the classification of up to 1,500 cc. The Rapid also supplied the wider rear axle.

The drivers, Z.Pohl, a well-known racing driver and a long distance driver, Ing. J.Hausman, were chosen for their experience. Both had skill and knowledge of similar cars in difficult conditions. Without hesitation they chose the most taxing route which carried the maximum number of bonus points and provided advantage for the best possible placing. The route went from Athens via Salonica, Sofia, Belgrade, Budapest, Vienna, Munich, Strasbourg and Dijon, Lyons, Avignon, Brignolles to Monte Carlo. For completing this 3,845 km (2,403 miles) journey without fault, drivers received 506 points. In comparison the routes starting from Tallinn and Bucharest carried only 503 points and from Stavanger and Umea 501 points and from John O'Groats 496.

Eighteen cars started in Athens and 14 reached the finish, 12 of them without any penalty points. The results showed that the Czechs chose the right route because all the three first places, after absolute results were declared, started from Athens. Pohl and Hausman reached Monte Carlo without penalty points with a considerable amount of time on their hands. However, in the eliminating test the handicap of the three-speed gearbox showed and despite all their efforts Hungarians E.Kozma and I.Martinek, who started from Tallinn with a 995 cc Fiat-Balilla and aided by its four-speed box, managed to overtake them. In the overall classification of both classes the much more powerful Ford, Delahaye, Renault and others scored at the top.

The magazine *The Motor* from February 4, 1936 confirmed the results of the Rally. A Škoda Popular with the starting number 54, gained 625.9 points and tied for second place with the 1,232 cc Triumph Gloria, driven from Umea by Miss J.Richmond and G.S.Brooks of Great Britain, in the 1,500 cc class and twentieth overall.

On the basis of the special Škoda Popular used in the Rally, Mladá Boleslav produced two series of about seventy cars called Škoda Popular Monte Carlo; 20 were made as roadsters with engines of 995 cc and fifty coupés with 1,385 cc engines.

The Popular's reliability was also proven in specific long distance events. These were not really of a sporting nature, but nevertheless very demanding. For instance in 1936, the enthusiastic Czech motor journalist F.A.Elstner and his wife Eva, prepared for a so-called 'hundred days in a small car'. They bought the Popular and took a ship to New York. Then they motored across the United States to Texas, around Mexico, through Arizona and California and all the way down to South America and back to New York, covering a staggering 25,000 km. The 'hundred days' really meant an actual driving time of only 47 days, with the Elstners averaging 530 km per day, a remarkable achievement for two drivers and their small machine. Once and for all the doubters were proved wrong. A small car was capable not only of staying long distances, but also of putting up good averages.

These facts were further underlined by yet another long trip, this time undertaken by B.J.Procházka and J.Kubiáš in a Škoda Rapid. Their aim was to circle the world, again in a small car and

The 1937 Škoda Popular OHV two door saloon had headlamps built into the front wings.

again in one hundred days. Their journey took them across Germany, Poland, the Soviet Union, Iran, India, Ceylon, China, Japan, then across the United States and, via western Europe, finally to Czechoslovakia. The non-stop San Francisco-New York stage was officially timed at 100 hours 55 minutes. The whole journey of 28,000 km took 97 days and received warm approval from the world's press.

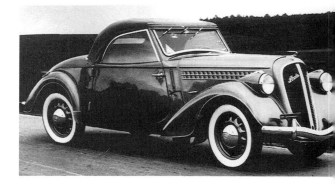

In 1937 the Populars, now with an added designation number IV and also called the Popular OHV, went into series production with overhead valve engines. They had the same cubic capacity as the side-valves but now in OHV form produced 27 bhp. The body design also improved using elements of streamlining. The headlamps were no longer free standing and became an integral part of the front wheel arches – a very advanced design for that time and this produced a pleasing, modern and well proportioned range of models including two door four-seater saloons as well as four-seater cabriolets, two-seater roadsters and delivery vans. In 1938 the engines went up to 1,089 cc (68 mm bore x 75 mm stroke) and 30 bhp. With an updated body this model was called the Popular 1100 OHV. Hydraulic brakes took the place of mechanical installation, a modern feature for its day.

The 1938 exports of the Populars and Rapids reached large number of countries including Belgium, India, China, Estonia, France, Italy, Yugoslavia, Hungary, Poland, Austria, Greece, Sweden, USSR, Turkey, USA, Argentina, Brazil, Bulgaria, Egypt, Finland, Holland South Africa, Norway, Spain, Siam, Switzerland, Uruguay and Romania. The photographer from the British magazine *The Motor* sent a picture of a Škoda Rapid roadster to his editors which was published on December 13th, 1938: 'Frisky and Škoda. A very attractive semi-sports two-seater Škoda spotted in Amsterdam. These cars are produced by the famous Škoda armaments concern in Czechoslovakia'.

By degrees, overhead valve engines were also installed in the other vehicle types and by 1938 the Rapid's new power unit of 1,563 cc produced 42 bhp. At the same time the Škoda Superb was upgraded to 3,137cc giving 85 bhp.

The old range of smaller commercial vehicles, the 104 and 206 were modernized in 1937. Instead of the 104 the model 918 was introduced. This was a one-and-a-half tonne truck with the 38 bhp engine of the Favorit. The two-tonne 915 replaced the 206, and was fitted with the 60 bhp engine of the Superb. The same unit, but with a longer chassis, was numbered 929. Exports were booming

LEFT **Škoda Popular OHV convertible roadster from 1937.**

CENTRE LEFT **Škoda Popular OHV publicity poster.**

BOTTOM LEFT **The 1937 Škoda Rapid 1.4 convertible coupé.**

RIGHT **Škoda Superb II touring limousine of 1937.**

again and in 1937 almost fifty per cent of Škoda vehicles were sent abroad. In the same year by way of proof of its exporting success, the company exhibited at the motor shows in Paris, Brussels, Geneva, Zagreb, Posen, Belgrade, Buenos Aires and Johannesburg.

In 1937 a particularly interesting technical solution well in advance of its time was applied to the Škoda 532 type, an aerodynamically shaped three-axle bus with a rear engine. Unusually, and perhaps with export in mind, the driver occupied a central seat. In those days, the Czechoslovak traffic rule was to drive on the left. This meant normally vehicles were made with right-hand steering, as in the United Kingdom to this day. Only when the Germans occupied Czechoslovakia in 1939 the rule of the road changed to the right. Sadly only a prototype of the 532 bus was manufactured; the approaching war stopped further development.

Various specific army vehicles – the 6ST6, 6STP6, and 6LTP6 – were made in considerable quantities and supplied to the Czechoslovak and other armies.

For the 1937 Monte Carlo Rally the factory prepared a special Škoda Rapid with an enclosed aerodynamic body. The engine and chassis were standard series, although a four-speed electric Cotal preselector gearbox was fitted after the last year's experience and the engine had a slightly increased output to 36 bhp. Pohl and Hausman chose Palermo in Sicily as their starting point from which 4,130 km (2,565 miles) were travelled before reaching Monte Carlo. The number of marks awarded for the route from Palermo was 500. The Škoda Rapid had starting number 120. Their journey went very smoothly and no troubles were encountered, although snow conditions in the Alps were treacherous that year. From the thirty

cars starting in Sicily only four reached Monte Carlo and among them, without penalty points, were the Czechs. After the final elimination test came the disappointment. Pohl and Hausman were classified second in their group, when the overall weight of the Rapid, 1,100 kg left the Škoda behind the lighter and stronger six cylinder 1,493 cc Fiat of 45 bhp, driven by L.V.Villoresi. The Škoda team tied with a 1,185 cc Hillman Minx driven by M.Gatsonides and a 1,496 cc Riley driven by the Innes brothers for the second place. However the final technical control discovered after a protest by the English competitors that the reflecting surface of the Škoda's rear view mirror measured 4 square cm less than the prescribed size, and this led to four penalty points bringing the total to 830.95. This loss of points resulted in the Czechs being downgraded to fourth place and twenty-sixth overall, which was still a fine achievement. Incidentally the Riley was also penalized for a similar offence and had to accept third place, behind the Hillman Minx.

The same year provided Škoda with more successes, this time in the Balkan Rally and the Nairobi to Johannesburg race. In the African adventure a 1935 Škoda Popular roadster of 995 cc, driven by Dutchmen Van Deburg and Van Vuuren executed this demanding event while outclassing much bigger cars such as a Ford V8, a Chevrolet, a Lincoln, a Bentley and many others.

In 1939 a Škoda Popular 1100 OHV driven by Uruguayan racing driver Victor Borrat Fabini, gained an absolute victory in one of the most difficult races in the world, through pampas and mountains, the South American Mercedes-Montevideo.

In the same year the Popular again became designated as the 995. The power unit was reverted to the earlier 995 cc engine of 22 bhp and had a new

ABOVE LEFT **The 1937 Škoda prototype 532 bus with six wheel chassis, rear engine and centre steering. Incredibly advanced, streamlined body design.**

LEFT **View of the smooth front of the 532 bus.**

ABOVE **Ing.Hausman and Z.Pohl team on their return from the 1937 Monte Carlo Rally in Prague with the Škoda Rapid.**

RIGHT **The Škoda Popular 1100 OHV.**

ABOVE **Škoda 606 D luxury coach for long distance travel with a Sodomka designed body from 1938.**

ABOVE LEFT **Škoda Popular 1100 OHV roadster from 1939.**

BELOW LEFT **Škoda Rapid OHV with a special two door aerodynamic body from 1939.**

body shape. For its time it was technically among the best in its class, even when compared to other European makes. This model continued in production until 1942 and endeared itself to many. Czech motorists referred affectionately to the Popular as Liduška, a young girl's name. In 1939 the Rapid OHV also received a new body shape. It was basically similar, but of course bigger than the Popular. The Rapid could be ordered with a specially streamlined body.

Rationalization was also introduced in the commercial sector and the OHV engine from the Rapid, the 1,563 cc of 42 bhp, was installed in a one tonne truck of the 100 type. The new 2,091 cc, 52 bhp engine later used in the next Favorit model was fitted to the 1.5 tonne type 150 truck. This vehicle was such a successful design that it was still produced for a number of years after the Second World War. Its modern design particularly showed up by placing the engine forward of the independent front suspension which comprised two superimposed leaf springs. The Superb's six cylinder

3,137 cc 85 bhp engine went into the type 256B truck, capable of carrying two and a half tonnes. This vehicle sold well.

The war clouds spreading across Europe in the late thirties finally persuaded those in power in Czechoslovakia that their anti-motoring attitudes had to change. Politicians actively began to support automobile development, especially in the commercial sector. The anticipated rise in demand provided further impetus to continue the modernization of the commercial and utility ranges of vehicles. The production of the older types 304, 306, 504 and 506 was run down and replaced by the diesel-engined models 404D and 606D. The heavy vehicles such as 706D, a more powerful version of the 606D, could transport up to seven tonnes. Their chassis were lowered and lengthened to be used for coaches.

The increasing production and design activity in Mladá Boleslav testified to an efficient organization with a modern and progressive outlook. The company was manufacturing good quality products which enabled low vehicle prices in increasingly competitive markets. It is not surprising that Škoda or ASAP, as the company was officially known, became the largest motor car manufacturer in Czechoslovakia. However, the outbreak of the Second World War in 1939 signified a repeat of the events in 1914 and Škoda's great plans for the future succumbed to an unknown fate.

9 How to ruin your automobile the Škoda way

THE LAUNCH OF the low priced Škodas opened the flood-gates to popular car ownership. To acquaint this new rabble of amateur enthusiasts with the arcane secrets of motor operation and routine maintenance, ASAP published a booklet in 1936 which came free with every purchase. The booklet was called 'How To Ruin Your Automobile Quickly And Without Much Effort (A Bit Of Irony For Those Who Do Not Bother To Read The Driver's Manual)'. Below we offer you the unabridged translation including all the illustrations:

'We who are engaged in the automobile manufacturing business can assure you that many of the cars which are brought to our notice are being ruined in a deplorably unprofessional way. They show a definite lack of proper education. Some owners manage, through trial and error, to destroy the engine quite efficiently, others to demolish the rear axle or the gearbox. However, many only manage to wreck the clutch; these people do get better results in ravaging the body, but anyone can manage that. Keeping the best interest of the service stations in mind, we decided to provide our customers with in-depth instruction on how to proceed systematically and effectively towards the destruction of their cars.

First rule: Never read the driver's manual. It was written by some pedantic egghead who, sprawled behind his desk concocts all kinds of useless rules. Nowadays, any child knows more about cars than these scribblers. Such reading would only wear you out and bore you to tears. Better go for a good detective story.

And now let us proceed, in an orderly fashion, with the instructions:

The engine is its master's servant, and nobody

Who needs to read the driver's manual.

can expect the master to serve the servant. There is no need to pay much attention to the engine. You are especially warned not to waste your precious time by daily cleaning. There are, as the rumour has it, fanatics who beside cleaning the engine, check and tighten the bolts on the engine and elsewhere, and pull at cables to check if they are secured in their clips. They top up the oil and even change it in the way the manual prescribes! Refrain from such foolishness! To keep the engine all spic and span is positively amateurish, and beside that, you deprive yourself of all the fun that awaits you on the highway where you can display in front of your friends your prowess in fixing the defects that the factory was unable to prevent. You may even get the opportunity to perform for their benefit and show them a faultless drive being towed at the end of a rope.

Under the bonnet there is a lot of unpleasant junk. The most revolting is the battery. There is no point in soiling your hands with it. The battery can-

It looks too schoolboyish if it is kept clean and polished under the bonnet.

not actually break down as there are no revolving parts inside and before it expires due to old age, you will have sold the car anyway. Some say the steering mechanism should be oiled from time to time. Not true! What is the use? The steering is not supposed to drip with oil and as long as it works, why fix it? Instances of a seizure due to lack of lubrication are rare indeed and one must never lose hope that catastrophe will be avoided and another driver inconvenienced instead. Besides, driving a car with dry steering is good for your health; it provides strong exercise for your arm muscles and your whole upper body. There is nothing else of importance under the bonnet although some cars, the Rapids and the Superbs, have a reservoir for the central lubrication hidden there. But it is not necessary to mess about with this nice little container. The oil inside is decreasing very slowly, and when it is gone, you are bound to notice the creaking. Ignoring the lubrication will also save you a lot of hard work, like buying the oil and pouring it into the reservoir.

Should you, however, insist on fussing with the oil, do it thoroughly so that the oil lasts longer: pour in enough so the oil shows well above the highest mark on the dip stick. The benefit of this action is two-fold: you will feel good about yourself for taking such good care of your property and if the car should break down due to faulty lubrication, no one can blame you. Changing the engine oil is another folly. Just consider how much you save if you simply top it up! You can always sell the car before anything serious happens. The felt disc in the oil filter does not have to be exchanged either. If you practise the suggested frugal method of lubrication, the new filter will become clogged with dirt again anyway in no time. From the outside nobody can tell whether the filter is clean or filthy, and the money you save can be better used for a couple of tickets to the movies or other pleasantries.

As far as engine tuning goes, it is only natural that you cannot be satisfied with the unimagin-

ative, uniform running provided by the factory. Seek to improve it. Take the jets out of the carburettor and using a point of a file, or a suitable nail, try to enlarge the apertures. Or else narrow them down a bit by hitting them with a few accurately placed hammer blows. You might well succeed, depending on what it was you intended to achieve.

Some say that the air filter has to be cleaned. It does not make sense, of course, that a cleaning device such as the filter, needs to be cleaned. If the air is clean, which is the case most of the time, the filter will stay clean too. Leave it alone. Consequently, the engine requires more fuel, but such trifling consideration does not bother a true gentleman. If the expense becomes excessive even for a gentleman's wallet, he can always blame the factory.

One other warning, this time concerning the belt running the dynamo. Ignore the instructions that suggest some kind of checking, adjusting and God knows what else. Forget it! A belt is a belt and as such it has to pull. Even if it should stop doing its job, not to worry – for in that case a scientific device will send you an automatic signal. That is the belt will start emitting a strong smell of burning rubber and will snap eventually. Should this scientific warning fail you will receive other, more subtle signals. The battery will lose its charge or the water in the radiator will start boiling. Then and only then, you better stop fooling around and really tighten the belt. Make it as tight as an A string, disregarding again the harangues of the driver's manual which in this age of advanced technology is superfluous anyhow.

When you happen to have some free time on your hands, spend it far from the madding crowd, in the bosom of nature, fiddling with the dynamo. You do not have to dismantle it completely – the smallish parts are difficult to retrieve from the grass. It should suffice to swap the cables. If St Christopher does not stand steadfastly by your side, this activity might provide you with all the joys of a long country ramble. But do not worry about such an unpleasant prospect until the dynamo

You can again enjoy the pleasures of walking.

Water-cooled engines are just one of those theories.

starts emitting fumes. A word of advice to those who reject long walks on principle: if you insist on researching the insides of your automobile bring along a good length of rope. It will come in handy should, by lucky chance, a friendly driver be passing by. Always remember to exclude the battery from your experiments, so that you can amuse yourself with listening to your wireless during the usually longish wait. This is precisely one of the reasons why your car was equipped with a wireless in the first place.

Just a few words about the radiator. You were instructed to keep it always full of water, and in winter to fill it with some mixture or other. But it is much more interesting to observe what happens when there is no water in the radiator. Try it. You may like it, and it does not come too expensive: a few hundred will do it. Only do not forget to bring along the rope and your friend with his car. You can enjoy the same experience with a water-cooled car, if you forget to cover the radiator on a frosty night.

Within the mess of entangled pipes and cables etc, you will find the accelerator link rod passing through two bearings and other carburettor mechanical linkages. Do not ever bother to lubricate the moving parts. What is the point? When they get dry and loose they emit a gentle rattle that provides a pleasant accompaniment to your driving. Also your

It is much better to slam the doors hard.

car will give the impression of long wear and tear and you will not look like an inexperienced beginner any longer.

Now let us get inside the car. The door has to be slammed properly at least three times. The neighbours appreciate it because it gives them enough time to reach their windows and to observe and comment on your driving skills. The door window breaks only rarely, but if you persist even that can be done. You might actually be able to get the glass replaced under the factory guarantee. That, of course requires a lot of persuasion and a loud voice.

Inside your car many strange things catch the eye. The most vexing is the notice saying: 'Do not exceed 50 kph during the first 1,500 km'. What nonsense! At the beginning, going uphill the car cannot drive any faster anyhow, owing to some kind of limiting gadget which was placed somewhere inside. And going downhill – what harm can that do to the car? All that gibberish about careful running-in is better ignored. A car well seized-up right at the start of its life is a joy forever!

On the dashboard there is a little light bulb that lights up when you insert the ignition key. After the engine has started the light is suppose to go out. If it does not light up at all, that is all right too. You do not have to worry about it. But if it does not go off, it may bother you. In that case the best thing to do is to unscrew the light bulb. You need not investigate why the light did not switch off. That will become clear soon enough. Surprise! Surprise!

Beneath the dashboard next to some levers and pedals, you will notice the fuel stopcock. You have to turn it on by hand because it cannot be done otherwise. But the best way to turn it off is to kick it shut with your boot. To alternate these two methods is very beneficial for the stopcock. There is also the speedometer drive spindle which should allegedly be greased. Nobody does it and in many cases the speedometer keeps working anyway.

Ever since man's tender years, a clock has been of great interest to him. Go ahead and take it apart, it is a pleasant experience, but do not forget to test the quality of the spring because a good spring cannot be broken, they say.

Somewhere in the rear there is the 'box with speeds'. Do not say gearbox – recognize the difference, how much more manly and experienced muddled technical terms sound. The box, as well as the rear axle casing, ought to be lubricated. When the petrol station attendant asks you whether you need to add oil to the gearbox and to the universal joint, just tell him to check it out. Then forget it. Nothing is going to happen right

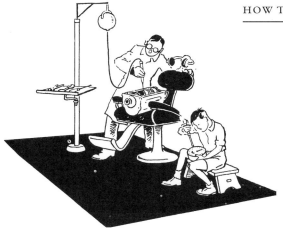

All those machines with little wheels were already interesting when we were boys.

away, only the little wheels will acquire a lovely bluish hue and the rest will come later. To replace the gear wheels is no big deal.

You can conduct a truly exciting experiment by trying to find out if it is possible to change into reverse gear while going full speed forward. You will prove that with some difficulty and a lot of racket this is within your power. And it is not excessively expensive, because, with luck, a few cogs and the box itself may survive.

Let us now turn our attention to the car's body. The most prominent features of the body are the doors with their handles and locks. When the car is new, nothing rattles. In order to preserve this blissful condition as long as possible, it is recommended to lubricate the lock mechanism and the leading edges. But please do not indulge in such folly! It is dangerous! Driving becomes so quiet that you could easily fall asleep. Better let it rattle a bit.

The rug and the seat covers do not need cleaning. They get dirty again very soon, and it is desirable to get rid of the pristine look as quickly as possible. You can hasten the process by storing

suitcases with sharp metal edges and baskets with ripe fruit on the seats. Spreading a blanket on the seat for your doggie to sleep on does not look elegant – and how much damage can a sweet puppy do? Do not hesitate to throw burning cigarette butts on the floor. You will prove that it is not so easy to set an automobile on fire.

When you have to push your car into the garage always lean heavily on both headlights. If they tend afterwards to focus more on the sky than the road, you can adjust them with a few smart blows of your fist. The light bulbs probably will not blow and if they do, the joy of paying a fine is worth it. If you push the car from behind do not lean on the spare wheel but on the smooth surface of the body. The few dents you make can be repaired in no time.

There are two opposite schools of thought concerning the car's paint. One opinion is that the car be kept as new and shiny as it was when it left the factory. This view is held mostly by ladies. The other persuasion has it, that a car must not look too conspicuously new. A well worn finish is therefore most desirable. It is not an easy task to keep your car shiny. The instructions call for a small amount of polish and a lot of elbow grease. The more convenient alternative is to use a harsh, strong abrasive paste and give the car frequently, if possible daily, a good rub. The shiny finish will be gone soon and this will give strength to your argument: the best way is to leave the car alone, wash it as little as possible and forget the polishing. Some say that unpolished paint loses its lustre, it cracks and chips, but what the heck! At least you did not wear yourself out.

In case you are a finicky owner, take this advice: drive only a little or not at all. That way in ten years your car will be still as good as new. When you have a few minutes to spare, switch the ignition on and listen to the quiet burbling of the engine. Should you hear any strange sounds, go and buy some special, supersensitive listening equipment. Then discuss the rattles with your friends and acquaintances and, if you are not a tinkerer youself, drive the car to your service station as often as possible. You will become the station owner's highly valued customer and revered benefactor.

Do not give in to what they say, demand that no sound should be heard, the engine benefits greatly by being taken apart daily. And when you listen to the music of your engine think of all the time you

Choose the right place to listen to the quietness of the running engine.

save on the wireless. It is only a pity that one cannot drive the wireless or the exchange could be complete.

In the effort to give a car a well seasoned look, the owners of cabriolets are at an advantage. All they have to do is to leave the dust covered car standing outside in a rainstorm and immediately afterwards to fold the dripping wet roof. Such a car will never look immaculate again. It is of course possible that the roof will refuse to unfold and will not look too good. It may help to wash it with good strong laundry soap, but if you are in a hurry you can try to use petrol. This procedure works faster and provides you with a valid excuse to throw the filthy roof away because now it has started to leak.

A few small repair patches on the roof gives a cabriolet, or even a saloon, some distinction. You can acquire this elegant look quite easily by stopping at a level crossing as close to the barrier as possible so that no other car can get ahead of you. The rest is done by the flying red hot ashes from the locomotive.

Stand tight to the rail barrier with your cabriolet.

At the rear of the car you will find the spare wheel. They say it should be used, especially in the summer months, because rubber that is not put to work, ages fast. You had better disregard such fairy tales. It is much more important to keep your spare in mint condition, just for display.

Now that we have dealt with the body, we can proceed to discuss the tyres, springs and brake cables. Tyres are easy to care for; pump them up with air until they are ready to burst and bounce on every bit of gravel on the road. Air is free, so pump in as much as you possibly can; you want to be rid of this chore for some time to come. Tyres which are filled according to regulations are no fun, the car does not go into exciting skids and driving becomes boring. Also such tyres last too long and you

Slam the brake hard, it will stop the car on the spot.

are deprived of the joy of shopping around for new ones and fitting them to the wheel rims. The wheel bolts were tightened at the factory, so do not bother to tighten them. Should they get loose, you are sure to notice the clatter and then you can tighten them whenever the fancy takes you.

Lubrication is done with a grease gun. You have to take the gun and crawl under the car – and what happens? You get all dirty! Why put yourself through such an ordeal? A bit of grease cannot make much difference and when the screeching becomes too awful you are sure to find someone who will fix the thing. It will not cost much. The bronze cases are so strong, they can take some punishment.

One thing however must never be neglected: the brakes. It is rather important that they work well. Certainly not for the sake of your, or even someone else's safety, but because they can be used to perform a number of spectacular tricks. The best one goes like this. You bring the car to the fastest speed and then slam on the brakes to see if the car will stop on the spot. For maximum enjoyment, repeat this when you feel like it. Eventually you might succeed in turning the car round or over without much effort. Brakes need a lot of exercise in order to become strong and sturdy. With perseverance the driver is bound to overcome the brakes and reap the rewards of his victory. For this type of exercise icy roads are best suited.

If your car has hydraulic brakes you have to top them up with special fluid from time to time. This fluid is outrageously expensive. Why waste your money on brakes? They are not called 'oil' brakes for nothing – surely you can use any kind of oil? Try some cheap brand. Just pour it in, that part is easy. Nevertheless, after a few days you will be paying a visit to your service man because the rubber parts of the brake system have become soaked in this oil and are sticky. At the service station you get the opportunity to watch and to learn everything about

Kerbing is so good for your tyres.

the workings of the brakes. This important knowledge is certainly worth the modest sum you pay for the repair and the new rubber parts.

Let us go over what we have learned. How does one drive in a truly stylish way? We are all adults here, so let me put it to you straight: winter or summer, rain or shine, do not ever bother to crank up your car. Instead arrange yourself elegantly behind the steering wheel, insert the ignition key and keep turning it till the engine starts. Now put your foot down, rev up and heat the engine fast. Rest assured that the bearings will not seize up! One can also drive with the choke or the selfstarter pulled out! Who has the time to wait for the engine to warm up? That is a joke! Just step on the gas, ram the first gear smartly in and release the clutch. The rear wheels will spin a little but the car will shoot ahead like an arrow and, believe it or not, even if you drive a family saloon, you will look exactly like Caracciola. Who says the rear tyres get worn in this process and the whole mechanism of the automobile is affected? Well, doesn't that sound a bit corny? A car like yours has to be resilient!

Let us proceed further. Changing up to second and third gear is done only after the valves start to rattle. Everything has to go one, two, three!

Racing the engine is such fun.

If the street is too narrow for turning just force one wheel up the pavement. When you are parking the car always push the wheels against the kerb as tight as possible. This alone will show the world what a first rate driver you are. Neither the kerb nor your tyres can voice their opinion. Do not miss any opportunity to honk your horn. The friends whom you pass will take notice as well as the traffic cop. (The fine is 20 crowns).

Straight after completing the running-in period, give the car a good fast drive. It stands to reason that since you drove carefully all the 1,499 km, as soon as you have reached 1,501 km the car is ready for anything. Sometimes the engine gets overheated but that can happen to people too. So who cares.

Furthermore, we might remind you that the ladies admire most those drivers who roar full

Garage owners need to make money somehow.

speed ahead and consistently slam on the brakes. To drive at an even pace may be easy on the car, but it is boring and somehow old-fashioned. A car must plunge ahead in high gear, slap, bang through the villages, over chickens, dashing into bends, brakes screeching – step on it, step on it! That is what we call driving – when death lurks behind every turn! Man is made to love challenge and danger.

If you keep faithfully to our instructions, everybody will be happy. You are going to experience the supreme driving pleasure with plenty of excitement and the service stations are going to prosper beyond their wildest expectations.

To sum up:

> *We have taught you what we knew*
> *now the rest is up to you:*
> *to keep in mind and follow through*
> *all we told you not to do!*

10 Carrosserie Sodomka

PERHAPS THE READER might consider that Carrosserie Sodomka is only of limited interest within the history of Laurin & Klement and Škoda cars. We believe however that Sodomka's involvement in the Czechoslovak automobile industry is certainly worth a mention. It produced special coachwork for a number of local manufacturers, to say nothing of creating splendid bodies on prestigious chassis such as Bugatti, Maybach, Rolls-Royce, Lancia, La Salle, Studebaker, Nash, Graham, Packard and others.

Josef Sodomka (1865–1939), the founder of Carrosserie Sodomka, started to produce horse-drawn carriages for the local trade in a tiny workshop in Vysoké Mýto in eastern Bohemia, during the last years of the nineteenth century, originally having been apprenticed as a wheelwright. Sodomka's workshop measured 92 square metres in which he managed to employ five workers. More space was added later and eventually the workshop became a factory making not only carriages but also horse-drawn wagons and sleds. The First World War brought Sodomka's manufacture to a virtual standstill as most of his employees were called up.

After the war, the making of horse carriages ceased and there was need to find new commercially viable fields to conquer. That was where Josef Sodomka Junior (1904–1965) came in. After finishing school, he took a course at the specialized coachwork school in Bohemia and put his new knowledge to good use by working not only for a number of local firms but also abroad. He realized quite early that his future lay in the design and construction of automobile bodies. In search of yet more experience he worked for Laurin & Klement during 1923–1925 and devoted all his time to im-

proving his acquired skills. Sodomka returned to Vysoké Mýto in May 1925 and set out to manufacture, in his father's company, bodywork for motor vehicles. It was a difficult task at first. The old-guard workforce were suspicious of his new ideas and activities.

With 14 workers and an enlarged factory, the first car bodies were built. To start with, wooden frameworks were built on Praga or Laurin & Klement chassis. The frames were covered in imitation leather, the use of sheet metal came later. All bodies were built to individual orders. In 1928 Sodomka built the first omnibus body and from then on this type of production formed a large part of the firm's order book.

Design and development continued, although new deliveries and ownership were limited. Contemporary sources state that only 45,403 vehicles (31,617 passenger cars) were registered in the whole of Czechoslovakia in 1929. In the same year Sodomka went into the production of cabriolet bodies. It was the cabriolet that became the com-

LEFT **One of the first carriages produced by Sodomka in 1896.**

TOP **Škoda 104 twelve seater omnibus with Sodomka body from 1929.**

ABOVE **The 1929 Škoda 4R faux cabriolet.**

pany's speciality. A particular feature was the use of a timber/artificial leather combination and two-tone colour schemes which were very popular.

The Sodomka design began by way of free-hand sketches from which construction drawings to full scale were developed. Often, wooden models about 400 mm long were made to validate the

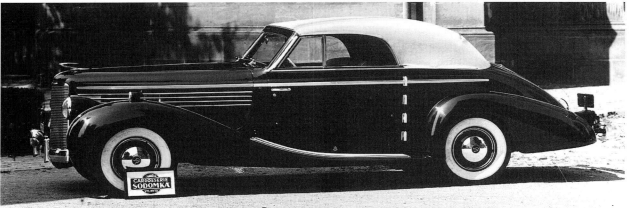

proportions and the overall styling concept. The full-size drawings formed the basic workplan for the woodworkers, panel beaters and upholsterers. Regrettably, only a few faded photographs remain from those early days. Between 1930 and 1931 thirty new car bodies were designed and constructed; additional income for the company came from repairs and reconstruction of the previously supplied models.

1932 was the beginning of real development for Carrosserie Sodomka and although most of the Czechoslovak economy was in the doldrums, some 50 or so special bodies were built in Vysoké Mýto and a slightly larger number repaired. This period brought significant change in the shape of passenger cars. The era of fashionable, as well as functional, streamlining brought wider front mudguards with built-in headlights, inclined radiator grilles, and front to rear flowing styling lines. Sodomka began to win *Concours d'Elegance* competitions with bodies on Walter, Tatra and other

TOP **Typical attractive Sodomka body on Škoda Superb 640 chassis, 1937.**

ABOVE **The mysterious La Salle convertible coupé said to have been delivered to Buckingham Palace in 1938.**

ABOVE RIGHT **Aero 50 coupé, 1938.**

BELOW RIGHT **Rolls-Royce town car from 1938.**

Czech manufactured chassis. While detractors, especially so-called experts, claimed that Sodomka styling took its inspiration from the French Carrossier Figoni-Falaschi, there was nonetheless enough individuality to stamp Sodomka's styling as its own.

The indigenous economic crisis now took a turn for the better and that was reflected in increased demand for specially bodied motor cars. Interest in Sodomka's work began to burgeon beyond the borders of Czechoslovakia, undoubtedly the result of

cars exhibited at various motor shows.

There was the story of the La Salle cabriolet said to have been ordered by the British Royal family perhaps intended as a gift for a member of another royal family. Much to the authors' regret, although the photograph exists, no confirmation of the story through the Royal Mews at Buckingham Palace has been forthcoming. The Sodomka records do, however, show this to be a fact. Perhaps this puzzle will never be solved.

There was also the Studebaker Commander chassis clothed with a beautiful cabriolet body and supplied to the head of a Middle Eastern country and many others. A contemporary bodied type 49 Bugatti is now proudly owned by a Swiss collector complete with Carrosserie Sodomka plaque. The famous Czech shoe magnate T.Bata had a travelling office built on a Ford chassis. New successes in coachwork competitions as far apart as Budapest, Basel, Nice and Monte Carlo added to the prestige already gained. Orders flooded in and the company premises had to be enlarged and more workers hired.

The technical press had nothing but praise for Sodomka coachwork. Above all, the famous Battista Farina, founder of Carrozzeria Farina, main-tained links with the younger Sodomka whose work he so highly appreciated. It should not surprise anybody that some of Farina's creations on the Lancia Aprilia chassis were reminiscent in some details of Sodomka's style.

Some of the Sodomka styling showed perhaps a degree of excess by covering the front wheels as well as the rear ones, but that extravagance appealed to the customers of the day; the vogue for streamlining was very much in fashion then. Sadly one particular project was never completed, nothing less than a roadster on a Rolls-Royce Phantom III chassis. The war put a stop to this order from a customer outside Czechoslovakia, although a coupé-de-ville on a 20–25 chassis was sold in Prague.

Other coachwork continued to be produced on bus chassis and special military vehicles and, surprisingly, gliders were also constructed between 1937 and 1939. In 1937 special orders for the production of trailers and caravans was undertaken and manufacture expanded right up to the beginning of the Second World War. During the war, instead of beautiful cabriolets and coupés, nothing but utility vehicles were built. Orders came from MAN, Ford, Mercedes, Praga, Škoda and others.

FAR LEFT **Luxury caravan for 5-6 persons, 1939.**

LEFT **Prototype of Škoda 1101 Tudor convertible coupé produced for the 1947 Prague Autosalon.**

Among the few exceptions to the utility output was a six-seater limousine on a Maybach SW 42 chassis intended for the government officials of the independent Slovak state.

1945 and the aftermath of war brought the continuation of bus and utility vehicle production on Škoda and Praga chassis. However, a renaissance of passenger car body manufacture started very quietly and slowly. Again, participation at motor shows became a business necessity and at the first post-war Prague Autosalon held in 1947, five passenger cars appeared on Sodomka's stand, among them two new Škoda 1101 cabriolets with disappearing tops and an elegant Tatra 57 limousine, which still exits today. The 5 to 6-seater two door Škoda Superb cabriolet showed obvious North American styling influence allied to European lines.

In 1948 the political situation changed dramatically. Czechoslovakia, along with other eastern European countries became a buffer-state to the Soviet communist regime. The Sodomka company was nationalized together with almost all the other important industrial concerns in Czechoslovakia, and became to be known as Karosa, Vysoké Mýto. The production programme was turned almost exclusively to bus and utility vehicles. Despite this, some interesting passenger cars were made and this departure from the rigid communist planning had to be justified for political reasons by the judicious earmarking of the special products for important political figures. A Tatraplan 600 was fitted with a luxurious cabriolet body and shown at the 1949 Geneva Motor Show where it gained a second place in the elegance competition. A considerable number of technical problems had to be solved in this design, particularly to ensure body stiffness. The car was ultimately to have been given to Stalin for his 70th birthday. Today it takes pride of place among the very interesting exhibits in the Tatra Museum in Kopřivnice, Moravia.

The nineteen-fifties saw the swan song of Sodomka–Karosa mainly because of Czechoslovakia's prevalent isolation from the new design ideas of the West. This isolation limited the progress of individualistic styling which Sodomka had developed so well in the inter-war period. Perhaps R.Jankel, a contemporary car designer, put it most succinctly when he said he would now like to build the sort of bodies Sodomka designed towards the end of the thirties. Bertone, the eminent Italian coachwork specialist, confirmed this view.

11 The world in conflict

CZECHOSLOVAKIA'S development as a nation was an outstanding achievement in those inter-war years. It must be remembered that prior to 1918 there were no political or administrative infrastructures other than those set by the Austro-Hungarian Empire. But against all odds, within the twenty years of the First Republic, Czechoslovakia achieved a fully developed democratic society and established a genuinely humane welfare system.

The republic quickly became one of the top ten industrialized nations in Europe, but in order to preserve this new-found prosperity it was vitally important to maintain good relations with her neighbours. From the first days of its existence, the new Czechoslovak nation had aimed for conciliation and understanding through the principles of collective security. Although there had been problems with Hungary, Czechoslovakia continued on an even diplomatic keel – until the end of the thirties, when Nazi expansionism exploded.

Despite Czechoslovakia's belief in international order, steps were taken to meet the potential danger. Military service was extended to two years and an extensive re-armament programme began. The army was rapidly re-organised and motorized, obsolete weapons were replaced and compulsory civil defence training was introduced.

By 1938, all Czechoslovakia was on the alert. Her four armies and reservists stood prepared and in September, as German pressure intensified, a general mobilization was proclaimed by President E. Beneš.

Backed by modern supply systems and efficient border fortifications, 1,250,000 highly trained army personnel took up arms in defence of their country.

All these preparations were in vain. In a weak attempt to appease Hitler, the four power conference in Munich, on September 28th, 1938, decreed that Czechoslovakia's border territories, the Sudetenland, should be ceded to the Nazis. Not a shot was fired. Four names on a piece paper signified the end of Czechoslovakia's sovereignty and by October 1st the German army occupied the Sudetenland.

Over 16,000 square miles of territory comprising 4,700 towns and villages with more than one-third of its population had been lost to a few simple strokes of a pen. The country had to surrender seventy per cent of its steel production, eighty per cent of its textile mills and its main railway network was severed by the new frontiers.

These new frontiers were so close to Plzeň that most of the Škoda workforce had to cross the border to get to the factory. The general situation became very difficult, but the country did its utmost to hold itself together. However, the new situation did not last long.

On March 14th, 1939, Hitler staged a coup in Slovakia, which became an independent puppet Fascist state. On the following day the rest of Bohemia and Moravia was occupied by the German army and turned into a Protectorate of the Reich, while Carpathian Ruthenia was invaded by the Hungarians.

Political life was stifled and the economic life of the Protectorate was subordinated to that of the

ABOVE RIGHT **Škoda 256 ambulance with Sodomka body, 1942.**

RIGHT **The multipurpose military tow truck Škoda RSO being tested on Radouč hill.**

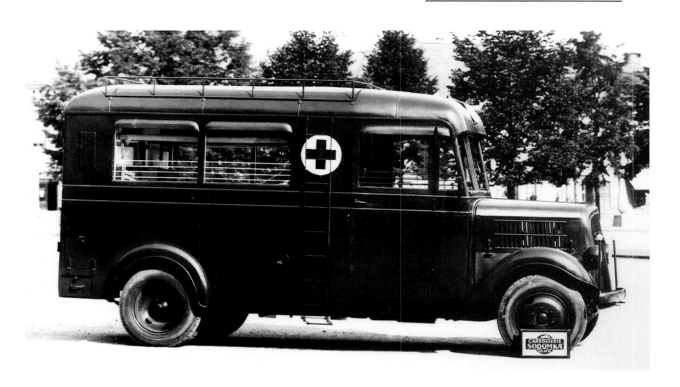

Reich. Its fate was sealed when a custom and monetary union between Germany and the Protectorate was introduced and a number of leading Czech banks and firms were taken over by the Germans without compensation.

Both the Plzeň and the Mladá Boleslav works came under Nazi directorship. From 1941, Škoda along with other large industrial concerns, like Steyr-Daimler-Puch, located in the lands occupied by the Third Reich, was forcibly incorporated into the Reichswerke Hermann Göring.

Sales of all new vehicles were governed by the laws of a wartime economy. In order to safeguard fuel supplies for military purposes drastic measures were taken to reduce the use of civilian transport. Only a very small number of new passenger and commercial vehicles came off the production line at Mladá Boleslav during the first two years.

From 1940 onwards the Favorit was given a 2,091 cc engine of 52 bhp and was designated 2000 OHV. Production of the Popular SV 995 continued until 1946, using up the large stock of spare parts from the original 1935 side-valve model. In 1940, a new Popular 1101 OHV model was introduced and fitted with a higher 32 bhp output engine of 1,089 cc – a benchmark engine that was to be used in future Škoda models. This car was in production until 1944. Few examples of the Superb 4000, with a 3,990cc engine of 96 bhp were made.

Production was concentrated on servicing the German war machine. Petrol engines designed for commercial trucks were re-designed to run on gas and were delivered from the factory with gas generators already fitted. Using the 3,137 cc engine a six-seater four-wheel drive military command car, Kfz 15, was derived from the passenger model Superb 3000 OHV.

The only civilian vehicle to remain in production was the commercial truck type 256G. This was fitted with a gas generator for wood or brown coal. Manufacture of military aircraft was also established.

In 1943 an interesting military tow truck prototype marked Škoda RSO was developed in Mladá Boleslav. The designation RSO was an abbreviation of Radschlepper Ost. This vehicle was to be destined for the Wehrmacht exploits in the Middle Eastern oilfields and the invasion of Soviet Union. The initiator of the project was Hitler and its constructor F. Porsche. In April 1943 the four-wheel drive truck was tested on Radouč hill near Mladá Boleslav. Porsche himself came to test his invention which had a 6,024 cc engine of 90 bhp, 1.5

F. Porsche, the designer of the Škoda RSO, at the wheel of his creation.

metre diameter wheels and a fuel consumption of 200 litres per 100km! However, the test became a disappointment to all present when it transpired that this particular design was unsuitable for its purpose. The main reason was the cumbersome and heavy wheels which did not provide adequate adhesion to the terrain surfaces, brought increased vibrations, broke up roads with the wheel blades and buried itself deeper into the mud. During further tests Hitler was present to inspect his project. Porsche suffered due humiliation when it became obvious that this vehicle could not go into series production.

The Plzeň works were now in full scale production for the Wehrmacht. This was very much against the wishes of the workforce, many of whom had been sent to the concentration camps, or even executed for allegedly sabotaging the manufacturing process. However, production continued on all kinds of military equipment, from aircraft engines, small and large calibre guns to light tanks.

Neither factory in Plzeň or Mladá Boleslav suffered serious bomb damage until the last days of the war. The Germans had even built a decoy plant from cardboard and plywood a few miles from the Plzeň factory. This trick worked a number of times, but on April 25th, 1945 the United States Eighth Army airforce unit dropped a massive payload on the real Plzeň works, almost totally destroying the whole complex.

On the last day of the Second World War, the day after Berlin had fallen, the remnants of the Luftwaffe operating in Czechoslovakia carried out a revenge bombing of the Mladá Boleslav works. Most of the factory was destroyed, including a treasure house of fascinating archive material.

THE WORLD IN CONFLICT

It is hard to understand why the order was given for the massive destruction of the Czechoslovak industry in the closing moments of the war. Many people agree that the reasons behind these actions were political rather than military. Peace came to Czechoslovakia revealing a greatly damaged industrial base, leaving her markets open to exploitation by foreign companies.

TOP **Panzerjäger Tiger (P) Elefant tank with two water-cooled Maybach V-12 11,867 cc engines producing overall 530 bhp designed by F.Porsche. Škoda, Plzeň supplied armour and gearbox parts.**

ABOVE **Pursuit tank 38 'Hetzer' made at Škoda, Plzeň for the Wehrmacht from 1944. After the war these tanks were supplied to Switzerland.**

12 Škoda behind the Iron Curtain

THE END OF THE bloody conflict signified the phoenix-like resurrection of the Mladá Boleslav works, despite the considerable damage inflicted upon it. Now peace-time production could start again and compete in local as well as foreign markets. However, decisions had to be taken very quickly and sensibly because the situation was quite unlike the aftermath the First World War. Motorized transport had become an integral part of modern life and new vehicles were in desperately short supply, while demand was overwhelming.

The Mladá Boleslav factory had been producing fine automobiles since the beginning of the century, but restarting manufacture was a monumental task. Many factory buildings had been destroyed, machine tools were incomplete because the Germans had taken a lot away during the war and many of the specialized personnel had lost their lives during the liberation, died in the concentration camps or at the hands of the Gestapo.

As soon as the situation in Czechoslovakia settled down, a new organization was founded in Mladá Boleslav. From March 7, 1946 Škoda was nationalized and split up into several independent companies: the Plzeň works, the mines, the rolling mills at Hrádek, the aircraft manufacturer Avia, the building construction firm Konstruktiva and the automobile factory in Mladá Boleslav. The Plzeň works, now named Škoda koncern, národní podnik, retained the production and repair service of heavy machine tools, boilers, locomotives, electrotechnical machinery, trolleybuses, tractors, trucks, armament products, ship equipment and parts, large steel castings, machinery for heavy industries and steam, coal and later on, nuclear power stations.

The Mladá Boleslav company was now called Automobilové závody, národní podnik – AZNP (Automobile Works, National Enterprise), but its long standing excellent reputation enabled it to keep the manufacturing marque of the winged arrow and the Škoda name. The name and the marque were also used by Škoda in Plzeň.

Nationalisation had considerable influence on the production programme. The manufacture of commercial vehicles was transferred out of Mladá Boleslav to other plants and what was left of manufacturing capacity at Mladá Boleslav concentrated on just one type of passenger car. The car was, of course, the Popular. It had reached such a high technical level during the 1940s that there was every reason to use it as the basis for the new production programme.

During the war a new car body had been developed in secret and the decision to use a four-speed gearbox was thought to enhance the Popular's appeal. By dint of hard endeavour, the devoted workforce produced a handful of post-war cars. These came on to the market as early as the autumn of 1945. At first, the new automobile was again called Popular but soon type numbering was reintroduced. The car was based on the war time model 1101 OHV and later became known as the Škoda 1101. It was similar to the original 420 Popular of 1933 but it appeared to be bigger, more powerful and better equipped. The works wanted to underline this image with the new model. The 1101 came in standard form as a two door, four-

ABOVE RIGHT **Škoda 1101 Tudor from 1946.**

RIGHT **Škoda 1101 P all-terrain model.**

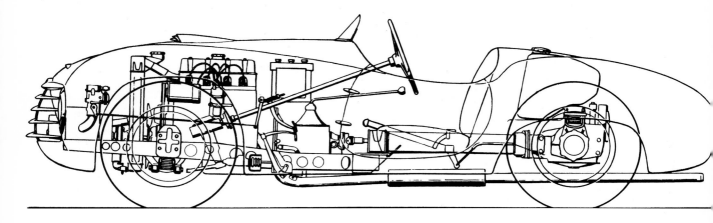

seater saloon. Since there was no Czech word to describe this body type it came to be called by the general public as the 'Tudor' (two-door). Van-type bodies and ambulances could also be supplied on the same chassis.

The Tudor was powered by an overhead valve four cylinder engine of 1,089 cc (68 mm bore by 75 mm stroke) providing 32 bhp. The four-speed box formed part of the engine block and since the wheelbase and track were longer and wider compared with its pre-war brother, a more capacious and comfortable body could be fitted. The pleasing radiator grille of the Tudor set a design precedent and a similar concept was later used by Renault. At the that time a special all-terrain vehicle called type 1101 P was built. This vehicle had the same chassis and engine as the Tudor and was used by the army and police force.

Alongside the Tudor 1101 a small series of the pre-war types was produced but only to use up existing stocks of parts. In the same way a few commercial vehicles such as the Škoda 256B became available and also several dozen of the 995 series Populars. Some of the pre-war Superbs, fitted with a new body, were also built.

In these very early days a new assembly hall was constructed to contain the press shop and body welding plant. Concentration on basically one type meant flow manufacture which obviously increased numbers with consequent savings in costs.

After a short space of time exports began again, closely tied to Škoda's previous reputation. The export figures soon exceeded the best attained before the war and the fame of the Mladá Boleslav works resounded again. Now hundreds of Škoda cars could be seen on the newly rebuilt roads. Indeed, by 1947, the arrow-winged motor cars were running not only in Europe but as far away as South America, Africa and Australia.

Cynics who remember those far-off days might well say that this was due to the world-wide shortage of vehicles. There was certainly some truth in this, but Škoda's commercial success was, without doubt, based on its cars' robust build and long life and, for the time, modern design and technology. In fact factory records show that some of the cars were going for thirty years or more, even in countries with very poor roads. If you find yourself driving in Czechoslovakia today the sight of a speeding Tudor in front of you should not come as a surprise.

In 1946 at the post-war elections the Czechoslovak Communist Party gained a large number of seats in the parliament. Participation in the Marshall Plan was accepted initially but, under pressure from Stalin, the Czechs were forced to withdraw from this favourable economic US aid programme. In February 1948, with the backing of the Soviet Union, the communists took over the already weakened but still democratic government. Czechoslovakia came under Soviet influence and the Iron Curtain divided Europe into the capitalist West and the communist East for the next forty-two years. These changes brought grave consequences both to the lives of the Czechoslovak people as well as to their working conditions and industries. The inevitable inaccessibility, distance and remoteness from the technological, material and political progress of the West resulted in reduced effectivness, productivity and quality of products.

A certain degree of competition motoring was meant to enhance the Škoda 1101's international reputation. A particularly noteworthy effort was the 24-hour event at the Belgian resort of Spa-Francorchamps in July 1948. Three standard, four-seater 1101s were entered. All three finished in line astern, having covered 1,972 km at an average speed of about 84 kph.

ABOVE LEFT **Configuration of the Škoda Sport, 1948.**

ABOVE **Václav Bobek in the Škoda Supersport, a supercharged competition racer with interchangeable engines for various events.**

Based on the 1101, two sports models were built called Škoda Sport. One had a special Rootes RO15 compressor which increased its power to 56 bhp. Both cars gained laurels in local racing events. In 1950 the Škoda Sport II racer was constructed based on the previous model but with a widened track and wheelbase. This car took part in the 24-hour Le Mans race in 1951. Also for the 1950 season two cigar shaped racing cars were made, again based on the backbone chassis and engine of the Škoda 1101. These cars were called Škoda Supersport. Their engines had V-shaped cylinder heads and with the Rootes RO15 compressor, 120 bhp at 6,000 revs was obtained. Later these cars were fitted with 1,221 cc engines with two RO15 and RO10 compressors which gave 160 bhp at 6,000 revs. In 1953 even more powerful engines were installed, the 1,490 cc which, with two compressors, achieved 150 to 180 bhp.

The 1101 was so successful that its manufacture was continued, although marketing conditions were changing due to more European automobiles being available to the general public.

From 1949 minor body changes, such as an at-tractive new radiator grille, were introduced to the Škoda Tudor range. The gear change lever moved onto the steering column as was the fashion of the time. More body styles became available which were fitted to the standard chassis, a four-door saloon body or an estate car could be ordered. A new two-seater roadster model was also included. These new models were designated as Škoda 1102.

In the early nineteen-fifties the technicians and designers at the Mladá Boleslav were set to prepare a new model based on the same concept, but with an updated chassis and engine. To keep up with current preferences the car was larger and had more power.

The new car, the Škoda 1200, went into production in 1952. It had a bigger bore at 72 mm but the stroke remained at 75 mm, with capacity rising to 1,221 cc and 36 bhp. Normally bodied as a four door four-seater saloon it was spacious enough to carry five people in comfort. It also became available as a van, ambulance and estate car. Again the public came up with a nickname – Sedan.

During the years of 1951 to 1953 a degree of co-operation was agreed upon with the old-established Moravian based automobile manufacturer Tatra, národní podnik. At that time the Mladá Boleslav works assembled a number of rear air-cooled engined passenger cars – Tatraplans T600 and an all-terrain light commercial truck, the Tatra 805, while the Tatra factory was being reorganized.

LEFT **Škoda 1102 roadster from 1949.**

BELOW **The 1952 Škoda 1200 Sedan four door saloon.**

RIGHT **Škoda 1200 taking part in the 1953 Monte Carlo Rally.**

In the late forties two former coachworks and vehicle manufacturing firms, Petera and Jawa, situated in the towns of Vrchlabí and Kvasiny were incorporated (as branches) into the main Mladá Boleslav AZNP enterprise. These branches manufactured special models such as the estate cars, ambulances and pick-ups. The main works in Mladá Boleslav concentrated on large saloon bodied car series. It became clear, however, that even with this expansion, the Mladá Boleslav establishment would have to be considerably enlarged in the near future.

Škoda cars were in so much demand in the nineteen-fifties that the works' capacity was fully utilized. Demand on the home market could only be satisfied by Škoda and Tatra production, the only remaining indigenous passenger car producers, and a limited number of imported vehicles. The

country had restricted hard currency resources and the national manufacturers had to keep up with the enlarged appetite for motoring by the Czech and Slovak public. Additional pressure for car supplies also came from the other Comecon countries.

Interest in Škoda cars came also from the West. The Škoda 1200 in passenger and estate (combi) form was exhibited for the first time at the London Motor Show in 1954 on the stand of a Škoda concessionaire, L.C. Rawlence & Co. Ltd of Lingfield, Surrey and later of East Grinstead. This firm handled the sales of Škoda cars in the United Kingdom from 1954 until 1957. From 1958 the Czechoslovak export firm Motokov together with Motor Imports Ltd took over the sales and also exhibited at the London Motor Shows. In 1966 Škoda (Great Britain) Ltd was established and looked after all the British business matters of the Czech parent company.

In 1953 several passenger car prototypes were constructed and designated the Škoda Spartak. It was perceived that the type 1200 was more suitable for companies' use and did not quite fulfil the aspiration of a people's car concept and a more acceptable solution was sought. The Spartak had a 995 cc engine of 30.5 bhp and a pleasing two-door body. When AZNP realized that a Dutch motorcycle company existed which used the marque Sparta, the Spartak label was dropped and others tried, such as Orlík or Rival.

A new model based on these prototypes was introduced in 1954, the type 440, which in the following years became the mainstay of the pro-

duction programme. With this motor car the works decided after all to revert yet again to the old type numbering system which dated back to the inter-war period. The 440 meant four cylinders and 40 bhp. Nevertheless the motoring public liked to use names and soon christened this model the Spartak, using the name of the prototype. The previously successful chassis construction design was maintained. The Spartak's 40 bhp was obtained by a redesigned intake manifold for its 1,089 cc OHV engine together with a modern down-draught carburettor. For its time the Spartak's body was very attractive and its standard equipment was better than most for contemporary vehicles. The 440 was reliable and long-lasting, and also very economical on fuel.

The biggest AZNP output from 1955 onwards consisted of the 440s and a limited number of cars based on the type 1200 now producing 45 bhp from a redesigned engine. Its designation changed to Škoda 1201 and was available in a number of body variations. Since both types had a number of interchangeable components, other vehicle types could be produced without impingeing on the rationale of production. Thus the Škoda 445 was created by using the 1201 engine fitted into the basic 440 model. The bodywork stayed practically the same.

Then came further design changes to the 440's 1,089 cc engine, with yet another re-worked inlet manifold, now with twin carburettors producing 50 bhp. This engine was installed into an attractive two-seater convertible body resulting in a new

ABOVE LEFT **The 1953 Škoda Orlík prototype ready to be shown at the Brussels Motor Show.**

LEFT **Škoda 1201 Sedan from 1956. This model had front indicators replacing the arm trafficators used in the previous type.**

ABOVE **Škoda 445 taking part in a British rally.**

TOP **Restored 1958 Škoda 1100 OHC driven around the Brooklands Track in March 1992.**

model, the Škoda 450, available with hard top and soft top roof option.

In 1958, a special racing roadster Škoda 1100 OHC was conceived. This racer was powered by a twin OHC version of the 1,089 cc engine, putting out a maximum of 92 bhp at 7,300 rpm with 9.5:1 compression ratio, having been based on the mass produced four cylinder engine from the Škoda 440

saloon. Combustion chambers were hemispherical with inclined valves at an included angle of 90 degrees, and two twin-choke 35 mm Jikov carburettors. Duplicate ignition systems were installed to give trouble-free operation. There were two sparking plugs per cylinder, each set having an individual magneto. These were directly coupled to the forward end of the camshafts which were driven by gear train. The engine was placed well behind the front axle, and, together with the five-speed gearbox, offset to the right of the chassis' centreline. The frame was of tubular construction, and body weight was kept down to 600 kg by using resin-bonded glass-fibre for all the panels except the bonnet. All independent suspension was by parallel wishbones with longitudinal torsion bars at the front, and swing axles with angled torsion bars and inboard brakes at the rear. The maximum speed was in the region of 250 kph. Only two of these roadsters were manufactured.

One of these racers, which were designed by Ing F.Sajdl, was brought over to Britain by a Czech student in 1969. A surprise find was made during its restoration when it turned out that the cylinder bore was 72 mm, bringing engine capacity from 1,089 cc to 1,221 cc, which were the basic Sedan engine dimensions: 72x75 bore and stroke, although this might have been done when the engine was worked on in the past. The restorers were impressed with the car: 'It was full of clever stuff, that engine, and half of our rebuild time was spent trying to fathom out how aspects of it worked'. Presently this valuable and unusual car is in a private collection. In 1960 two racers named Škoda 1100 OHC Sport were also built and their design based on the earlier 1958 model. The main difference was in the body form made as a two door coupé with a hardtop roof.

In 1959 certain front suspension modifications

ABOVE LEFT **Škoda Octavia from 1959.**

LEFT **Škoda Felicia together with Škoda 422 from 1929 and Škoda 120 L Five at Brooklands Clubhouse, March 1992.**

ABOVE **Škoda Octavia Touring Sport.**

were introduced to the 440, 445 and 450 models. Until then there had not been any fundamental changes to the basic design system. The wheels were attached to a transverse leaf spring and two pivoting arms which also served as part of the hydraulic shock absorbers. In the new system a pair of suspension arms either side, with coil springs containing telescopic dampers, looked after the front end. Some minor changes to the body were also incorporated and these modified types reverted to model names. It seems that the creative people at AZNP could not make up their minds in which direction to proceed. It was acknowledged that the general public preferred cars with proper names rather than numbers, and if there were just model numbers people almost naturally invented their own names.

Thus the new car model based on the previous 440 type was now called Octavia (the 'eighth') because that was its position in the range of Škoda's one-litre models development – Popular 420, Popular 995, Popular 995 OHV, Popular 1100 OHV, Tudor 1101, Sedan 1200, Spartak 440 and Octavia.

The 445 became the Octavia-Super and the two-seater roadster 450 became known as the Felicia (Latin for happiness). The 1961 prices for Octavia and Felicia in the United Kingdom were £589 and £785 19 shillings and 2 pence respectively, with £50 extra for Felicia's hard top.

These attractive Škoda models were followed by the Octavia TS (Touring Sport) but the body and chassis remained practically the same as the base model Octavia. The 50bhp twin-carburettor Felicia engine powered the TS and the equipment was adapted to a sporting drive. Performance potential of the Octavia Super engine was also increased by fitting a higher lift camshaft, new inlet and exhaust manifolds, twin carburettors, bigger valves and higher compression. In 1961 this more powerful 1,221 cc engine was installed in the Felicia and Octavia and in this modified form they became Felicia Super and Octavia TS 1200. The AZNP engineers developed two basic benchmark engine designs of 1,089 cc and 1,221 cc sharing the same stroke of 75 mm and these were used successfully in various versions and modifications in Škoda models for almost thirty years.

At this time agreements were reached to assemble Škoda cars abroad using Octavia chassis and terrain vehicle type body. The 'Trekka' was manufactured in New Zealand and the 'Skopak' in Pakistan.

In the 1961 Rallye Monte Carlo two Škoda Octavia TSs proved their stamina by finishing first and second in the 1,001–1,300 cc series production class. Finns Keinanen and Eklund drove the winning car achieving sixth overall place among 305 starters. The second Octavia TS was driven by Norwegians Gjolberg and Martinsen who finished twentieth overall.

An increasing marketing requirement for multifunction vehicles brought the factory to produce the Octavia Combi, an estate car with four seats on the Octavia Super chassis. The vehicle had a useful load capacity of 400 kg and a horizontally divided rear door and was made until 1966. The 1202 came into production and was a further development of the type 1201 but had a bigger body. Some detail changes were made which were also carried out on the other models. The 1202 was available as an estate car, delivery van, pick-up and other commercial versions.

In these lively expansionist days of the fifties the Mladá Boleslav works could not quite manage to cope with the demand for its vehicles, even when using all possible production reserves. Clearly this situation needed a radical solution, for the home market and foreign orders needed fulfilling. The decision was taken to build a large new factory complex close to the existing works. Here production could be organized according to the most modern methods. It was to be a factory which could handle a considerable increase in production and accommodate the manufacture of new models as and when it was required.

To achieve this ambitious project technicians and engineers were sent abroad, charged with the task of gleaning detailed knowledge of the most modern European vehicle plants and to make contact with the manufacturers of the most up-to-date automobile manufacturing machinery and equipment. This was almost a repetition of the situation in the twenties when the factory was substantially rebuilt and extended. However, the task in hand was infinitely more complicated. Not only because an entirely new works needed to be built, but because elaborate mechanization and automation had to supersede traditional automobile production practices.

In 1960 the new project slowly began to take shape and much activity became apparent close by the old works. The new complex was built on a 800,000 square metres site. Its axis was a central boulevard of 1,500 metres in length with a number of specific buildings on both sides, while the main production was concentrated in four vast halls. In total, the new factory comprised more than forty buildings. These contained facilities for component manufacture, stores, energy, management and

ABOVE **The 1961 Škoda 1202 prototype.**

BELOW LEFT **Škoda Octavia Combi from 1961.**

RIGHT **Škoda's new plant in Mladá Boleslav manufacturing the 1000 MB model.**

social installations. A rail link of 10 km length was constructed alongside with a complete marshalling yard. In the grounds of the complex road network extended for 13 km. For the production tooling, reliable manufacturers were selected who had already supplied such equipment to other major vehicle producers. This obviously meant that the new Mladá Boleslav factory not only wanted to ensure more effective production but also needed to maintain high quality. The production and machine tool park was ultimately supplied by 134 different manufacturers from fourteen countries, apart from the domestic suppliers. The new works also contained metallurgical facilities at variance with the old factory system. In this way AZNP became independent of outside suppliers. The factory's rated production capacity was designed for up to 500 cars a day.

A.Kuba, in his book *Veteran Cars*, described the manufacturing process. 'In the new plant the manufacture of automobiles was divided into two basic production blocks. In the first one, mechanical car components were made and assembled. This block consisted of a cast iron foundry, an aluminium pressure-casting plant, forge, and machine shops. The second unit included a body construction shop and final assembly line, supplemented by a small welding shop and an electroplating line.

'The production of a car would start in the grey and malleable cast iron foundry. The moulds and cores were made in the moulding shop. Metal was melted in electric furnaces and molten metal poured in the moulds on casting tracks. Castings were transported either to the cleaning shop or to tempering furnaces. In the aluminium pressure-casting plant, special cast alloy was melted in electric induction furnaces and the molten metal distributed to individual die-casting machines. The raw pressure castings were transported either to the cleaning shop or to furnaces for temper ageing. In the forge, bar stock was first cut or sheared in the preparation department and then distributed to individual forging units, each consisting of a heating unit, a forging press and a trimming press. After trimming, the forgings were heat-treated in furnaces. Finished castings and forgings moved to machine shops and to the transfer lines. These were arranged according to the automobile's main assembly groups, and inter-connected directly with assembly lines. The production included front axle, engine, gearbox and rear axle component parts. Parts of bar stock were made on automatic bar lathes. Gears were made in the gear cutting shop and refined in the hardening hall.

'The assembly lines ran through the bay centres. The front axle, which was assembled first, was then hung on a conveyor running along the bay. The engine assembly line fed into the engine testing hall. The assembly of the gearboxes and final drives involved testing in sound-proofed halls. At the end of the bay the engine, gearbox, rear axle and torque arms were assembled into a complete driving unit. This unit was picked up by the inter-block conveyor and transported to the final assembly line.

'Body production was independent. Sheet stock from storage was transported to the shearing shop for cutting to required shapes. The blanks were fed to the respective press lines consisting of huge body presses in medium and small size press halls. After inspection, the large pressings were transported to intermediate storage in the body shop while a portion of the pressings moved to the electroplating shop for chromium coating. The pressed parts of sub-assemblies were welded on lines in the small welding shop. After welding, they were painted in the paint shop and transported to their respective destinations in intermediate assembly lines, machine shops, or final assembly line in the body shop. The parts which had to be chromium plated were ground in the grinding shop partly on automatic grinders, partly by hand, and after plating in two automatic electroplating shops they were moved to the body shop for final assembly.

'In the body shop, pressings from intermediate storage were welded step by step into larger sub-assemblies adjacent to the main assembly lines. The body skeleton was first welded at the bottom supporting part on Lanquepin welding lines and then finished on three other lines. Then the skeleton was transferred to three body finishing lines where wings, doors, bonnet and boot lids for engine and luggage compartments were provisionally attached. The body thus assembled entered the paint shop where it was firstly degreased and phosphatized. Then the underside was dipped in anticorrosive paint and, after drying, once more sprayed with primer. Immediately after the antivibration compound was applied to the underside, the body moved to three finishing enamel lines. From the paint shop, the body proceeded to the upholstery line first to receive the electric installation, hardware, upholstery and then to be glazed. The upholstery was prepared in the adjacent upholstery shop. The finished body was then automatically transferred to the final assembly line to be mated with the drivetrain, etc.

'From the machine shops, the inter-block conveyor (the total length of conveyors amounted to 11 km) carried front axles and power train units, taking on complete wheels with tyres fitted in the separate tyre department while passing through the body shop, to the proper position on the final assembly line. Power units and front axles were carried on a special underground conveyor for mounting on the bodies from below. Each car leaving the hall was tested on rollers. After adjusting the headlight beams and the steering geometry, the car moved to the dispatch hall and left the factory either by rail or road.'

This new factory complex was of course intended for completely new ranges of Škoda automobiles of the latest design.

13 *The rear-engined Škodas*

THE BASIC DESIGN parameters of Škoda cars did not materially change for thirty years: from the advent of the Škoda 420 – Popular in 1933 to 1964. This design was based on a backbone frame and independent suspension all round with swing axles at rear. The main differences concerned the engines, various body designs and sizes and improved equipment. At the time when the main factory expansion and rebuild was being considered a great deal of new design research was undertaken. Since the biggest commercial success had been achieved with small, four-seater popular cars, it was decided to continue with this traditional basic concept. Research and development began with three series of prototypes: front engine with rear-drive, front engine with front-wheel drive and rear engine with rear-wheel drive. Now comparison tests were needed not only from the point of view of technical concepts, but also for research into economic manufacturing processes. After extensive testing and development, the solution decided on was the rear engine, rear-wheel drive layout and this became the principle for the new Škoda model.

The passenger compartment would be situated within the two axles and thus be least exposed to shocks from uneven road surfaces and provide most comfort. Similarly a good weight distribution between front and rear was achievable. There was no need for a propeller shaft, car weight was decreased and the floor tunnel eliminated achieving a flat floor. Very importantly, the rear engine installation facilitated a modern monocoque chassis/body construction.

After more tests, a water-cooled engine was preferred to an air-cooled one. The water-cooled engine had a better specific output and was quieter running, with the undoubted plus of an easy-to-install heating system.

Last but not the least were the examples of other successful rear engine designs of the Tatra cars since 1933, the Volkswagen Beetle, the Renault 4CV and Dauphine, Fiat 500 and 600 and Porsche 356. These must have convinced Škoda's designers that they were on the right track.

After all, Škoda were running prototypes with rear engines as early as 1932. Quite a number of automobile manufacturers decided to adopt this layout at that time and yet again in the nineteen sixties. It was considered the best arrangement, combining optimum road holding with real comfort for the car occupants. Even the very first motor cars at the end of the last century had their engines at the back.

The first new four-seater Škoda 1000 MB (MB stood for Mladá Boleslav) left the gates of the new factory in 1964. It had a water-cooled OHV four cylinder engine of 988 cc inclined about 30 degrees from the vertical to lower its installation height. This was mounted behind the final drive gear. It had a pressure-die-cast aluminium cylinder block with inserted wet liners and a cast iron head with wedge shaped combustion chambers. With a bore and stroke of 68 mm, the power output came to 48 bhp at 4,750 rpm. Deliberately, a modest compression ratio of 8.3:1 had been chosen to enable it to run on 84 octane fuel. A down-draught Jikov carburettor supplied mixture to the engine and was positioned upright, left of the engine. The radiator was fully shrouded and provided with a large nine-blade fan. The drive train to the transverse swing axles consisted of a single-plate dry clutch, four speed and reverse synchromesh gearbox, bevel

LEFT **The 1968 model of Škoda 1000 MB.**

BELOW LEFT **Škoda 1100 MBX de Luxe, 1967.**

RIGHT **Škoda 1000 MB/F3 racer displayed, in front of Tatra 87, in the National Technical Museum in Prague.**

differential gear and spiral gear drive. Rear wheels were suspended on long fabricated trailing arms with rubber pivot bushes and transverse tubular half-axles, ball-jointed at their inner ends. Inside these tubes were live drive axles, jointed at the differential-gear end. Springing was by conventional coils with rubber bump stops and telescopic dampers ensured comfort on the poor road surfaces of the time. Front wheels were suspended on unequal-length wishbones with coil springs and dampers and there was an anti-roll bar to counteract roll. Steering was by worm and nut and hydraulic brakes were fitted.

The standard all steel pontoon body was a four door saloon type built round a supporting structure consisting of a reinforced floor, wheel arches, door pillars, scuttle and roof. To these were attached outer panels which could be removed for repairs. Maximum speed was 125 kph, average fuel consumption 7 litres per 100 km.

The 1000 MB models were built at the rate of 435 units per day and the derivatives of this model continued in production until 1969. The basic 988 cc engine of the 1000 MB type allowed further increases in cylinder sizes and additional upgraded models followed. In 1966 came the two door version, the Škoda 1000 MBX, with a twin carburettor engine and higher 52 bhp output. The body had retractable window pillars which, in a car of this size, was a rather exceptional and expensive design: but only a small number was made. Its twin carburettor engine was then installed in a four door body version model called 1000 MBG.

The engine was then increased to 1,107 cc by enlarging the bore from 68 mm to 72 mm and was fitted into a new model Škoda 1100 MB from 1967. The engine produced 54 bhp and ensured better flexibility and higher acceleration. Another improvement followed shortly with the 1100 MB de Luxe with 8.5:1 compression ratio. Its maximum speed was 135 kph and acceleration 0 to 80 kph in 13 seconds. The roofline and rear part of the body was redesigned. The new Škoda models were usually introduced to the general public at the autumn motor show and international industrial fair held in the Moravian capital Brno which always attracted a large number of visitors eager to find out what new surprises Mladá Boleslav had managed to come up with.

Apart from the standard series manufacture of MBs, special sports versions with much higher performance in power and speed were produced in order to participate in various racing events. Their design was indicated by the high number of excellent results. In the 1966 Raid Polski, for example, almost four fifths of the 20 car makes did not complete the very demanding course. In the end only 11 cars finished, out of which three were Škodas, two taking fourth and fifth place in the overall classification. In the *Internationale Österreichische Alpenfahrt* Škoda 1000 MBs gained first and third places in their class. In 1968 again special 1100 MBs were made in A2 version and achieved the best results for Škoda so far. In the *Alpenfahrt*, which formed part of the Rally Championship for European Manufacturers, the drivers O.Horsák and Ing. J.Motal gained first place in the 1,150 cc class and a special Alpine prize for the fastest times in the speed stages. Out of all manufacturers crews the Škoda team was also placed at the top. Thus AZNP Mladá Boleslav claimed an absolute victory for this event.

Other specials were produced for Formula 3 circuit racing. The Škoda 1000 MB/F3 was built for the sports seasons of 1966 to 1968, mainly driven with honours by Czech racing drivers V.Bobek the elder and M.Fousek. It had a standard Škoda 1000 MB engine (adapted in accordance with international sports regulations appendix J), situated ahead of the rear axle. Bore and stroke were adjusted to 72x61.3 mm to give 998 cc. Maximum output was 90 bhp at 8,600 rpm. The engine block, as usual, was alloy with inserted cylinder liners and a cast iron head. The crankshaft with nitrided journals was supported on three plain bearings. Connecting rods were in forged steel and cast aluminium pistons had two L-shaped piston rings. A Weber 40 DCOE downdraught carburettor and two fuel pumps were fitted. The radiator, oil cooler, oil tank and battery were placed in front of the car. The chassis was a ladder-type frame of welded Cr-Mo tubes. Independent suspension was by means of trapezoidal wishbones and the rear axle was located by two torque arms at each side. Coil springs with concentric telescopic shock absorbers were accommodated inside the frame. Steering was by rack and pinion. The cigar shape body was easily detachable and made in resin laminated fibre-glass. Maximum speed was 210 kph. This monopost racing car is now exhibited in the National Technical Museum in Prague.

Further accomplishments followed and brought the Norwegian driver J.Haugland world-wide prominence. He won almost every competition he attended in the nineteen-seventies and eighties, be it in the Norway Rally or the RAC Rally held in Britain or in other important motor sport events.

In 1969, when Škoda first officially participated in the RAC Rally, Škoda dealers M.Hinde and N.Davies of Britain came first in Group 2 (up to 1,150 cc) with a Škoda 1100 MB. From then on Škoda never looked back in this world-class 4-day rally. It had been established in 1932, staged in November of each year and from 1974 sponsored by the British banking house Lombard North Central. J.Haugland took eight winning trophies in his classification, the most successful of all the Škoda drivers. To date Škoda have achieved an astonishing 18 class wins in 20 years of taking part!

More radical changes came in 1969 when the

ABOVE **M.Hinde and N.Davies with the Škoda 1100 MB after their class victory in the 1969 RAC Rally. The beginning of a rallying legend.**

RIGHT **Škoda 100 from 1969.**

BELOW RIGHT **Škoda 1203 minibus prototype, 1969.**

Škoda engine was again upgraded and the suspension design improved with the advent of new Škoda types 100, 100L and 110L. Until August 1969, when their production ceased, 419,540 of 1000 MBs and 23,000 of 1100 MBs were made. The initial release of the new models was delayed due to a large fire which occurred during the factory summer holiday break. On Tuesday August 12th, 1969 the fire started in one of the workshops and quickly spread throughout the plant becoming one of the most devastating in the history of the Czechoslovak industry. The damage was estimated at 320 million crowns and resulted in a temporary loss of 55,000 square metres of production area. Nevertheless the factory was speedily put back in order and production of the new models started as soon as August 25th.

The Škoda 100 and 100 L had the same engine as the 1000 MB of 988 cc and the rear suspension by swing axles. Front suspension was trapezoidal and all wheels suspended by coil springs with double acting telescopic shock absorbers. The steering was still by worm and nut. The main technical improvements from previous models were front wheel disc brakes, the front axle held in self-lubricating bearings and a twin circuit hydraulic brake system. Changing to the use of disc brakes brought the redesign of the king pins for which the engineers used enlarged bearings for longer life. The maximum speed was 125 kph and fuel consumption was 7 litres per 100 km. The body and

ABOVE LEFT **The 1970 Škoda 110 R Coupé.**

LEFT **Škoda 1100 GT prototype with a specially designed body by the Prague research institute UVMV.**

ABOVE **John Haugland in his first factory prepared Škoda 110L Rallye in the 1971 *Alpenfahrt* winning his class.**

RIGHT **Special Škoda 110 L Rallye in the 1975 Ecce Homo race, Czechoslovakia.**

interior of the car was substantially redesigned and modernized. The model 110 L differed by having the stronger 1,107 cc engine fitted which was used previously in 1100 MB type. The compression ratio was increased to 8.8:1 with the power output reaching 53 bhp at 5,000 rpm.

In the Škoda branch factory in Vrchlabí the type 1202 continued to be made and from 1969 production started of a minibus designated as the Škoda 1203.

Exactly a year after the introduction of 100 and 110 L, in August 1970, a new Škoda 110 R 2+2 seater coupé came from the production line in the Škoda branch factory at Kvasiny. This branch specialized in Škoda sporting models. In the years 1959 to 1964 they made almost 15,000 Škoda Felicias and Felicia Supers and between 1970 and 1981 56,000 Škoda 110 R Coupés. The 110 R Coupé had the 1,107 cc engine but with an output of 62 bhp, which was more becoming for a genuine sporting model.

Also in 1970 came the 110 LS, a wolf in sheep's clothing with the standard saloon body but having the more powerful engine from the coupé. In the same year and for real sporting events the manufacture of limited numbers of Škoda 110 L Rallye and later of Škoda 120 S Rallye cars began. These cars were derived from standard models and were designed with special attention to safety and a high level of driveability in order to participate in the most arduous long distance rallies, cross country

ABOVE **The factory team Škoda 120 S.**

RIGHT **T.Didlick and P.Titterton in a Škoda 120 S participating in the A.P. Stages Rally.**

trials and hill-climbs. The 110 L Rallye had a 1,107 cc engine of 73 bhp (the factory team cars had a 1,144 cc engine of 100 bhp), special sets of headlamps and foglights, anatomically formed seats, sports steering wheel, tripmaster and a host of other small modifications to body and suspension. Its derivative, the Škoda 120 S had a newly designed four cylinder OHV engine of 1,173 cc, both bore and stroke of 72 mm and an output of 64 bhp. The factory team cars had 1,295 cc engines giving 120 bhp at 7,500 revs.

Using the series production passenger cars with more powerful engines fitted for sporting events was a tough way to gain valuable knowledge of construction and correct dimensioning and design of automobile parts. Under the testing conditions it was possible to ascertain the driving characteristics of series-produced automobiles and the longevity of their components. That was the main reason for AZNP's decision to keep on taking part in sporting activities.

Škoda's determination to prove the stamina of its products was richly rewarded. In 1971, in ten various local and European competitions, Škoda reached ten victorious positions. In that year the Czechs participated in 35 races and rallies out of

THE REAR ENGINED ŠKODAS

which they gained 64 first places in classes or groups and absolute victories, 48 second and 29 third positions. In the RAC and Scottish Rallies the Škoda 110 L came on top in its class.

In 1969 Škoda achieved the figure of one million vehicles manufactured. To illustrate how fast the subsequent manufacture developed, it is sufficient to say that half a million automobiles of Škoda types 1000 MB to Škoda 110 L were made by the spring of 1970, three-quarters of a million by the beginning of 1972 and one million by August 29th, 1973 at 10 o'clock in the morning. The production figures which illustrate the increase in manufacture show this progress very clearly:

1964: 18,653	1969: 118,441
1965: 63,601	1970: 128,109
1966: 80,000	1971: 134,158
1967: 97,450	1972: 141,654
1968: 100,000 plus	

The success of Škoda passenger cars in various sporting events continued in 1973 when 52 first, 21 second and 16 third places were achieved. In the Baltic Rally, through Denmark, Sweden and Germany, the Škoda team also gained a victory. J.Jelínek and S.Kvaizar, in a Škoda 120 S, battled through to absolute first place in the Wartburg Rally held in East Germany.

For the 1974 season Mladá Boleslav prepared two special super sports coupés, the 180 RS and 200 RS. These became experimental prototypes for the future type 130 RS. The 180 RS had a 1,774 cc engine of 155 bhp and the 200 RS a 1,997 cc power unit giving 163 bhp. In that year the first Škoda Rally was organized. The Škoda Team participated there and in another 41 events gaining 59 first, 38 second and 20 third places. In the 1974 RAC Rally J.Haugland in the 120 S came first in his class. In the 1974 Circuit of Ireland Škoda cars were also victorious.

The sporting successes continued to affect sales very positively and production went up in ever increasing numbers. In 1973 616, in 1974 629, and in 1975 650 cars were made daily. In 1973 seventy

LEFT **The 1974 Škoda 200 RS of 163 bhp.**

BELOW LEFT **Škoda 105 Estelle from 1976.**

RIGHT **J.Haugland and R.Saunders in Škoda 130 RS competing in the 1977 Lombard RAC Rally.**

BELOW RIGHT **J.Haugland driving the 130 RS in the 1981 Norway Winter Rallye.**

itially with 112 bhp at 7,250 rpm and later 120 bhp at 8,000 rpm and 129 bhp at 8,500 rpm. The clutch was centre sprung of 190 mm diameter. The four-speed gearbox had different ratios but was of series manufacture. The transmission also had different gearing and a limited slip differential could be obtained to special order. The rear suspension with inclined swing axles had coil springs and adjustable telescopic shock dampers. The front suspension was similar to the type 110 R, with longer suspension arms and modified steering. Power assisted brakes were fitted and water cooling with a pressure radiator were positioned in the front of the car. The body was a modified and lightened version of the 110 R. The body panels were made partly from aluminium and partly from glass reinforced laminate. Maximum speed was between 150 and 170 kph, acceleration from 0 to 100 km 9 to 12 seconds, fuel consumption 14,7 litres per 100 km.

The cars prepared by the factory for competitions were further improved to achieve higher performance as permitted by regulation J of FIA. For the following seasons, modified springs, shock dampers and anti-rollbar were planned. The rear suspension stops were to be absorbed by the shock dampers. The modified fan, distribution and shaped inlet and exhaust passages were to provide more power.

In 1975 Škoda scooped 23 first, 16 second and 16 third place medals. In circuit races and hill-climbs 23 firsts, 15 seconds and 13 thirds out of 61 starting positions were added to the trophy collection, proving the 130 RS to be a very competent sporting machine.

In 1976 new types rolled out of the factory gates at Mladá Boleslav. The first Škoda Estelle models 105 and 120 had the rear engine concept based on the previous 100 and 110 models, but the body design was changed including some minor alterations. The petrol tank was moved to a position above the rear axle, the radiator was placed forward in the front of the car for better cooling and changes were made to the dashboard and interior trim. The 105 had a four cylinder engine of 1,046 cc, 68 mm

per cent of production was exported.

For the 1975 sports season, the new release was the special sports models 130 RS Rallye and 130 RS Racing. In their eight years of existence these cars became the most triumphant sporting vehicles Škoda had ever produced and were one of the best sports cars in their class.

The sports coupé Škoda 130 RS (production type number 735) was derived from the 110 R and the 120 S with the intention of producing a high performance car to compete in automobile competitions. It had a four cylinder OHV engine with a three bearing crankshaft and a pressure cast alloy cylinder block which had a light alloy cylinder head, replacing the traditional cast iron one, with separate inlet and exhaust passages for each cylinder. Twin Weber 40 DCOE 2 carburettors, a bore of 75.5 mm, stroke 72 mm providing a cubic capacity of 1,289 cc, with a compression ratio 10.5:1 in-

bore and 72 mm stroke achieving 46 bhp output and a maximum speed of 130 kph. The 120 had the larger engine of 1,173 cc, initially giving 52 bhp and in later models 58 bhp.

In the meantime the racey 130 RS continued to reap rewards in sporting events. J.Haugland was first in his class with the 130 RS in the 1976 and 1977 Lombard RAC Rallies. In fact, in the 1977 Rally all first three places in Class 4 of up to 1,300 cc were taken by the Škoda 130 RS. After its many victories, the 130 RS was nicknamed the 'Czechoslovak Stratos' adopting the name from the similarly consistently successful and famous rally winning Lancia Stratos.

One of the most prized Škoda triumphs was the two first places gained in Group 2 in the 45th Rallye Monte Carlo in 1977.

Three Škoda 130 RS cars were entered with V.Bláhna/L.Hlávka, M.Zapadlo/Ing. J.Motal and S.Kvaizar/J.Kotek as their crews.

Škodas provided a surprise from January 22nd to 28th for the onlooking experts and journalists when they observed that the Czech cars and crews managed to keep pace with other, more experienced drivers of world-renowned makes. And the tyres which they used were not Michelin, Pirelli or Dunlop but the Czech made Barum 'rubbers'. In the penultimate stage, the Kvaizar/Kotek car fractured its oil sump and had to retire. If it had not been for this accident, all three Škodas would have been among the remaining 60 cars (out of 177) for the final stage.

However, the last two Škodas managed to make up this loss by coming first and second in the final stage. The French driver C.Laurent who came third in his Autobianchi A112 in Group 2, commented in an interview published in the French magazine *L'Equipe*: 'It was impossible to beat the Škodas because their factory had prepared them so exceptionally well. Even their servicing was perfect and Škodas proved themselves resilient and reliable. We had no hope against them'.

L.Hlávka, a member of the winning crew described the rally: 'This competition was of the highest quality. Not only because of the excellent drivers and cars but because of the perfect rally organization. Throughout the rally there was not one occasion on which we needed to adjust our timing to that of the timekeepers. All the controls and speed tests were totally objective and the rules were very strictly followed. We witnessed how the Finnish driver Markku Alén was disqualified. Until then he was one of the contenders to overtake the leading driver, the Italian Sandro Munari. Alén got

off at the start of the speed stage Moulinet-Col de Turini and after only one kilometre his electrics gave up. He repaired the damage, returned to the start and wanted to drive off again. At that point ensued a great row. Hundreds of Italian supporters demanded his re-entry, Alén was driving a Fiat, on the other hand hundreds of Frenchmen whistled and shouted for disqualification – the French do not like Italian cars. The organizers would not bend the rules and did not let Alén re-start. They took his card away and that was the end...

'Not even in a football stadium do so many people get together as in some of the attractive places along a rally route. Onlookers stand along the road like a live barrier with 300 metre ravines behind them. On the other side of the road the stony slopes create a natural amphitheatre, which is 'sold out' to the last seat.

'Of course, we did not escape without problems. In the penultimate stage we got into one of the special stages at around the 3 km mark out of the total of 16 km, and we punctured one of the front tyres. We decided against changing and continued with the flat one. On the final 2 km level stretch to the finish we were doing a speed of 100 kph and the flat tyre began to disintegrate with large bits of rubber flying off. But we made it to the end.

'The second puncture happened during the last night of the rally on the fourth section of the stage. Then we lost the rear tyre and that one we had to change. While still driving we got out of our seat belts, switched off the ignition and I prepared the tools. We stopped, jumped out and got to work. At that moment we were being overtaken by Zapadlo's Škoda who started 2 minutes behind us. Seeing us hard at it he went on. At the finish Zapadlo was surprised how quickly we managed to carry out the change. The last night brought another unpleasant event in the run up to the start. The drive of the tripmeters broke and as there was no time for repair we had to use stopwatches and maps...

'We were glad to see the great interest in Škodas expressed by spectators and experts. This interest increased with every day of the rally. Most of the attention came from the tyre specialists who, at the finish of one of the speed stages, literally surrounded our car. We made seventh best time and the leader Munari came only 21st which gave everyone a bit of a shock. They all wanted to see what our Škoda was wearing. I think that it was not only the Škodas but also their Barum tyres which were the focus of attention.

1983 Škoda advertisement for the 120 LE.

Good Luck to the Skoda Team on the 1983 RAC Rally from Skoda Great Britain Ltd and their UK network of Dealers

THE RALLY WINNING MONEY SAVING CONSTANTLY SURPRISING SKODA

There's a nice surprise in store for you with the '83 Skodas.

Britain's top value for money car has been the Lombard RAC rally Class 1 winner 10 times in the last 10 years. And this year's tough new models offer better value than ever.

Money Saving 120LE package includes:–
∗1.2 litre, 4 cylinder engine ∗Improved fuel economy ∗Rack and pinion steering ∗Dual circuit servo assisted brakes.

∗British 5J x 13 alloy wheels ∗British Radial ply tyres ∗Laminated windscreen.

∗Heated rear window ∗British black impact moulded bumpers incorporating twin fog lamps.

∗Fully reclining front seats with adjustable head restraints and British inertia reel seat belts.

∗Carpeting throughout ∗Childproof locks on rear doors.

∗Fold down individual rear seats and

much more – The 120LE **£2,748** (illustrated below).

Every Skoda is backed by:–
∗Free 24 months unlimited mileage warranty ∗Special low cost insurance scheme for Skoda owners ∗Full anti-corrosive body protection ∗Over 260 dealers nationwide.

∗The Skoda Parts and Service Complex covering 18 acres in Kings Lynn.

∗RAC rally-proven reliability.

Test drive a winner today – the Skoda range from... £2,378

†Recommended retail prices for the Skoda range (ex works including seat belts, car tax and V.A.T., but excluding delivery, number plates and road fund tax) are 105S £2,378.29, 120L £2,509.10, 120LE £2,748.30, 120LS £2,889.09, 120LSE £3,148.22, Rapid £3,388.67.
Skoda (Great Britain) Ltd., 150 Goswell Road, London EC1. Tel: 01-253 7441.

157

'I experienced the normal human fear when we trained for the first time in the Alps on roads barely 3 metres wide, where on one side there were vertical stone walls and on the other a deep ravine waiting for us. And there was no barrier or bollards. Driving to the limit on such roads was not a very pleasant task. It was interesting that at night, when one did not see the ravines, although we knew they were there from the practice runs, the driving went much better. What the eyes could not see, the brain did not react to. It was obviously different when we took such a route first nor was it the same going for the second time. One had to get used to situations very quickly...

'To manage twelfth place overall we had to drive quite a few kilometres. 6,500 km in preparation for the rally itself, plus 350 km of the second stage from Monte Carlo to Gap plus 350 km on the return trip to Monte plus the main part of the competition which measured 1,600 km. Then there were 680 km of the most difficult sections during the last night. The total count of kilometres to be driven came to 11,030! The night section of the rally could only be taken by the best 60 cars. It was a pity that our third team car of Kvaizar/Kotek, who ended their main rally run 250 km before the finish, could not be with us.

'When we received the rally route directions, initially it seemed that at some sections the average speed required was rather sedate. Despite the winding road, according to the map we had to average 52 kph. However that was a great miscalculation. All the time we had to keep up with the clock, because the track in places climbed for several kilometres to the height of 2,000 metres above sea level and then plunged back to sea level again. All this on a road which at the start was dry, got wet after the first bend, then was covered in snow and, below the mountain summit, turned to smooth ice. Then we had the reverse order back to sea level. Choosing the right tyres required a magician. Not every crew managed the correct choice. In one of the speed sections of the last night, our rival Zapadlo decided to be shod with the long studded tyres. It was too late when he found that the short studded ones were more appropriate and he lost about a minute against our time. Until then we were about level.

'Monte Carlo is well known for its casinos and this competition certainly is a great gamble. Tyres, servicing, weather, other competitors: all these bore some relevance and were valuable playing chips for those who are the masters of their craft. The very able manage to battle through among the other contenders for victory. In the end, it is only the little things that decide who makes it to the top: the ability to go full blast where reason tells you to take the foot off the throttle. That is when the roulette wheel comes into play. For out-and-out victory you need a bit of luck'.

On the basis of such long-standing successes, in 1978 it was decided that Škoda should participate in the top competitions. At the end of the season this decision paid off when in the overall classification announced by the *Federation Internationale de l'Automobile* that, after the final results, the Škoda 130 RS was placed third after Alfa Romeo Sud and Fiat 128 coupé. 8 wins were gained in 24 starts. When Škoda took part in sporting events it almost always brought excellent results. In the Rallye Boucles de Spa, Kvaizer and Kotek were sixth in overall classification and Bláhna and Hlávka were seventh. In the class up to 1,300 cc Kvaizar's crew was declared the winner. In the Swedish Rally, held between February 10th and 12th, Haugland and Holmes were ninth overall and won their class. In the Yugoslav Rally Kvaizar/Kotek were first overall and Bláhna/Hlávka second. And so it went on.

The 1978 Lombard RAC Rally route was staged around Birmingham. Three factory crews took part from Škoda: Zapadlo/ Motal, Bláhna/Ing. Raichl, Kvaizar/Kotek all in 130 RSs and additionally the Czech team was complemented by the British Škoda Dealer Team T.Didlick/P.Titterton in a Škoda 120LS.

The Škodas were equipped with Goodyear tyres of various designs depending on the predominant type of road surface on each stage. The 3,000 km long route included 76 special stages. In the first special stage Kvaizar caused a great surprise when he gained eighth best time, placing himself 7 seconds in front of drivers like Waldegaard, Mikkola 8, Vatanen 4, Clark 10, Munari 3, Brookes 7, and others.

The rally was divided into 3 main stages. The first one, around Birmingham, had 9 special stages and measured 550 km. The second stage, the so called 'Scottish', lead up to the north via Scarborough, Middlesborough and up to Moffat and back to Birmingham. The course was 1,500km long and took a day, a night and a day amounting to 36 hours with a 3 hour break. It included 38 special stages. The third, 'Welsh' stage, measured approximately 1,000 km and had 29 specials and again took over a day, night and day ending in Birmingham.

One could not practice for the special stages and drivers went into them 'blind'. The reason for this was that the frequently used public roads which could not be closed for practice purposes. That was why the stages were usually run on private property, in parks and on woodland tracks. It was true that some stages were repeated from year to year on the same track but those were few and the organizers changed even those by arranging them to be driven in reverse order. Some specials were only 4 or 5 miles long, while others were 22 miles or more and these were really tough. Kvaizar and Bláhna admitted that by the end of the demanding stages they could not see for perspiration streaming into their eyes. Such tests decided not only the quality of crews but also of machines.

Fiat, Vauxhall, Toyota, Triumph were hit by defects and nobody was without difficulties. That also applied to the Škoda team. Right on the first night stage they suffered a great loss. Straight in the first special stage the Zapadlo/Motal Škoda broke its halfshaft which meant the end of the competition for a very able crew. The other Škoda crews also had problems and the team of mechanics divided into 5 groups earned their pay twice over. Their best opportunity came when the Kvaizar/Kotek car had to have the gearbox changed three times in addition to repairs to the chassis. All that extra work had to be done outside the normal service duties such as checking the state of engine, oil, water, front and rear suspension, adjustments to the brakes and changing discs and tyres. The Bláhna/Raichl Škoda 130 RS went on without problems up to the middle of the competition when they suddenly stopped without any sign of oil pressure and a seized fuel pump. For twenty minutes Bláhna tried to mend the defects and finally managed to reach the service point. Even then it looked like a certain retirement, but the mechanics saved the day and Bláhna was able to continue within the given limit of time loss which was 60 minutes maximum. At that time he was third in the class. After every special stage he tried to improve his position behind the second Toyota Levin driven by T.Katsuka/ D.Webb. In the end the Czechs led them by almost 7 minutes and finished second, 645 minutes 3 seconds behind the winning pair Kvaizar/Kotek with their time of 614 minutes 38 seconds. Bláhna's result was really astonishing.

Right from the beginning Kvaizar drove at a high and concentrated tempo. From the first special stage he led the 1,600 cc class and kept his position, even with all the defects which gave him no rest right up to the finish. That is what competition driving is all about.

In 1981 the Škoda 110 R Coupé was substituted by a new model, the 120 Garde, which was named

for export as Škoda Rapid. This was also a 2+2 two door coupé body. The car was developed from a prototype S743 and built in Kvasiny. The engine and gearbox were made in Mladá Boleslav, the rear axle and suspension came from BAZ Bratislava and the body and assembly were completed in Kvasiny. The major improvement from the previous models was the redesign of the rear independent suspension, to remove the consistent and until then frequently criticized oversteer experienced with Škoda rear engine cars. This was done by adopting a semi-trailing arm arrangement with the swing axles. That formed a complete assembly with the right and left drive shafts and their universal joints. The 1,173 cc engine of 58 bhp achieved at 5,200 rpm, and had a compression ratio 9.5:1. Together with the gearbox, this completed the power-train. The front suspension was also independent and the steering was modernized by using rack and pinion. In the second half of 1983 the types Škoda Estelle 105/120 (in the new M series) received improved functional and aesthetic touches. In the same year improvement to the Škoda 120 range continued with the installation of a new type of distributor, the fitting of a diaphragm clutch, widened tracks, rack and pinion steering, full-flow oil filter, a redesigned braking system, modifications to the gear-

Škoda 120 LS in the 1984 Rallye Škoda.

box and changes to the exterior and interior of the car body. Also fitted were a new system limiting exhaust emission to conform with more stringent regulations, an air cleaner with automatic temperature control for the fuel mixture intake and protected ignition cables.

In 1984, from the branch factory in Kvasiny, the Škoda 130 Rapid coupé went into production with a 1,289 cc OHV engine of 75.5 mm bore by 72 mm stroke with 58 bhp output and five-speed gearbox, wider track and an inclined rear axle with increased suspension travel. Another new Škoda model, the 120 LX, was based on the 120 LS and also had the new widened rear suspension. The Škoda 120 GLS and LX were fitted with a five-speed gearbox as standard. The 120 GL type had an improved production number L engine installed.

Then came the introduction of the Škoda 130 L saloon with the 1,289 cc engine. This was fitted with the proven semi-trailing arms rear suspension with the inclined swing axles and the wider track adopted from the Rapid. In the same year, 1984, came similar improvements to the rest of the Škoda model range, thus the 130 L, 120 LX and the Rapid had the same rear suspension arrangements which notably improved their roadholding. That allowed the dynamic capability of the engine to be used safely to its full advantage. Servo-assisted dual circuit brakes fitted only into Rapids until then, were also included in the 130 L model.

For sporting occasions the Škoda 120 LS replaced the 130 RS but from 1985 a new 130 LR took over the duty of bringing more racing trophies back to Mladá Boleslav.

Prior to the changes made to the rear suspension design in 1982, Škoda rear engine models received rather poor press coverage from the hardened motor journalists in the United Kingdom. The main criticism focussed on the way the cars handled in certain driving conditions and because of the weight distribution at rear. The rear engine made the cars less stable than was desirable. Unkind and rather unjustified stories spawned by comedians circulated round the country. Often, however, the Škoda owners got their own back as, for example, the story telling of the dream of a lifetime which appeared in the London *Times* recently.

A journalist was asked to look after a stored Porsche for a friend while he was on holiday. As a reward, the grateful owner urged him to take the 911 Carrera out for a spin. The Porsche was tentatively backed out of the garage for a drive around the Hertfordshire countryside when disaster struck as a complete electrical failure brought the Porsche

to a standstill. That was bad enough, but the first help to arrive came from the driver of a rival marque, a Škoda, who kindly and smugly helped push the Porsche to the side of the road.

The Czechs were intent on continuing with the Tatra/Volkswagen concept of rear mounted engine cars which achieved good traction and a simpler layout. They decided not to abandon or alter the basic design but tried to solve its deficiencies by sensible improvements. The introduction of the semi-trailing arm rear suspension arrangement and rack and pinion steering seemed to solve the main problems. Suddenly the distinguished motoring journals were full of praise of the new Škoda models, mentioning the acceptable prices being offered to the general public outside Czechoslovakia.

From 1986, United Kingdom headlines read: 'Back on the Road to Success', 'Škoda 120 L – Bargain of the Year', 'What Handles Like a Porsche, Costs Only £4,200 and Is More Fun Than a GTI?'. Journalists were heralding a new era for Škoda. Suddenly the press could not stop singing Škoda's praises and recommended the Czech-made cars to the young, the middle aged and the elderly as the best value for their money.

The *Nottinghamshire Observer* of January/February 1986 issue put forward its opinion on the 130 Rapid Coupé: 'Do you realize, you could buy a brand new Škoda every two years and never see any repair bills again? Ideal for first-time new car buyers, as a workhorse second car, for retired people who want economy with the peace of mind that goes with a two-year guarantee. It's an excellent little car, and superlative value for money. Highly recommended'.

The *Buying Cars* of November 1989 said of the Škoda 120L: 'The car itself has all the virtues you could want. At the money, the 120L in particular, has to be the British bargain of the decade'.

One of the later models, the Škoda 136 Rapid Coupé (or the 135 RiC with fuel injection combined with Walker 3-way catalytic converter), gained almost cult following. The *Autocar & Motor* magazine of September 28th, 1988 described the newly released 136 Rapid Coupé in very approving tones. The most surprising was their comparison of a Škoda Coupé driving experience with Porsche 911 handling. For the 136 Rapid model AZNP made improvements to the 1,289 cc 62 bhp engine, by fitting a high compression eight-port alloy cylinder head to the alloy block. Another new feature was that the inlet manifold was water heated for improved starting. The body design was of pleasing proportions and had easy flowing lines. Many accessories could be obtained from specialist dealers to enhance its looks and comfort.

'Even discerning drivers... are going to be surprised by its character and charm. Modestly stylish, it is practical, its doors shut with a nice clonk and it has a useful level of equipment. More importantly, in an era of sameness, it offers a genuinely different driving experience. There's no better way to learn about every angle of handling...' ran the verdict from *Autocar & Motor*.

The loyalty to the Škoda marque and its fierce defence by drivers of the Czech-made cars was reflected in the great number of people joining the Škoda Owners' Club, which was founded in 1962 and is one of the largest single marque motor car clubs in the United Kingdom. The club magazine, *National Newsletter*, is full of interesting correspondence describing drivers' lives enriched by their reliable family friend, the Škoda automobile.

The Škoda Trophy was founded in Britain in the middle of the nineteen-eighties, a one-make rallying championship. This competition was so popular that in time it developed into the second largest event after the Peugeot Trophy. It not only gave the opportunity of testing the quality and reliability of Škoda cars but also established a breeding ground for the advancement of driving skills and abilities of young keen British drivers and became a stepping stone for the driving talent and selection and nomination to participate in prestigious international sporting events.

The popularity of Škoda resulted in the rising figures of sales at home and abroad. The export figures to Great Britain alone were impressive: 1987 – 12,000 units, 1988 – 16,000 units, 1989 – 13,000 cars out of 45,500 exported into western Europe.

In rallies and hill-climbs almost every event was successfully concluded by the Mladá Boleslav contingent. J.Haugland and R.Saunders in a 130 LR came first in their class and ninth overall in the 1985 National Breakdown Rally based that year on the city of Bradford. The rally was 250 miles long in 50 stages.

In the 1986 San Remo Rally, L.Křeček and B.Motl were first in their class and sixth overall. S.Kvaizar and J.Janeček were second and ninth overall. Both crews drove the 130 LR. To have two Škodas in the first ten places when only 38 finished out of 118 starters was quite a triumph.

Markku Alén, the well-known Finnish driver, said at the end of the gruelling Acropolis Rally, when a little Škoda 130 LR driven by Křeček and

TOP **The elegant Škoda 136 Rapid in profile.**

ABOVE **More advertising emphasis on Rally success.**

Motl romped in to the finish 14th overall: 'The Škoda is an excellent car. If it had more power, it would give us a lot of trouble. Škodas are a surprise, they have staying power, they are fast and they hold the road perfectly. It really is an excellent car'. In fact in 1986 alone Škoda won 24 class victories in

LEFT **Škoda 130 LR under full power in the 1985 National Breakdown Rally.**

BELOW LEFT **Škoda 130 L in the second round of the 1988 Škoda Trophy Championship driven by R.Platts and I.Young.**

RIGHT **Škoda 130 LR being prepared for the 1985 Lombard RAC Rally in the special workshop in Mladá Boleslav.**

Europe including outright victory on the Turkish Rally where Škoda beat top works rivals with twice the engine size and finished ahead of a Peugeot 205 T16 turbo four-wheel drive and a Metro 6R4 with 400 bhp. Other class successes followed in the Rally of 1,000 Lakes and the Rallye Boucles de Spa.

In the 1987 Rallye Monte Carlo J.Haugland and P.Vegel finished first in the 1,300 cc class and fifteenth overall. In the Lombard RAC Rally Škoda class victories continued throughout the nineteen eighties. Škoda gained laurels every year in that decade except in 1984 when its crew came second and in 1987 when Haugland lost the premier position by just two seconds. Škodas defeated, in some cases by almost an hour, Vauxhall Novas, Ladas, MG Metros, Opel Corsas, Toyota Starlets, Citroën Visas, Peugeot 205s, Talbot Sambas, Suzukis and other distinguished makes.

The only cars left ahead of Škodas in overall classification were almost without exception four-wheel drive, super and turbo-charged fibreglass bodied machines. Their production shape was just about visible but all the rest had very little in common with series manufactured cars. Peugeots, Metro 6R4s and Lancias boasted of four times the power. Škodas, on the other hand, had 1,289 cc push-rod engines that used the normal standard engine block and much else that was used in series manufacture including a production-steel body. In the 1986 Lombard RAC Rally, for example, the only cars finishing in front of Škodas in Group B

were either turbo-charged or over two litres capacity and all had over twice the engine power. The four Ford Sierra Cosworths had 290 bhp 16 valve twin cam turbo-charged engines and all failed to reach the end!

Haugland was the hero in most of the rallies in which the Škoda team participated. The special skills possessed by a successful rally driver and what it takes to make it triumphantly to the finish are quite difficult for laymen to appreciate. In the *Škoda Standard* magazine, P.Young described Haugland's driving technique in the 130 LR when preparing for the 1986 Lombard RAC Rally in the Forest of Dean, which revealed something of the magic of competing.

'We reach the start of the pre-rally shake-down stage and John pulls over, puts two wheels on the grass verge and keeps the throttle at a steady 3,000 revs...'We cannot go just yet, it needs more time to warm,' explains John. Minutes tick by...'Let's go!' The Škoda snicks into first, and we roll up to the line. There are dark pines on either side. Ahead, wet reddish brown slime, a straight of 200 yards or so, easing into a long left hander, and we watch Salonen's Peugeot blast off the line, four-wheel drive and turbos all forcing this projectile of over £100,000-worth of technology down the track and into the corner.

'A timekeeper by my door shouts out the seconds, but he has ignored the fact that this Škoda is left hand drive, and John can only try to catch sight of the digital watch through the misty windscreen...Suddenly we are away!

'That familiar Škoda engine, on full song at once, wheels biting, up to 40 mph and John is reaching for second, hell that was some getaway! Not much wheelspin, just an engine on the cam delivering all of its goods and now John is holding on to the gear lever, ready for third and just steering with his left hand, first a flick to the right and still steering with his left hand...Just a flick to the right, now left, and we are powering into the long left hander, without a hint of lifting off, and with only a hint of a drift. We had cut across from the right hand verge to clip the grass on the left and we felt the nearside front wheel rise up and over a clod of earth and the still howling Škoda engine never relents. So that is how it's done! When you have only 1,300 cc, you never ever lift off.

'But now I know what's coming and I can remember the next bit when getting a ride with Markku Alén in his Lancia an hour ago. Bloody hell, doesn't he realize that at the bottom of the hill, there's an S-bend. That is why there are so many people watching the action. A streak of blue and red anoraks merge into a blur of ribbon as we flash downhill like something from the top of an Austrian Alp on a ski slalom course, flicking right here, up against the bank, now left, and John's window is now the only way of looking where we are going, and there's a gigantic pile of sawn up logs just dumped by the side of the track, covered in spectators. And the little all-singing-and-dancing Škoda is sliding round. I did not see those logs, sitting terrified in Markku's bucking Lancia. But here in the Škoda, with all the noises and familiar sounds of a

car I knew, this was much more worrying!

'Still he drives one handed, using all of the track, through the S-bend and out down the next straight, up to fourth, now fifth, back to third, now fourth, over the brow, and here we go, that orange triangle! Yes, it's caught out John as well, and he's still got his foot hard down as the corner looms. Has someone changed the direction of that arrow? What looks, at first, like a long open left is a hard, sharp hairpin, and John is tap dancing over the pedals, braking, on, off, avoiding front lock-up, now back on the power, instantly tweaking the back out of line with another dose of bhp, braking and keeping the revs up at the same time, cutting deep into the corner, talk about late braking – 'There is a mighty ditch on my side, John'; but he is not into reading my thoughts, just yanking the hand brake. And now going for first gear. The engine is howling away again, 6,000 revs, now 8,000, into second, the mud is now so wet here, it's pouring slime up over my side-window, and we are truly flying.

'Deep into the forest, the distinctive sound of the howling Škoda causes a parting through a gaggle of spectators walking down the track, all the time rocks hammer at the floor, and the vibrations of the fully lightened shell all combining with the straight-through exhaust and two heavy-breathing Webers to produce a raucous sound that punches a hole through the gloomy mist.

'Down hill, over flints as big as your fist, dabbing the brakes, through a gate and over a cattle grid. Finally we stop! Just three seconds slower than the Lancia. Even when switched off, the screaming crescendo still rings in the ears'.

J.Haugland celebrates his 100th international class win with J.O. Bohlin after the 1988 Lombard RAC Rally.

14 The new era

IN 1983 AN INTENSIVE activity began in the research and development department of AZNP Mladá Boleslav. The decision was taken to embark on a totally new and modern design to replace the ageing and now obsolete concept of the rear engined, rear wheel driven cars which had been in continuous production for the previuos 19 years. At AZNP it was felt that now was the time to start to follow the mainstream automobile concept of front wheel drive coupled with engine position in the front. Obviously this was a radical change which would require a new car body form and major re-tooling of a number of components. However the well, proven all-alloy engine unit of 1,289 cc, 75.5 mm bore and 72 mm stroke was retained for the new model.

The directors at AZNP decided to go abroad for advice on the design of certain major elements of the new model in order to obtain a car which would withstand the rigourous world of market competition. For the body design the Czechs turned to the Italian studio of Bertone, for suspension engineering to Porsche of Germany and Lucas Girling of United Kingdom saw to the front disc-brake arrangement.

Škoda not only designed a totally new product, but thoroughly prepared its manufacture. In 1988 Škoda invested in new assembly lines, installing a welding line of 102 robots which put it on a level with any modern West European car plant. Other areas of production such as the finishing process had been upgraded and the potential factory productivity was increased to 800 cars a day.

In 1988 the series production of the new model started and a year later the Favorit 136 was launched in western Europe and the rest of the world. The tradition of the name was continued, adopting the designation from the Škoda Favorit manufactured in the nineteen thirties. The Favorit's all-alloy OHV engine with its 9.7:1 compression ratio, was equipped with electronic ignition and a Pierburg twin-choke carburettor. The output at 5,000 rpm was 61.7 bhp. Maximum speed was 150 kph. The Favorit had a five-seater, five door hatchback body. The 136 model range consisted of four basic types which differed according to the levels of equipment and interior trim: Forum, 136 L, 136 LX and 136 LS. In 1990 an estate version, Forman LS and Škoda Pick-up, together with the newest low compression engine Favorit 135 LS

N.Bertone visiting Mladá Boleslav in 1988.

TOP **Škoda Favorit 136 L.**

CENTRE **Škoda Favorit Forman LS design proposal.**

ABOVE **J.Haugland participating for the last time in the 1989 Lombard RAC Rally driving Škoda Favorit 136 L.**

and GLS types were put on the market.

Right from its launch the new Škoda model was very well accepted by the general public though many regretted the inevitable demise of the rugged rear engine models which, by then, had established an enthusiastic following. The new Favorit won universal praise from motoring journalists. *The Daily Telegraph* liked the way the Favorit handled, the *Autocar & Motor* commented that 'One thing hasn't changed and that is Škoda's enviable reputation for producing value-for-money cars. The most striking aspect of the Favorit is its size... none of its European competitors gives so much metal for the money'. *The Daily Express* found nothing to dislike. 'Škoda has made a great leap forward with the new Favorit'. The *Autocar & Motor* in the November 28th, 1990 issue summarized its verdict on the 136 LX: 'It can be compared directly with any obvious opposition, irrespective of country of origin. The Favorit rides and handles well, turns into corners eagerly and functions as a complete package without quirks. It is comprehensively equipped and looks like it should stand the test of time. It is well developed and can even be fun to drive. It offers masses of features for the money, and underneath the obvious value-for-money image, it is a thoroughly engineered car with a pleasing, willing nature'. The *What Car* magazine chose the Favorit Forum as the winner of the 'Best Budget Car of the Year' in its 1991 Awards.

The new car did not fail the Škoda's well-established reputation in rallies and sporting events. In the 1989 Circuit of Ireland a Favorit won its class and came eighth overall. In the legendary Lombard RAC Rally the Favorit 136 L, driven by the Czech drivers P.Sibera and P.Gross, came first in the showroom class group N to record Škoda's 17th class win in this event. No other car manufacturer in the history of the RAC Rally has collected so many class wins, and no other manufacturer has won so many classes so consistently. In the 1990 Lombard RAC Rally, Škoda just missed the class trophy but consoled itself with the first prize in Manufacturers' Team finishing ahead of Ford and Mitsubishi. In the 1991 Rallye Monte Carlo, Sibera and Gross won their class and came 25th overall in their Škoda Favorit 136 L.

The early winter of 1991 provided Škoda with a triumphant confirmation of the reliability of the new Favorit and finally convinced any remaining critics among the general public by winning its class and finishing 20th overall in heavy competition in the Lombard RAC Rally. The now familiar duo of Sibera and Gross did it again in their

TOP **The Group N Škoda Favorit 136 L driven by G.Anderson and A.Rands in the 1990 Cartel International Rally.**

ABOVE **S.Wedgbury and N.Petrusic in the Favorit 136 L in the 1990 Lombard RAC Rally finishing third in their class.**

factory 110 bhp six-speed Favorit 136 L, the lightest car of the competition, weighing only 794 kg. After successfully completing the most demanding British rallying event, Sibera confirmed: 'This car is maximum everywhere'. He was not joking.

Towards the end of 1989 came other events which had enormous influence on the future of

Czechoslovakia and AZNP – Škoda of Mladá Boleslav. In November of that year the so-called 'velvet revolution' was staged in Czechoslovakia. After fourteen days of bloodless unrest Czechoslovakia came back from the cold to join the previously lost but now newly found European democratic tradition. The stable and tolerant

Czechoslovak attitudes founded in the inter-war period and never quite forgotten, even in the darkest moments of the communist rule, have re-emerged. The personal freedom and free market forces were established. Under the old system, virtually all profits gained from product sales went to the Czechoslovak government. Škoda produced cars at a cost of 50,000 crowns, sold them for 85,000 but was allowed to keep only 700 crowns of the profit. In the new situation all the profit will stay with the manufacturer.

Privatisation of small and large nationalized companies has started to take place. Company after company has negotiated and found West European partners with which to enter the new era.

The Mladá Boleslav automobile works, as well as the Škoda concern in Plzeň, came to the attention of foreign companies and investors. AZNP, having been turned into a joint stock company and named Škoda, automobilová a.s. (Škoda automobile joint stock company) began discussions for a possible partnership with four competing western firms, Volkswagen, General Motors, Renault–Volvo consortium and BMW. Škoda needed money for further investment and the selected partner would have to put up a substantial amount of hard currency to let Škoda develop and expand its manufacturing base and export markets. Škoda planned to double its output to 400,000 cars a year and wanted to develop a new engine as well as manufacture engines for other car makers. Škoda was searching for a partnership, not a takeover, and the competition among the four contenders was surprisingly fierce.

Meanwhile the Plzeň concern, also turned into a joint stock company, had been negotiating with the German firm Siemens, the Swedish/Swiss consortium Asea-Brown-Boveri, the British/French joint venture GEC/Alsthom and the American Westinghouse company which were all interested mainly in a stake in the transport and power generation units of the company. A great deal of attention was also shown for the whole concern by the old Škoda partner, Schneider, and also by Mitsubishi of Japan.

Towards the end of long discussions and bargaining for the Škoda automobile company two firms came out on top: VW and Renault–Volvo. Finally, despite many high level visits by French officials it was announced in December 1990 that Volkswagen would be Škoda's new partner with a planned investment of DM9.5 billion. Mr Carl H.Hahn, the VW chairman, confirmed that the Czechoslovak marque Škoda was to be the bridgehead for Volkswagen's operations in all of central and eastern Europe and further afield.

The long negotiations in Plzeň came to an end in January 1992. Siemens, the German electronics and electrical group together with its partners Krupp and Krauss Maffei were recommended to take control of the transport division of the Škoda concern. The deal, under which Siemens acquired 51 per cent of the transport business, was valued at US$105 million. The joint venture, named Škoda-Transport, planned to continue supplying the former Soviet Union with electric locomotives and producing suburban trains and underground railway carriages. Earlier, in November 1991, Siemens also won the race to control Škoda's power generation division valued at US$170 million. Under the terms of the Siemens agreement a new joint stock company, Škoda-Energo, would be formed, with the Germans and a French company Fromatone, holding a two thirds stake in the new firm. For both ventures, Siemens had offered its Czech partners guarantees to maintain employment and retain research and marketing facilities.

The establishment of western markets, cooperation and joint ventures has already brought results. A new electrically powered Favorit prototype was produced in the Plzeň concern's branch factory in Ejpovice in 1991. This car was produced together with the Swiss firm Fridez Solar AG. Cruising speed is designed at 60 kph, maximum speed is 75 kph and travel distance of up to 80–100 km. The recharging time is 8 hours and electrical consumption 20 kW per 100 km. The series production was planned to start late in 1991. The new electrically powered Favorit was shown to the public at the 1991 Brno Trade Fair and the Prague Autosalon in October 1991 and was intended for export to Switzerland.

The future of the Škoda will undoubtedly be very different from anything which the company has been through in the past. We can only hope that the winged arrow symbol, following on the long tradition and uninterrupted manufacturing experience of transport products since 1895, will fly and keep triumphantly on course into the twenty-first century and beyond.

Technical Information

Laurin & Klement Motorcycles

Type	Year	Capacity cc	Bore/Stroke mm	Power bhp	Brakes	Max. Speed kph	Notes
A	1898	184	60/65	1.25	front	40	
B	1899	240	66/70	1.75	front	45	
CT	1900	331	75/75	2.5	front	45	tandem
BZ	1901	331	75/75	2.5	rear	50	
BZN	1902	353	75/80	3	rear	50	
BZP	1902	331	75/75	2.75	front	45	
L75	1902	353	75/80	3	rear	50	
L80	1902	502	80/100	3	rear	60	
L85	1902	633	85/108	3.5	rear	65	military
LW	1902	633	85/108	4	rear	65	water cooled
CC	1903	491	65/74	3	rear	65	twin cylinder
CCD	1904	615	70/80	4	rear	75	twin cylinder
CCR	1904	812	75/92	5	rear	85	twin cylinder
CCRW	1905	812	75/92	5	rear	85	water cooled twin cylinder
CCCC	1905	570	55/60	6	rear	75	four cylinder

Laurin & Klement Passenger Cars

Type	Year	Capacity cc	Cylinders	Bore/Stroke mm	Power bhp	Cooling	Max Speed kph	Wheelbase mm	Track front/ back mm	Notes
A	1905–11	1,005 1,105	2	80/100 80/110	6–7	water	45	1,920 1,800	1,190/ 1,190 1,150/ 1,150	open two-seater
B	1906–13	1,399	2	90/110	9	water	45	1,920	1,150/ 1,150	open two-seater
C, C 2	1906–16	2,278	2	110/120	10–12	water	45	2,630	1,300/ 1,300	four-seater
D	1907	3,391	4	95/120	18	water				four-seater
E	1907	4,562	4	110/120	28	water	70	3,800	1,590/ 1,545	four-seater
B 2	1907–17	1,595	2	92/120	8	water	45	2,600	1,300/ 1,300	four-seater
F	1907–18	2,438	4	84/110	14	water	60	2,700	1,300/ 1,300	four-seater
FF	1907	4,876	8	84/110	45	water	90	3,160	1,320/ 1,320	open six-seater
BC	1907–08	1,885	2	100/120	10	water	60	1,920	1,150/ 1,150	open two-seater
FC	1908	2,238	4	84/110	14–16	water	60	2,130	1,300/ 1,300	sports model
FC Semmering	1908	3,485	4	86/150	50	water	120	2,130	1,300/ 1,300	racer
BS, BS 2, BS 4, BSC	1908–11	1,399	2	90/110	10	water	45–75	2,160	1,200/ 1,150	open sports model
G, G 2, G 4, GC	1908–13	1,555	4	75/88	12	water	55	2,600	1,200/ 1,200	passenger, sports model
FCR	1909	5,674	4	85/250	100	water	120	2,540	1,330/ 1,330	racer
EN, ENC 4 ENM	1909–11	5,702	4	110/150	33–45	water	85	3,500	1,420/ 1,370	
L, LC 4, LC 2	1909–17	3,684	4	95/130	25–36	water	75	3,170	1,350/ 1,350	
ENS, ENSC 4	1910–11	7,363	4	125/150	60	water	90	3,500	1,420/ 1,370	luxury passenger
FN	1910–15	2,660	4	84/120	18–24	water	65	2,700	1350/ 1350	

Type	Year	Capacity cc	Cylinders	Bore/Stroke mm	Power bhp	Cooling	Max Speed kph	Wheelbase mm	Track front/ back mm	Notes
GDV, GDVC, GDVT, GDVR, GDVF	1910–17	2,660	4	84/120	18	water	60	2,510 2,685 3,050	1,350/ 1,350	open taxicab
S.2	1910	1,520	2	100/100	10	water	60	2,150	1,200/ 1,200	prototype
K, Kb	1910–21	4,252	4	95/150	32	water	80	3,170	1,375/ 1,350	passenger and sports
LK	1911–12	4,084	4	100/130	25	water	50	3,170	1,350/ 1,350	Knight engine
S, Sa, Sb, Sc	1911–14	1,770	4	70/115	14–16	water	60–70	2,325 2,688	1,200/ 1,200	
DN	1912–19	2,881	4	84/130	25	water	70	3,070	1,370/ 1,350	two- and four-seaters
RK	1913–15	4,712	4	100/150	50	water	95	3,170	1,375/ 1,350	Knight engine
Sd, Se, Sg	1913–15	1,847	4	70/120	20	water	65	2,788	1,200/ 1,200	
O	1913–15	2,715 2,614	4	80/135 80/130	30	water	65	3,150	1,340/ 1,320	
M, Mb	1913–18	3,817	4	90/150	40	water	80	3,200	1,350/ 1,350	luxury passenger
MK, 400	1913–25	3,308	4	90/130	40	water	80	3,200	1,365/ 1,365	Knight engine
OK	1914–15	2,412 2,614	4	80/120 80/130	30	water	70	3,150	1,300/ 1,300	Knight engine
T	1914–20	1,198	4	67/85	12	water	60	2,400	1,100/ 1,100	
Sh, Sk	1914–23	2,064	4	74/120	24	water	70	2,788 3,050	1,200/ 1,200	
Sil, Sm, Sp, 210	1916–25	2,412	4	80/120	25–30	water	65–70	3,120 3,220	1,200/ 1,200	
Md, Me, Mf, Mg, Mh, Mi, 300, 305	1917–24	4,712	4	100/150	50	water	85	3,200	1,350/ 1,350	
So, 200, 205	1920–25	2,412	4	80/120	25	water	65	3,150	1,260/ 1,260	
MK 6, 445, 450	1921–25	4,962	6	90/130	60	water	80	3,650 3,200	1,365/ 1,365	Knight engine
A, 100, 105, 110	1922–28	1,791	4	72/110	20	water	80	2,950	1,250/ 1,250	

Type	Year	Capacity cc	Cylinders	Bore/Stroke mm	Power bhp	Cooling	Max Speed kph	Wheelbase mm	Track front/ back mm	Notes
150	1922–25	1,460	4	65/110	20	water	85	2,950	1,300/ 1,300	Knight engine
350	1924–27	3,498	6	78/122	50	water	110	3,400	1,400/ 1,450	Knight engine

Laurin & Klement Commercial Vehicles:

Type	Year	Capacity cc	Cylinders	Bore/Stroke mm	Power bhp	Cooling	Max Speed kph	Wheelbase mm	Track front/ back mm	Notes
E	1907	4,562	4	110/120	28	water	35	3,800	1,590/ 1,545	1.5 tonner, omnibus
H, HOP, Hos	1907–08	5,918	4	116/140	32	water	26	4,135	1,800/ 1,800	4 tonner, omnibus
FO, FOF, FOZ, FL	1908–12	2,438	4	84/110	16	water	35–40	2,840	1,300/ 1,300	light omnibus
DL, DO	1909–15	4,503	4	105/130	25	water	16	3,400 4,000	1,550/ 1,550	2 and 3 tonners omnibus
FD, FOD	1909–16	3,402	4	95/120	22	water	25	3,200	1,340/ 1,340	1–1.5 tonner, omnibus
HL, HO	1910–13	7,363	4	125/150	40	water	25	4,100	1,660/ 1,700	6 tonner
HLb	1912–15	7,964	4	130/150	40	water	25	4,100	1,660/ 1,700	6 tonner
MS	1914–17	5,911	4	112/150	40	water	20	3,600	1,400/ 1,400	2 tonner
Md, Me, Mf, Mg, Mh, Mi, 300, 305	1917–24	4,712	4	100/150	50	water	85	3,200	1,350/ 1,350	van, fire truck, military vehicles
500,505	1923–25	4,712	4	100/150	35	water	40	3,100 4,300	1,640/ 1,670	2 tonner, bus
540, 545	1923–27	5,911	4	112/150	40	water	35	4,000	1,400/ 1,400	4 tonner, bus

Škoda Passenger Cars:

Type	Year	Capacity cc	Cylinders	Bore/Stroke mm	Power bhp	Cooling	Max Speed kph	Wheelbase mm	Track front/ back mm	Notes
Škoda-Hispano-Suiza	1925–29	6,597	6	100/140	100	water	125	3,690	1,450/ 1,450	luxury passenger made in Plzeň

Type	Year	Capacity cc	Cylinders	Bore/Stroke mm	Power bhp	Cooling	Max Speed kph	Wheelbase mm	Track front/ back mm	Notes
110	1925–28	1,791	4	72/110	25	water	85	2,950	1,250/ 1,250	
120	1925–29	1,944	4	75/110	30	water	80	3,100	1,300/ 1,300	
360	1926–28	3,969	4	95/140	55	water	100	3,400	1,400/ 1,400	luxury six-seater
4 R	1928–30	1,944	4	75/110	32	water	90	2,950	1,380/ 1,380	
6 R	1928–30	2,916	6	75/110	50	water	100	3,460	1,380/ 1,380	
422	1929–31	1,195	4	65/90	22	water	75	2,600	1,300/ 1,300	
860	1929–31	3,888	8	75/110	60	water	110	3,570	1,400/ 1,400	luxury six-seater
430	1929–32	1,661	4	72/102	30	water	80	2,800	1,360/ 1,360	
645	1929–32	2,492	6	72/102	45	water	100	3,025 3,375	1,360/ 1,360	
650, 651	1930–34	2,704	6	75/102	50	water	110	3,025 3,375	1,360/ 1,360	luxury six-seater
430 D, 431, 432, 433	1930–36	1,802	4	75/102	32–36	water	80	2,900, 3,075, 3,135	1,360/ 1,360	
633	1931–34	1,792	6	65/90	33	water	100	2,775	1,300/ 1,300	
932	1932	1,498	4	72/92	30	air		2,750	1,250/ 1,240	rear engine prototype
637	1932–33	1,961	6	68/90	37	water	110	3,100	1,300/ 1,300	
933	1933	800	2			air				rear engine prototype
420	1933–34	995	4	65/75	20	water	85	2,430	1,150/ 1,150	new small car concept
420 Popular I 0.9	1933–34	903	4	65/68	18	water	85	2,300	1,050/ 1,050	
637 D, 637 K, 639	1934–35	1,961	6	68/90	45	water	125	3,000, 3,200	1,320/ 1,320	luxury six-seater
420 Rapid I	1934–35	1,195	4	65/90	26	water	90	2,450	1,150/ 1,150	
Superb 640 I	1934–36	2,492	6	72/102	55	water	110	3,300	1,320/ 1,360	six-seater

Type	Year	Capacity cc	Cylinders	Bore/Stroke mm	Power bhp	Cooling	Max Speed kph	Wheelbase mm	Track front/ back mm	Notes
430D III, 433	1934–36	1,802	4	75/102	40	water	100	3,135	1,360/ 1,360	
Popular II 1.0	1934–36	995	4	65/75	22	water	85	2,300	1,050/ 1,050	
935 II	1935	1,995	4	84/90	55	water		3,200	1,250/ 1,300	rear engine prototype
Rapid Six	1935	1,960	6	68/90	50	water		2,620	1,150/ 1,170	sports and aerodynamic
Rapid 1.4 II and III	1935–38	1,385	4	70/90	31	water	100	2,550	1,170/ 1,220	
Popular Sport Monte Carlo	1935–38	1,385	4	70/90	36	water	125	2,570	1,100/ 1,200	sports special
Popular III	1935–38	995	4	65/75	22	water	85	2,430	1,050/ 1,100	
Superb 640 II	1936–37	2,704	6	75/102	60	water	110	3,300	1,320/ 1,360	six-seater
Favorit 904	1936–39	1,802	4	75/102	38	water	95	3,050	1,250/ 1,320	
926	1937	2,500	4			air				military terrain prototype
Popular IV OHV	1937–38	995	4	65/75	27	water	100	2,440	1,050/ 1,140	saloon, roadster, cabriolet, van
Sagitta	1937–39	844	2	80/84	15	air	70	2,100	1,000/ 1,050	
Superb II 913	1937–40	2,916	6	75/110	65	water	120	3,300	1,320/ 1,360	six-seater
Rapid 1500 OHV, 922	1938–42	1,563	4	72/96	42	water	110	2,650	1,250/ 1,300	
Popular 1100 OHV	1938–42	1,089	4	68/75	30	water	100	2,440	1,160/ 1,200	
Superb OHV	1938–46	3,137	6	80/104	85	water	120	3,300	1,320/ 1,420	
Rapid 949	1939	3,137	6	80/104	60	water	95	2,930	1,350/ 1,400	on generator gas
Rapid 2200	1939	2,199	6	72/90	60	water	115	2,880	1,330/ 1,400	
Popular SV 995	1939–46	995	4	65/75	20	water	85	2,200	1,150/ 1,150	Liduška
Superb 4000	1940	3,990	8	84/90	96	water	130	3,400	1,460/ 1,500	passenger and military
Favorit 2000	1940–41	2,091	4	80/104	52	water	110	3,050	1,300/ 1,320	passenger and military

Type	Year	Capacity cc	Cylinders	Bore/Stroke mm	Power bhp	Cooling	Max Speed kph	Wheelbase mm	Track front/back mm	Notes
Popular 1101 OHV	1940–44	1,089	4	68/75	32	water	110	2,440	1,160/1,200	
Superb 3000	1942–43	3,137	6	80/104	81	water	100	3,300	1,620/1,620	military
Kfz 15	1942–43	3,137	6	80/104	80–85	water	100	3,300	1,620/1,620	four-wheel drive military
Rapid	1945–47	1,563	4	72/96	42	water	110	2,650	1,250/1,250	
Superb	1946–49	3,137	6	80/104	85	water	120	3,300	1,320/1,420	luxury limousine
1101 Tudor	1946–51	1,089	4	68/75	32	water	110	2,485	1,200/1,250	two-door saloon, coupé, roadster, van
1102 Tudor	1949–52	1,089	4	68/75	32	water	110	2,485	1,200/1,250	two, four-door, coupé, roadster, van
1101 P	1949	1,089	4	68/75	32	water	110	2,485	1,200/1,250	terrain and military
1101 Sport	1949	1,089	4	68/75	42, 56	water	150	2,150	1,250/1,200	2 special racers
1101 Sport II	1950	1,089	4	68/75	56	water	175–200			special racer for Le Mans race 1951
Supersport	1950–53	1,089 1,221 1,491	4	68/75 72/75 78/78	73–120 160 150–180	water				special racers
1200 Sedan	1952–55	1,221	4	72/75	36	water	105	2,685	1,250/1,320	four-door saloon, van, ambulance
972	1951	1,221 1,491	4	72/75 78/78	45, 52	water	75–80	2,200	1,350/1,350	military amphibian
973	1952	1,491	4	78/78	52	water				military ambulance, communications van
Spartak Orlík, Rival	1953	995	4	65/75	30.5	water				prototypes
440 Spartak	1954–59	1,089	4	68/75	40	water	110	2,400	1,210/1,250	saloon
976	1956	988	4	68/68	40.5	water	115	2,250	1,250/1,250	prototype

Type	Year	Capacity cc	Cylinders	Bore/Stroke mm	Power bhp	Cooling	Max Speed kph	Wheelbase mm	Track front/ back mm	Notes
1201 Sedan	1956	1,221	4	72/75	45	water	100	2,685	1,250/ 1,320	saloon, van, ambulance
445	1957–59	1,221	4	72/75	45	water	115	2,400	1,210/ 1,250	
1100 OHC	1958	1,089	4	68/75	92	water	250			2 special racers
450	1958–59	1,089	4	68/75	50	water	125	2,400	1,210/ 1,250	roadster-cabriolet
Octavia	1959–64	1,089	4	68/75	40	water	115	2,400	1,210/ 1,250	saloon
Felicia	1959–64	1,089	4	68/75	50	water	130	2,390	1,210/ 1,250	roadster-cabriolet
Octavia Super	1959–64	1,221	4	72/75	45–47	water	118	2,390	1,210/ 1,250	
Octavia TS	1959–64	1,089	4	68/75	50	water	125	2,390	1,210/ 1,250	
1100 OHC Sport	1960	1,089	4	68/75	92	water	250			2 special racers/ hard top roof
Felica Super	1961–64	1,221	4	72/75	55	water	135	2,390	1,210/ 1,250	roadster-cabriolet
Octavia TS 1200	1961–64	1,221	4	72/75	55	water	125	2,390	1,210/ 1,250	
Octavia Combi	1961–71	1,221	4	72/75	47	water	125	2,390	1,200/ 1,250	estate
1202	1961–73	1,221	4	72/75	47	water	100	2,685	1,250/ 1,320	estate, ambulance
1000 MB	1964–69	988	4	68/68	48	water	125	2,400	1,280/ 1,250	first of the series rear engine models
1000 MB/F3	1966	998	4	72/61.3	90	water	210			F3 racer
1000 MBX	1966–69	988	4	68/68	52	water	130	2,400	1,280/ 1,250	
1100 MB	1967–69	1,107	4	72/68	54	water	135	2,400	1,280/ 1,250	
1203	1968–81	1,221	4	72/75	47	water	100	2,685	1,350/ 1,350	minibus, camper van
100	1969–77	988	4	68/68	48	water	125	2,400	1,280/ 1,250	
110 L	1969–76	1,107	4	72/68	53	water	135	2,400	1,280/ 1,250	

Type	Year	Capacity cc	Cylinders	Bore/Stroke mm	Power bhp	Cooling	Max Speed kph	Wheelbase mm	Track front/ back mm	Notes
1100 GT Coupé	1970	1,138	4	73/68	75	water				prototype, UVMV body
100 Racing	1970	988	4	68/68	90	water		2,400	1,280/ 1,250	racing model
110 L Rallye	1970–72	1,107	4	72/68	73	water		2,400	1,280/ 1,250	sports model
110 L Rallye	1970–72	1,144	4	73.2/68	100	water		2,400	1,280/ 1,250	factory team rally car
110 R Coupé	1970–80	1,107	4	72/68	62	water	145	2,400	1,280/ 1,250	sports model
110 LS	1970–76	1,107	4	72/68	62	water	145	2,400	1,280/ 1,250	
Spider 720	1972	1,500	4		150	water				racer
120 S	1972–75	1,173	4	72/72	64	water				sports model
120 S Rallye	1972–75	1,295	4	75.7/72	120	water				factory team rally car
180 RS	1974	1,774	4	82/84	155	water				OHC sports coupé prototype
200 RS	1974	1,997	4	87/84	163	water				OHC sports coupé prototype
Spider 733	1975	1,790	4		180	water				racer
105 L, S Estelle	1976–84	1,046	4	68/72	46	water	130	2,400	1,390/ 1,350	
120 L Estelle	1976–84	1,173	4	72/72	49–52	water	140	2,400	1,390/ 1,350	
120 LS, GLS Estelle	1976–84	1,173	4	72/72	58	water	145	2,400	1,390/ 1,350	
130 RS Racing	1975–79	1,289	4	75.5/72	112–130	water	200	2,400	1,445/ 1,448	racing model
130 RS Rallye	1976–83	1,289	4	75.5/72	112–130	water	200	2,400	1,445/ 1,448	sports model rally car
120 LS	1981–84	1,173	4	72/72	105	water				rally car
120 Garde/ Rapid	1981–84	1,173	4	72/72	58	water	145	2,400	1,390/ 1,350	
120 L, LE, LS, LSE, LX, LXE, GL, GLS Estelle 2	1983–89	1,173	4	72/72	49–52	water	140	2,400	1,390/ 1,350	

Type	Year	Capacity cc	Cylinders	Bore/Stroke mm	Power bhp	Cooling	Max Speed kph	Wheelbase mm	Track front/back mm	Notes
105 GL Estelle 2	1983–89	1,046	4	68/72	46	water	130	2,400	1,390/1,350	
130 Rapid	1984–89	1,289	4	75.5/72	58	water	155	2,400	1,390/1,350	coupé
130 L, GL	1984–89	1,289	4	75.5/72	58	water	150	2,400	1,390/1,350	
130 L	1984–89	1,289	4	75.5/72	75	water		2,400	1,390/1,350	sports model
130 LR/B	1984–89	1,289	4	75.5/72	125	water	200	2,400	1,440/1,445	rally car
135 Rapid	1987–90	1,289	4	75.5/72	58	water	160	2,400	1,390/1,350	coupé
136 Rapid	1987–90	1,289	4	75.5/72	62	water	155	2,400	1,390/1,350	saloon
136	1987–90	1,289	4	75.5/72	62	water	145	2,400	1,390/1,350	saloon
135	1988–90	1,289	4	75.5/72	58	water	140	2,400	1,390/1,350	saloon
125	1988–90	1,173	4	72/72	52	water	135	2,400	1,390/1,350	saloon
135 RiC Rapid	1988–90	1,289	4	75.5/72	55	water	140	2,400	1,390/1,350	catalytic converter fuel injection
Favorit 135 L	1988–	1,289	4	75.5/72	58	water	150	2,450	1,415/1,380	first front-wheel drive front engine model
Favorit Forum, 136 L, LX, LS	1988–	1,289	4	75.5/72	62	water	150	2,450	1,415/1,380	
Favorit 136 L	1988–	1,289	4	75.5/72	80–105	water		2,450	1,415/1,380	rally car
Favorit Forman LS	1990–	1,289	4	75.5/72	56	water	140	2,450	1,415/1,380	estate
Favorit Pick-up	1990–	1,289	4	75.5/72	56	water	135	2,450	1,415/1,380	
Favorit/Fridez Solar	1991–				13.2kW			2,450	1,415/1,380	city electrocar Ejpovice
Favorit Electro II	1991–				13.2kW					city electrocar UVMV
Favorit 135 LS, GLS	1991–	1,289	4	75.5/72	58	water	140	2,450	1,415/1,380	Škoda marque positioned centrally on the bonnet

Škoda Commercial Vehicles (manufactured in Plzeň and Mladá Boleslav):

Type	Year	Capacity cc	Cylinders	Bore/Stroke mm	Power bhp	Cooling	Max Speed kph	Wheelbase mm	Track front/ back mm	Notes
C Zug	1915	20,309	6		150	water				Daimler engine mixte system 32no
U	1922	7,479	4	115/180	50	water				train tug
Sentinel	1923–29	10,518	2	171/229	70					steam engine 3, 5, 7 tonners
115	1925–27	1,791	4	72/110	20	water	40	3,050	1,400/ 1,420	1.5 tonner
550	1926–28	6,786	4	120/150	50	water	35	4,000	1,414/ 1,628	5 tonner
125	1927–29	1,944	4	75/110	25	water	60	3,120	1,300/ 1,300	1.2 tonner
504 504 N	1928–33	4,849 5,517	4	105/140 112/140	45 55	water	40	4,065	1,820/ 1,800	5 tonner, bus
506, 506 N, 506 T	1928–38	8,276 7,274	6	112/140 105/140	75 60	water	60 60	4,065	1,790/ 1,800	5 tonner, bus
154	1929–31	1,944	4	75/110	32	water	60	3,120	1,300/ 1,300	1.5 tonner
104	1929–37	1,661	4	75/102	30	water	60	3,030	1,360/ 1,360	1 tonner, bus
304, 304 N	1929–39	4,849	4	105/140	50–52	water	45	3,665	1,786/ 1,725	3 tonner, bus
306, 306 N	1929–39	7,274	6	105/140	67–75	water	55	3,825	1,786/ 1,725	3.5 tonner, bus
206	1930–39	2,704	6	75/102	52	water	70	4,300	1,420/ 1,490	2 tonner, bus
606 D, 606 DN	1930–40	8,553	6	110/150	100	water	50	4,065	1,840/ 1,860	6 tonner, bus, diesel
404 D, 404 N, Nd	1930–44	5,702	4	110/150	67	water	50	3,845	1,820/ 1,745	4 tonner, bus, diesel
206 D	1931–38	2,916	6	75/110	60	water	90	3,800	1,420/ 1,490	2 tonner, bus, diesel
354	1933–35	4,862	4	105/140	55	water	40	3,685	1,835/ 1,725	
656 D	1934–36	8,553	6	110/150	105	water	50	4,850 + 1,250	1,860/ 1,920	6.5 tonner diesel

Type	Year	Capacity cc	Cylinders	Bore/Stroke mm	Power bhp	Cooling	Max Speed kph	Wheelbase mm	Track front/ back mm	Notes
406, 906	1934–37	8,553	6	110/150	100	water	60	3,846	1,830/ 1,845	
806 DT	1935	8,553	6	110/150	105	water	50	4,150 + 1,300	1,840/ 1,860	8–10 tonner 3 axles diesel
806 DTS	1935	11,781	6	125/160	135	water	65	4,150 + 1,300	1,840/ 1,860	8–10 tonner 3 axles diesel
254	1935–43	3,770	4	100/120	60	water	60	3,800	1,550/ 1,540	2.5 tonner diesel
918, 104 II	1936–40	1,802	4	75/102	38	water	70	3,175	1,360/ 1,370	1.5 tonner
903	1936–43	3,137 2,916	6	80/104 75/110	73 60	water	100	2,500 + 920	1,400/ 1,400	military six-wheeler
532	1937	7,983	6	110/140	108	water	80	4,000 + 1,150	1,850/ 1,850	rear engine aerodynamic bus
536	1937	11,781	6	125/160	140	water	75	4,800 + 1,250	1,900/ 1,900	rear engine bus
915, 929	1937	2,916	6	75/110	60	water	65	4,300	1,420/ 1,490	2 tonner
100	1939–40	1,563	4	72/96	42	water	80	2,900	1,460/ 1,360	1 tonner
150	1939–41	2,091	4	80/104	52	water	80	2,900	1,500/ 1,420	1.5 tonner
256 B, 947, 948	1939–47	3,137	6	80/104	80–85	water	80	3,800 4,300 4,800	1,530/ 1,540	2.5 tonner
706, 706 DN	1940–43	8,553	6	110/150	110	water	55	4,400	1,915/ 1,890	7 tonner, bus, diesel
706 G	1940–43	8,553	6	110/150	70	water		4,400	1,915/ 1,890	7 tonner, on generator gas
RSO	1943	6,024	4	115/145	90	water	15	3,000	1,820/ 1,720	military tug truck
256 G 957	1943–46	3,619	6	80/120	60	water	60	3,800	1,530/ 1,540	Imbert generator

Subsequent Škoda commercial vehicles were manufactured in other factory branches in Prague (Avia) and Liberec (LIAZ).

RAC Rally, Great Britain Results of the Official Škoda (GB) Ltd Participation:

Year	Placing	Crew	Car Type	Classification	Notes
1969	1st	M.Hinde/ N.Davies	Škoda 1100MB	Group 2 Class 2 up to 1,150cc	151 starters 69 finished London
1970	5th	P.Titterton/ J.Chitty	Škoda 110L	Group 1 Class 1 up to 1,150cc	196 starters 67 finished London
1971	1st	J.Haugland/ A.Antonsen	Škoda 110L	Group 2 Class 1 up to 1,150cc	231 starters 104 finished Harrogate
1972	1st	T.Sveinsvoll/ O.M.Evje-Olsen	Škoda 110L	Group 2 Class 3 up to 1,300cc	192 starters 80 finished York
1973	not entered				
1974	1st	J.Haugland/ A.Antonsen	Škoda 120S	Group 2 Class 4 up to 1,300cc	190 starters 83 finished York
1975	1st, 15th overall	J.Haugland/ F.Gallagher	Škoda 120S	Group 2 Class 4 up to 1,300cc	236 starters 104 finished York
	2nd	V.Havel/ D.Kirkham	Škoda 120S		11 works teams entered, only two finished.
	3rd	M.Zapadlo/ P.Hortek	Škoda 120S		2nd Manufactuers Team after Vauxhall
1976	1st, 16th overall	J.Haugland/ F.Gallagher	Škoda 130RS	Group 2 Class 4 up to 1,300cc	200 starters 104 finished Bath
1977	1st	J.Haugland/ R.Saunders	Škoda 130RS	Group 2 Class 4 up to 1,300cc	180 starters 67 finished London
	2nd	M.Zapadlo/ J.Motal	Škoda 130RS		2nd Manufacturers Team after Ford
	3rd	S.Kvaizar/ J.Kotek	Škoda 130RS		
1978	1st, 20th overall	S. Kavaizar/ J.Kotek	Škoda 130RS	Group 2 Class 4 up to 1,600cc	168 starters 61 finished Birmingham
	2nd, 24th overall	L.Bláhna/ M.Raichl	Škoda 130RS		
1979	not entered				
1980	not entered				

Year	Placing	Crew	Car Type	Classification	Notes
1981	1st	J.Haugland/ J.O.Bohlin	Škoda 120LS	Group 1 Class 1 up to 1,300cc	151 starters 54 finished Chester
1982	1st	G.Kalnay/ M.Eckhardt	Škoda 130RS	Group 2 Class 10 up to 1,300cc	149 starters 63 finished York
	2nd	J.Haugland/ J.O.Bohlin	Škoda 120LS		1st in Manufacturers Team Prize
	3rd	L.Křeček/ B.Motl	Škoda 120LS		
1983	1st	L.Křeček/ B.Motl	Škoda 120LS	Group A Class 5 up to 1,300cc	129 starters 61 finished Bath
	2nd	J.Haugland/ J.O.Bohlin	Škoda 120LS		Škoda Team was the only team to finish the rally
	3rd	S.Kvaizar/ M.Eckhardt	Škoda 120LS		(Team not officially entered)
1984	2nd	L.Křeček/ B.Motl	Škoda 120LS	Group A Class 5 up to 1,300cc	120 starters 52 finished Chester
	3rd	J.Haugland/ J.O.Bohlin	Škoda 120LS		
1985	1st 20th overall	L.Křeček/ B.Motl	Škoda 130L	Group A Class 5 up to 1,300cc	155 starters 62 finished Nottingham Class winner by 53 min.
1985	1st	J.Haugland/ J.O.Bohlin	Škoda 130LR	Group B Class 9 up to 1,300cc	
1986	1st	L.Křeček/ B.Motl	Škoda 130LR	Group B Class 9 up to 1,300cc	150 starters 83 finished Bath
	2nd	J.Haugland/ M.Eckhardt	Škoda 130LR		Křeček had 51 min. 51 sec. better time than the winner of the 1,600cc class
1987	1st	P.Sibera/ P.Gross	Škoda 130LR	Group B Class 9 up to 1,300cc	165 starters 85 finished Chester 1st in Manufacturers Team Prize
1987	2nd	J.Haugland/ J.O.Bohlin	Škoda 130L	Group A Class 5 up to 1,300cc	Haugland second by just two seconds!

Year	Placing	Crew	Car Type	Classification	Notes
1988	1st, 16th overall	J.Haugland/ J.O.Bohlin	Škoda 130L	Group A Class 5 up to 1,300cc	178 starters 87 finished Harrogate Haugland 18 min. 33 sec. in front of second Vauxhall Nova. 100th international win by Haugland
1989	1st	P.Sibera/ P.Gross	Favorit 136L	Group N Class 1 up to 1,300cc	187 starters 83 finished Nottingham
1990	2nd	J.Haugland/ P.Vegel	Favorit 136L	Group A Class 5 up to 1,300cc	175 starters 94 finished Harrogate 1st in Manufacturers Team Prize ahead of Ford and Mitsubishi. Wedgbury received special prize for highest placed first time competitor
	3rd	S.Wedgbury/ N.Petrusic	Favorit 136L		
1991	1st, 20th overall	P.Sibera/ P.Gross	Favorit 136L	Group A Class 5 up to 1,300cc	151 starters 82 finished Harrogate 2nd in Manufacturers Team Prize
	2nd	K.Williams/ V.Cann	Favorit 136L		

Škoda Tractors Manufactured in Plzeň:

Type	Year	Capacity cc	Cylinders	Bore/ Stroke mm	Power bhp	Fuel
HT30	1928–33	4,849	4	105/140	36	kerosene
HT18	1929–39	2,424	2	105/140	18	kerosene
HT25	1930–34	4,849	4	105/140	33	kerosene
HT33	1931–37	8,868	4	142/140	40	kerosene
HT33S	1936–37	8,868	4	142/140	55	petrol
HT20	1937–40	2,758	2	112/140	20	kerosene
HT40	1937–39	5,517	4	112/140	40	kerosene
HT20D	1941–42	2,660	2	110/140	22	diesel
HT40D	1941–42	5,321	4	110/140	44	diesel

Archive, production and other sources vary considerably in technical details. The above tables were compiled using best possible information available.

Bibliography

Magazines and newspapers
Auto
The Autocar
Autocar & Motor
Auto Express
Auto & Moto Veteran
Autosport
Buying Cars
Classic Cars
Classic and Sportscar
The Car
Hispano-Suiza Society
Markt Klassische Automobile und Motorräder
The Motor
National Newsletter (Škoda Owners' Club)
Škoda Standard

Trade Literature
Laurin & Klement, Mladá Boleslav
Škoda, Mladá Boleslav
ASAP, Mladá Boleslav
AZNP, Mladá Boleslav
Škoda, automobilová a.s.
Škoda, koncern, Plzeň a.s.

Archives
Karosa, a.s., Vysoké Mýto
National Technical Museum, Prague
The Royal Automobile Club, London
Škoda, automobilová a.s., Mladá Boleslav
Škoda, koncern, Plzeň a.s.

Books
Babuška, A., Od laurinky ke Škodě 1000 MB, Nadas, Praha 1967
Branald, A. Dědeček automobil, Albatros, Praha 1986
Čech, J., Mellon, J.E., Czechoslovakia, Land of Dream and Enterprise, Czechoslovak Ministry of Foreign Affairs, London 1944
Couper, M., Rallying to Monte Carlo, The Sportsmans Book Club, London 1957
Dvořáček, Ing I., Veteráni na našich cestách 1, 2, 3, Pressfoto ČTK, Praha
Fersen, von H.-H., Klassiche Wagen I, Hallwag, Bern und Stuttgart 1971
Hausman, Ing J., Kovařík, M., Vteřiny za volantem, Nadas, Praha 1968
Janáček, F., Čtení o Škodovce, Museum Škoda, Plzeň 1978
Janáček, F., Největší zbrojovka monarchie 1859-1918, Novinář, Praha 1990
Jíša, V., Škodovy závody 1859/1965, Práce, Praha 1969
Kieselbach, R.J.F., Stromlinienautos in Europa und USA, Verlag W.Kohlhammer GmbH., Stuttgart 1982
Kovařík, M., Svět velkých závodů, Novinář, Praha 1984
Kuba, A., Atlas našich automobilů 1, 2, 3, Nadas, Praha 1988-90
Kuba, A., Automobil v srdci Evropy, Nadas, Praha 1986
Kuba, A., Veteran Cars – Catalogue, Národní Technické Museum, Praha 1974
Margolius, I., Henry, J.G., Tatra – The Legacy of Hans Ledwinka, SAF Publishing, Harrow 1990
Meisl, C., Four Wheels on my Basket, Bookmarque, Minster Lovell 1991
Minarik, Ing S., Automobily 1966-1985, Nadas, Praha 1987
Norbye, J.P., The Complete History of the German Car, Portland House, New York 1987
Pinczolits, F., Austro-Daimler, Weilburg Verlag, Wiener Neustadt, 1986
Řepa, K., Premiery nadšení, Nadas, Praha 1989
Seper, H., Österreichische Automobil Geschichte 1815 bis Heute, ÖRAC, Wien 1986
Spremo, M., Atlas našich automobilů 4, Nadas, Praha 1991
Stechmiler, R., Peukert, O., Loučková, D., Naše automobily včera, Mladá Fronta, Praha 1957
Štilec, B., Mocek, A., Vznik a vývoj továrny Laurin & Klement v Mladé Boleslavi, AutoAlbum, Brno 1986
Štilec, B., Mocek, A., Od prvních škodovek po osobní automobily 105/120/130, AutoAlbum, Brno 1986
Tulis, J., Carrosserie Sodomka, AutoAlbum, Brno 1989

Chronology

1839 Emil Škoda is born in Plzeň on November 18th.

1856 Waldsteins establish ironworks in Sedlec near Plzeň.

1859 Larger premises consisting of boilershop, forge, carpentry and machine shops are founded in Plzeň.

1865 Václav Laurin is born in Přepeře near Turnov on September 27th.

1866 Emil Škoda starts to work for the Waldsteins and becomes director.

1868 Václav Klement is born in Velvary on October 16th.

1869 Emil Škoda buys the Waldsteins' machine factory becoming its sole owner.

1871 Plzeň factory is enlarged including a casting shop.

1872 General reconstruction of the Plzeň works.

1876 Škoda factory establishes first agencies at home and abroad.

1882 New forge is built.

1884 Building of Škoda steelworks commences.

1886 The production of steel begins, first attempts at armour plating material, obtaining of licence to manufacture machine guns to the design of K.Salvator and von Dormus. First guns are produced. Direct rail connection into the works.

1888 First gun carriage made for 15 cm calibre gun.

1889 First gun barrel made of 7 cm calibre.

1890 Special workshop established for armament manufacture.

1893 Škoda machine guns are supplied to the Austro-Hungarian army.

1894 Laurin & Klement founded in Mladá Boleslav.

1895 Laurin & Klement company is registered in Vienna. Manufacture of Slavia bicycles begins.

1896 New armament factory is built in Plzeň.

1897 Škoda delivers its first navy gun of 15 cm calibre to the Austro-Hungarian army.

1898 Klement travels to Paris to study motorcycle manufacture.

1899 E.Škoda in Plzeň becomes a joint stock company and is called Škodovy závody, a.s. v Plzni.
Laurin & Klement commences production of Slavia/Republic motorcycles.

1900 Emil Ritter von Škoda dies on August 8th.

1901 Economic crisis begins. Podsedníček second in Paris-Berlin race on a Laurin & Klement motorcycle.

1902 Economic crisis continues. Klement first and Podsedníček second in Arlberg hill-climb on Laurin & Klement motorcycles.

1904 Toman second in the *Coupe de France* held on Dourdan circuit.
Economic situation improves. In Plzeň, J. Gunther becomes managing director of the works.
K.Slevogt is appointed as a designer at Laurin & Klement.

1905 Vondřich wins the first recognized world motorcycle championship *Coupe de France* at Dourdan. Overall economic recovery.
Škoda works visited by Austro-Hungarian Emperor Franz Josef I.
Laurin & Klement commences manufacture of automobiles.

1906 Austro-Hungarian army orders 1,200 gun carriages for field guns of 8 cm calibre from the Škoda works.

1907 Laurin & Klement becomes a joint stock company.
Laurin & Klement produces a type FF, a first eight cylinder engine motor car in Austria-Hungary.

1908 O.Hieronimus replaces Slevogt as the Laurin & Klement motor car designer.
Count Kolowrat is taken on as a Laurin & Klement factory racing driver.
In December Hieronimus establishes a speed record on type FC at Brooklands.

1909 Karel Ritter von Škoda becomes managing director of Škoda works in Plzeň.

1910 Škoda, Plzeň builds the first steam turbine of 5,000 bhp.

1911 Laurin & Klement ceases the manufacture of motorcycles.
Hieronimus leaves Laurin & Klement to work for Warchalowski, Eissler & Co.

1912 Laurin & Klement receives the Thurn-Taxis Trophy.

1913 Laurin & Klement takes over RAF and the licence to manufacture Knight sleeve-valve engines.

1914 Austria-Hungary declares war on Serbia on July 28th. The First World War starts.

1915 Catastrophic shortage of fuel and food.
Both Plzeň and Mladá Boleslav works busy supplying the Austro-Hungarian army with armaments.
Porsche designs and supervises construction of the C-Zug for Škoda.
Large calibre guns produced at Škoda.

1918 On October 28th the new Czecho-Slovak Republic is declared.
The First World War ends.

1919 On September 25th Škoda comes into partnership with Schneider et Cie.

1920 First steam locomotive is produced in Plzeň.

1922 Hieronimus dies at Ries hill-climb on May 8th.

1923 Škoda winged arrow trademark is designed in Plzeň.
Škoda begins manufacture of Sentinel trucks under licence.

1925 Škoda takes over Laurin & Klement on July 20th.
Plzeň concern commences the manufacture of Škoda-Hispano-Suiza automobiles under licence.

1927 First electric locomotive is produced in Plzeň.
Count Kolowrat dies in Vienna on December 4th.

1930 On January 1st Akciová společnost pro automobilový průmysl (ASAP) is set up in Mladá Boleslav.
Laurin dies in Mladá Boleslav on December 4th.
First signs of world economic crisis affecting Czechoslovak industries.

1932 Motor company is established by Škoda and Praga, but only survives three months.
Škoda produces rear air-cooled engine prototypes.

1934 Economic situation is improving.

1936 Škoda Popular second in its class in Rallye Monte Carlo.
Elstners' hundred days in a small car.

1938 Klement dies in Mladá Boleslav on August 13th.
On October 1st Sudetenland is annexed to Germany after the Munich conference.

1939 In February Schneider et Cie resigns as Škoda partner.
On March 15th the rest of Czechoslovakia is occupied by Germany.
Protectorate of Bohemia and Moravia is established. Škoda is under German direction from September 1st.
Second World War begins.

1941 Škoda is forcibly incorporated into Reichswerke Hermann Göring.
Armament manufacture continues in Plzeň and Mladá Boleslav.

1945 Plzeň factory is bombarded by USAAF with devasting effect on April 25th.
Mladá Boleslav plant is decimated by remnants of Luftwaffe on May 9th.
Plzeň is liberated by the USA armed forces. Mladá Boleslav and Prague on the other hand, welcome the Soviets.
End of the Second World War.

1946 Škoda concern, Plzeň is established as national enterprise company.
Mladá Boleslav factory becomes Automobilové závody, národní podnik (AZNP).

1948 In February in Czechoslovakia a Communist coup is staged and the country is incorporated into the sphere
of Soviet political influence.

1960 Large reconstruction of the Mladá Boleslav works.

1961 Škoda Octavia TS wins its class in the Rallye Monte Carlo and is placed sixth overall.

1964 AZNP introduces its first rear engine models in series production.

1968 In January A.Dubček becomes head of the Czechoslovak state and his government introduces 'socialism with human face'.

On the night of August 20th/21st the Soviet Union armed forces invade Czechoslovakia to reimpose their rule.

1969 Škoda officially participates in the RAC Rally and wins its class. This success is repeated from now on every year of Škoda's entry apart from 1970, 1984 and 1990.

1987 J.Haugland and P.Vegel in a Škoda win their class in the Rallye Monte Carlo.

1988 AZNP commences series production of front engine, front-wheel drive cars.

1989 In November as a consequence of the 'velvet revolution' Czechoslovakia embraces a truly democratic statehood after 42 years behind the Iron Curtain. Manufacture of rear engine models ceases.

1990 Škoda, koncern, národní podnik, Plzeň is made into a joint stock company.
AZNP becomes a joint stock company named Škoda, automobilová a.s.
Volkswagen of Germany incorporates Škoda, Mladá Boleslav into its group of companies in December.

1991 P.Sibera and P.Gross win their class in a Škoda Favorit in the Rallye Monte Carlo.
Škoda, koncern, Plzeň a.s. signs joint venture agreements with the German industrial firm Siemens.

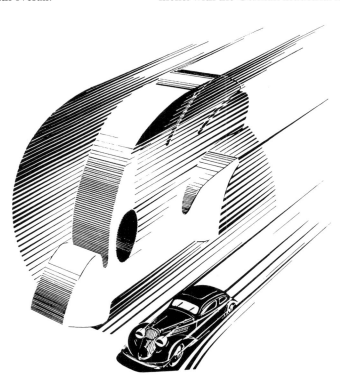

Index